GOING AS FAR AS I CAN

GOING AS FAR AS I CAN

the ultimate travel book

Duncan Fallowell

First published in Great Britain in 2008 by
PROFILE BOOKS LTD
3A Exmouth House
Pine Street
Exmouth Market
London EC1R 0JH
www.profilebooks.com

Frontispiece illustration 'Cheltenham Doorway' © Tony Ogle

1 3 5 7 9 10 8 6 4 2

Typeset in Transitional 551 by MacGuru Ltd
info@macguru.org.uk

Printed and bound in Italy by
Legoprint S.p.A, Lavis, Trento

The moral right of the author has been asserted.

A CIP catalogue record for this book is available from the British Library.

Hardback ISBN 978 1 84668 069 4
Paperback ISBN 978 1 84668 125 7

To Elisa

DUNCAN FALLOWELL'S PREVIOUS BOOKS

Novels
Satyrday
The Underbelly
A History of Facelifting

Travel Books
To Noto
One Hot Summer in St Petersburg

Other
April Ashley's Odyssey
(with April Ashley)
20th Century Characters
(interviews of unusual or celebrated personalities)

Contents

Light Jazz

It's black outside, as black and solid as coal, but inside all is white and clean, although the glass of white wine I had with my dinner was a mistake, one measly glass and a headache for the rest of the journey. Nurofen didn't work at all. I'm not a sleeper in public places and couldn't sleep on the first leg, distracted by the remote drill in my head and also by a boy in the window seat to my left. His tummy button, glinting with a few golden hairs, was exposed as he sprawled asleep, oh yes, he was asleep all right, one of those who can do it anywhere. I've slept with people like that – you lie awake for hours thinking about life, about them, about it, while they've moved effortlessly on to the next phase. It's beautiful to contemplate someone asleep beside you, but it's painful too because it means you are the less happy one.

We dumped down for a couple of hours at Singapore where I had a shower, followed by French onion soup from a cauldron. Despite air-conditioning, the airport was sultry. The terminus had recently been redecorated and the result was vile: brightly flecked carpet clanging horribly in the head. Since it's a major stopping point for exhausted travellers with hot eyeballs, someone should tell them, but people tell less and less these days, frightened to speak up and say what they really feel. The whole world is increasingly cowed by fears of retribution. Oh hell – in order to get back on to the plane I have to join a very long queue and go through the whole security and boarding process again –

The tummy-button boy swivels his blue eyes on to me and says 'It's more important to get some sleep on the second leg than on the first,' whereupon he adjusts the time on his watchface and falls asleep again. Obviously he's an experienced long-hauler, so after the second air-dinner (we've had two consecutive nights divided by a non-existent, theoretical day), I drop half a tranquilliser and in due course harvest four triumphant hours of kip on the tiltback. When I resurface the boy is gently disentangling his crotch with a large hand. He says 'These seats are not comfortable. The new ones go flat; five feet eight inches long in business, six feet six in first class.' I search those eyes for any flirtatious twinkle. Not a chance. I'm in the presence of sub-zero efficiency. It seems flirting has succumbed to the new puritanism too. Flirting is now called sexual harassment. I stumble off for a pee, passing in the galley the stewardess, who is having a snack. 'I'm flying on to Auckland after this,' I tell her proudly.

'What, in one hit?' she asks.

'Yes.'

'All three legs?'

'Mmm.'

'My God! Make sure you take *plenty* of vitamin C when you arrive. And have a shower at Melbourne. They've got great facilities.'

I wish she hadn't said 'My God'. Am I doing the wrong thing then? The longest flight in the world in one three-leg hit? Will I have a heart attack or a clot on the brain? A squishy sensation tells me the plane has landed in Melbourne, where the airport clock says it's 4.45 in the morning. I toddle across to the Qantas Business Lounge but it doesn't open until 5.30 a.m., so I go for a groggy meander on soft auto-legs and end up buying a litre of Stolichnaya vodka at the Duty Free. My vision slurps along the wine possibilities as pains shoot erratically behind my eyes. No rosé. One of the things I want to find is a rosé. In London, Margaret Harvey said 'When you arrive in Auckland, contact Bob Campbell. He's their top wine man. He'll put you right on rosé. And remember – get a cancer hat.'

'A what?'

'A cancer hat. The Cancer Society sells them in chemists. They're very cheap. And you want sunscreen.'

'What factor?'

'The highest factor. On your face especially.'

'Right.'

'And in your ears.'

'My ears?'

'And back of the neck.'

'I don't take my top off any more.'

'And remember.'

'What?'

'It's a no-worries society.'

The Qantas Business Lounge, when eventually it swings open its plate-glass door, is large and empty and fitted out with muted fabrics and plain eye-lulling carpet. Despite the crackle of my headache, I feel weightless. The shower-room is marbled and its shelves are stacked with thick white towels. Suddenly my nose starts to bleed, which is fortunate. Throughout my life I've made too much blood for my own good, resulting in nosebleeds at critical moments. If these have been preceded by a headache, which often they have, it is relieved. So my headache drains into the basin, drop by crimson drop, and at last my being becomes suffused with what has so far eluded it: the quiet thrill of escape.

In the main lounge a breakfast buffet is being laid along sleek glass shelves. The view through the giant window is of empty runway, empty green turf, empty blue sky, framed like the opening of an arthouse film in which nothing moves for long moments. I scoop some Bircher muesli, whatever that may be, into a bowl and add several pear halves. There is no one here from the previous two legs of the journey. The sense of flying yet further on, further than anyone else, further even than the sub-zero boy, makes me feel alone, yes, but also rather cocky. As I wander from magazine to tea-dispenser to plate-glass window with its abstract view, quietly killing the empty hours, I sense that even weariness is at a distance and my back is upright and my head is erect. So here we are again, on another voyage of the mind and body, chucking oneself across impossible distances to a destination that is merely a beginning. Must remember my back exercises. Don't want to conk out halfway through the trip.

∼

My American friend took me out for dinner on my birthday, as she had done many times before; only this time it was different because she was dying. It was the last dinner she ever had in a public place and we went to the Notting Hill Brasserie.

'I've left you some money in my will,' she said.

'I know.'

'It's not enough to make a difference. But it's enough for a book.'

'For me a book is a difference. And I know the book.'

'You do? What is it?'

She'd ordered steak but was cutting off small pieces, pushing them about with a fork, couldn't really get it down. It was the cancer.

'I want to travel as far as I can.'

'My goodness. Why?' she asked.

'So that I need never travel again. Anything afterwards will just be mooching about. Because I'll have cracked the planet, finally solved the terrible mystery of distance, and can relax. I want to travel so far that if you go any further you start to come back again. Which means going to New Zealand.'

Suddenly she was animated. 'I've always wanted to go there!'

'And what's *your* reason?' I asked her.

'To see those prehistoric lizards with the third eye. Don't you want to see those?'

Oh yes. Once the instinctive reason had established itself there were other reasons for going. Lizards – yes. Why not. And I'd discovered that on the very day I was born in London in 1948, Laurence Olivier and Vivien Leigh and the Old Vic Company were in the middle of a tour of that most distant of lands. I became fascinated by the idea of seeing what I could recover of their forgotten theatrical tour, of those faraway times, of that broken decade the 1940s.

'It's as though by going as far away as possible I may be able to revisit the lost world of my boyhood on the opposite side of the Earth. I know that sounds stupid.'

'It doesn't sound stupid at all,' said Bunny. Her eyes were moist. She'd love to be coming with me. In our time we'd had some great jaunts together. 'Didn't Einstein say that time and space were really the same thing?' she continued. 'You go. Go as far as you can. It's the only place worth going to.'

'And I want to go there to … ' I was going to say 'to breathe' but I checked myself. I have an image in my head of standing on the beach of a bay. It is warm not hot. The only building is a little cabin in the background, and friendly forest comes right down to the sand. And I don't have a care in the world. That's my dream.

'Do you want some pudding, Bunny? Have some ice-cream.'

'They've given me two months, Duncan.'

~

Bump. Lurch. Judder. Rattle. We're safely down. Auckland.

The taxi-driver from the airport is Samoan and he talks about money – any aspect of it excites him into rapid speech – while I frown out of the window at mudflats, green bluffs and strange shaggy trees. The buildings are small and low and have a look of impermanence. Even the houses, when we come to them, have this temporary look and appear like holiday homes. We hit traffic jams. Another reason for coming all this way was to escape traffic jams but here they are, one after another, on the approaches to the city. Closer in, we hit a clutter of flyovers and, well, the Samoan says this is the centre of town. It looks like a ... I don't know what it looks like. Not my idea of a town. The streets are very wide and everything is new and tinny and spreads in a disorderly manner; there are no old buildings – they must have knocked them all down. There are no people walking about. And now the traffic too has vaporised. Where have all the cars gone? Tower-blocks reach for the sky like forced celery, which is very surprising after the lowness of the buildings along the route. I guess that having been low for so long, the locals now want to be high.

The Hilton Hotel on Princes Wharf is not high but long, boaty and white, and surrounded by water on three sides. Everything about it is unreal and futuristic. The staff in particular are so well made that they might have come newly minted from a factory. My bedroom has an enormous creamy bed while the bathroom, lined with stone and steel, is almost as big as the bedroom, but doesn't have a bidet.

Sliding back a wall of glass I walk on to the balcony and look down at the water, which is eau-de-Nil in full light, turning to gun-metal green in the shadows of the quay. In the foreground is a harbour with ships, cranes and sheds. On the far side of a broad channel, low cliffs are speckled with villas, and beyond that the concave slopes of a volcano rise silently out of the sea. The volcano is uninhabited and of brooding green.

The Indian porter who brought up my bags said 'This is a beautiful country. No pollution, no immigrants.' He was from Goa. I lived in Goa for a while in the mid-Seventies and remember the ferryman who used to take one across the river between Baga and Anjuna beaches.

'There's a bridge there now,' says the Indian porter, 'a very ugly one.' His complexion gleams through his modesty.

'I know. A cement box-bridge. I went back for a look.'

Nod out at 10 p.m. or so, but am awake again at 3.30 a.m. Yes, I was a beach bum in Goa and in other places. Being a beach bum is probably my most natural mode if the temperature's reasonable, a beach bum with a stack of high-culture books. I raise my head from the skewed pillow and reach across for a slug of Stolly, a quarter chip of Zopiclone, and eventually the sound of the Arabian Sea slapping the Goan coast is heard and forgotten and heard again and lost again, the waves rising like rolls of cellophane, the distant concussion coming and going like nostalgia, like the memory of every warm and quiet beach one has ever known, of every molten reflection in a sunny land, the endless repetition of the unique, wave upon wave …

≈

Vivien Leigh was born in Darjeeling in India in 1913 and Laurence Olivier was born in Dorking in Surrey in 1907, and at the time of their antipodean tour of 1948 they were the most famous married couple in the world. It was astonishing that they should turn up in its remotest country, staging three lavish productions:

Shakespeare's *Richard III*, Sheridan's *The School for Scandal* and Thornton Wilder's *The Skin of Our Teeth*. Vivien Leigh had starred in *Gone with the Wind* and Olivier had starred in just about everything else. Their relationship was always empassioned and rocky – Vivien was highly strung and would eventually go bananas, Laurence was a control freak. Leading the Old Vic Company, the most prestigious theatre company of the age, they visited Auckland, Wellington, Dunedin and Christchurch. Rapturous on-stage acclaim was tempered by yells emanating from their dressing-rooms, and Olivier ended the tour in hospital while Vivien twitched and wondered what the hell it was all about.

∼

Wake at 9 a.m., refreshed. Jetlag? What jetlag? The sky is grey. All the buildings have canopies over the pavement, plain slabs sticking out, so that you can never look up at a building because the canopy is in the way. This means that 'architecture' begins at a level hidden above one's head, while on the ground the street becomes a gloomy shelter for pedestrians. There is a huge march today against GM crops down Queen Street, the main shopping stretch, but the other streets are vacant, tranquil, desolate.

I'm still trying to work out why the city demolished itself, and a book of sepia photographs in a secondhand bookshop – down narrow stairs into a basement – records a splendour of cupolas, pediments and volutes, thoroughfares lined with ornate shipping offices and insurance companies one after another, the mercantile palaces of the Empire put up in stone and built to last. There is nothing left – an odd building here, another there, screaming with pain and isolation in no man's land.

The bookseller raises a bespectacled face from the corner desk and asks 'Where are you from?'

'London.'

'Just arrived?'

'Yes.'

'And your first call is to a secondhand bookshop?'

'Yes. Actually I'm looking for the St James Theatre.' (This is where the Oliviers gave their Auckland performances.)

'Doesn't ring a bell, I'm afraid. I'm from Manchester. But I arrived a long time ago.'

'What brought you all this way?' I ask.

'The usual,' he replies.

'The usual?'

'A woman.'

The street tilts sharply upwards. I'm on Prince's Street – now that rings a bell – the Grand Hotel should be along here some-where – you see, I did do a bit of research before leaving … Oh … Here it is. And here it isn't. What's happened? This is very odd. A fragment of façade survives with 'Grand Hotel' carved into the stone but that's all and a tower-block has been glued on to it. The resulting malformity is empty, with a large TO LET sign on the outside. My stomach plunges. As I shall learn, there are no grand hotels left in Auckland. All pulled down.

At the brow of the hill the rebuilding stops and something of long-ago eddies in the atmosphere. A bell-tower with pillars in white stucco shines through leaves. The air quickens. A breeze fingers my hair, which has grown very long, right down to my shoulders in fact. Why I let it grow again, after so many years with it short, I don't quite know except that I definitely wanted to, perhaps to see if I could, perhaps as another attempt to recover the past, perhaps in the hope that I'd end up living on an antipodean equivalent to that golden Goanese beach of my twenties.

A board tells me I'm about to enter Albert Park, which is in the sort of condition I remember from the London parks of my boyhood. A third-world ethos has entered English life – that crime is inevitable, that corruption is the name of the game, that illiteracy is nothing special, that cheating is essential, that social violence is par for the course, that litter is normal, that parks and other public spaces are vandalised – but before I am able to give way to dismal thoughts on the wrecking of my homeland, I find myself hailed and uplifted by Queen Victoria. It is remarkable how so many generations after her death she retains the power, wherever you come across her, of bringing comfort. The dear old thing's incarnation here is in bronze and was unveiled, it says, in 1899, and the lawns are just as bright and green, the edges just as neatly clipped, and the urns just as packed with floribunda as they were in that imperial heyday. As for the trees, they've come on wonderfully and their limbs writhe in wild gesticulation across the blankness of skyscrapers. The park is almost empty but a woman pushing a pram says to her husband 'I thought you said it would be quiet.'

Buried out of sight behind evergreens is a Georgian villa in cream stucco with caramel dressings and a balustrade along the roof. The sunken lawn in front of it was presumably laid for tennis in the old days and is trying to recover from a marquee whose recent removal is betrayed by a large anaemic rectangle. Though now for the public, the garden still feels private, with blackbirds in song and sparrows popping from branch to branch. A notice reads *Old Government House Lawn. Passive recreation only. No ball games or frisbees.*

There are yellow spring flowers of an obscure kind at the base of a massive tree trunk and among them a plaque is studded into the earth, explaining that the enormity branching overhead is a flame tree: *Erythrina indica*. This specimen was planted by Sir George Grey, who was Governor here in the middle of the nineteenth century, and at present it is leafless with blossoms shut tight. The English loved to plant flame trees in their warmer colonies, suggesting passions which, denied at home, might flourish far afield. The first I ever saw were when driving into Rangoon from the airport along a boulevard lined with detached residences of the classical kind. A thrilling sight those enflamed gardens, one after another, so redolent of sticky afternoons in tropical places, passionate adulterous kisses and choked rebukes. I wonder if they are still there, splashing the shuttered mansions on the outskirts of Rangoon in the midday sun. Even then the dust was gathering, and Sarah Moffet and I sat in the bar of the Strand Hotel, which overlooked the Irrawaddy, sipping Singapore Slings at twilight and watching a rat investigate the skirting board with its snout.

~

Two fat men are approaching in brand-new stetsons, sunglasses, blue jeans, white trainers, and their bumfreezer jackets are zipped up, emphasising huge bellies. One of them sports a bracelet. And the more I try not to look at them, the more I fail. Would these be Auckland homosexuals? Or country farmers doing the town? It's impossible to tell. The air comes springing fresh off the water, and these two, even on a cloudy day, are exposed in sharp relief under a torrent of light. Suddenly I realise that everything since my arrival has existed in this exaggerated clarity, foreground and background equally discernible as in a Pre-Raphaelite painting. There is no escape from the acute image, the vivid panorama. Although I am disorientated and drained by having been thrown to the other side of the world, my perception nonetheless is not allowed to dull; the local geography insists that I walk upon a surface of breathtaking brilliance.

The two fat men notice my looking at them and I get a clench of apprehension because in London, the most cosmopolitan of all cities, the city of strangers, people walking the streets are afraid to look at each other. Who knows what you'd get, a shaft of abuse, a smack in the mouth, a knife, a mugging, or just your anxiety returned twofold? For a Londoner, a street without venom is an anomaly. But here I must try to learn that I need not be afraid. They nod, they smile, and say hullo. 'Yes, possums are so destructive,' remarks the braceleted one to his companion as they pass by. I don't think he was referring to me.

Where is the bloody St James Theatre? I've been searching for it in guidebooks and on maps, in lists, brochures and newspapers. Not a mention. We, by the way, would say 'St James's' but one quickly notices that here they don't use the possessive apostrophe, which is discomfiting, and I shall reintroduce it in some cases – the light is very bright indeed – obviously, like so much else, the St James Theatre has been demolished – itchy eyes – jzjzjzjz – look, my line is breaking up – maybe I do have jetlag – jzjzzz – I need to go back for a rest –

~

The overwhelming impression of this city is disconnectedness. Nothing is connected visually to anything else. The tummy-button boy said 'The second night is the worst. And even the third and fourth. The first you arrive knackered and sleep through. But the second night your old biorhythm reasserts itself. You wake up in the small hours and can't sleep at all.'

Yes, I awoke at 4 a.m. after three hours' sleep, tried to snooze, but hopeless, there it was again: clarity, bags and bags of clarity. Should I have a chip of Zopiclone? Not much point, since a highly resonant growl from the harbour was penetrating my earplugs – a red ship called *Indian Reefer* doing something vital to itself. So I arose at eight and made tea. Several cups later, my nose is pressed to the glass and I'm looking across water to that settlement which I know to be Devonport flickering on silver foil. The volcano, called Rangitoto Island, dominates the scene languorously in its wide-spreading skirt. Its dark covering of vegetation could pass for volcanic ash in this light, and where it sinks below the waves is at present hidden by a belt of smokey mist. Two canoes – one fluorescent orange, the other fluorescent lime – skim across the foreground. I feel like crap. Perhaps a shave would help.

Well, I've just had that shave. My whole face is sore. I switch on a stronger light and look more attentively. It's red with sunburn. There's a definite line at the base of the neck where the T-shirt began. Those few hours walking round town yesterday, with an overcast sky, and I'm sunburnt! The ferocity of those rays is absolutely terrifying. Margaret Harvey said get a cancer hat, but the Aucks weren't wearing cancer hats. Apart from those two stetsons, there was hardly a head-covering to be seen. This is their spring and they want to enjoy it.

The phone rings. Whoever it is I'll ask for help. It's Jenny Nagle, the distributor of my books, and she tells me that the largest hole in the southern hemisphere is near Nelson. 'It's called Howard's Hole. You can't miss it.'

'I'm sure you can't. Who was Howard?'

'I don't know. What do you think of us so far?'

'I feel this is not a redneck country.'

'No, it isn't. We buy more books per head than anyone else except the Norwegians.'

A *bookish* population – with the largest hole in the southern hemisphere. There's something odd about the southern hemisphere in general. Name for me ten important events that happened below the Equator. There you are, you see, you can't. But I'm not here for important events. Quite the opposite – I'm here for tranquility. And it's mostly sea anyway. In the southern hemisphere everything tapers into the sea.

Jenny and I arrange to meet, since we've never met before, and

in the bathtub her question comes back to me. What do you think
of us so far? Already I've noticed they can be rowdy, these people,
without being violent. That's unusual. They sing out loud and it
doesn't arouse suspicion. They don't look over their shoulder, or
yours, before looking you in the eye. Yes, they look you right in the
eye and on the other hand you're never quite convinced that
they've seen you. The women seem very confident. The girls can
be outrageous, rushing at you while waving a chunk of fast-food,
squealing inanely, and lots of them have lesbian haircuts and they
don't do cleavage. But however high-spirited, it all takes place
somehow in slow-motion.

   I should've had a shower not a bath because the bath weakened
me and I'm drifting again, drifting past a group of art deco buildings which are so charming and speak of a happy ice-cream society
before the Second World War, and I pause on the rim of the wide
road waiting for the traffic lights to change and then march across
directly towards a poster which is pasted on to a derelict Victorian
building, a pretty pile mutely readying itself for obliteration, and
the poster coming into focus reads Black Rebel Motorcycle Club
One Show Only! I bought this band's first album, maybe I'll go
along, oh, it was October the 9th, which was my lost day in the sky.
But I notice something else. Black Rebel's venue was – the St
James Theatre! It must exist after all. But where, where? No
address on the poster. Is one supposed to know? Actually I don't
have jetlag in the sense of cotton wool in the head. That clarity
keeps right on going, varnishing every second, leading me by the
nose. That's what's so disconcerting, the inability to fade. Drat – I
forgot to ask Jenny about my own red neck.

   What time is it? A boy has come in to turn down my bed. His
eyes might have been inked by a Persian miniaturist, so elegant are
their lines. He is Indian like the other one – but from Fiji – and
with a South African accent. I ask him how he came by it and he

says he was at school up the road with South Africans. A lot of white South African families have come here. He says it's because South Africa now has such a high murder rate. My head swivels to the window, drawn by lightning over the black water which is followed almost at once by torrential rain. Dragging the glass door open, I walk out on the balcony to view the waterfront. The skyscrapers glow and steam in the night like computer-generated special effects, their multi-coloured lights fractured into vivid, random smudges. When I turn back in, the room is empty and there is a chocolate on my bed.

~

Jetlaggerama, yes, waking up fully hard with a start at 3 a.m., adrenalin coursing at all levels, damp with sweat, longing for a pee, plus vivid bits of dreams here and there – or are they recollections? – the one about the man who went mad trying to kiss his own elbow. These rushes at the wrong time, presumably it's what menopausal women go through. I inspect my face in the bathroom, pressing my naked body against a whole wall of mirror. Redder and redder. This sunny planet is a murderous machine. It's like nothing I've known before and I feel in mortal danger.

    … I phoned directory enquiries. The St James Theatre is listed and I got the number but nobody answered when I rang. I phoned enquiries again and they said its address is Queen Street, so I walked the length of Queen Street until I came to a department store called Smith & Caughey. I entered Gentlemen's Outfitting on the ground floor and isolated a young assistant who looked up at me with cherubic eyes and said no, he didn't know where the St James Theatre was. Not wishing to leave it at that I fandangoed for a second and indicated the upmarket spaces about us and he told me that although the Smiths had gone, the Caugheys were still very much there and the only reason that the shop has survived in its original building is that the family owns it outright, otherwise the rent would be prohibitive. As he explained these things the young man's expression was of such Walt Disney innocence and good intention that I was tempted to give up the St James Theatre and saunter among the beachwear and cancer hats chatting him up – but I lacked the vigour to deviate.

As I persisted up the second half of Queen Street, which is very steep, giant Corinthian columns grew beyond a large demolition site. Surely this must be it, the theatre standing like a white Roman temple at the top of the hill, defying the bulldozers, a copy possibly of the Theatre Royal Haymarket. But it wasn't it; it was a Baptist chapel. Disheartened I turned about and began the descent, and at the Town Hall made further enquiry and was politely referred to a huge modern cinema bulging like a polythene bag where an attendant said yes, it's across the road, and I said but I've been across the road quite a lot and they said that's right, you can't see it, it's behind some shops and anyway it's always locked up.

So I staggered back over the road again and, well, yes, I did this time make out among the junk food outlets a pair of dirty golden pillars supporting filthy glass doors. Peering closely one could see into a mean foyer with crowd-barriers stacked up against one wall. Not a soul there. Everything shut, dingy, dead. A tap on my shoulder and I jumped. An oriental girl asked 'Can you help me open my shop, please?' It was lunchtime. Why the shop was opening then God knows, but she was very short and the keyhole was very high, so I unlocked it for her and asked 'Is there ever anyone in this building?'

'Round back. Entrance round back,' she said. So I found myself in Lorne Street round back, facing a second grotty entrance, but this time there were decorative lightbulbs on the canopy, and beneath my feet were the letters 'St James Theatre' in black mosaic. My fatigue lifted in a flash.

Another oriental female emerged from one of the tall doors and tipped a bucket of water into the gutter near my feet. 'Can I come in and look?' I enquired. She straightened up and answered 'I go ask.' The next moment a woman of European make, about forty, skinny in tight blue jeans, stood in the doorway. She looked at me and said 'Yes?' She was severe but not unfriendly. I said 'How do you do.' Strictly speaking 'How do you do' is what you say when you're being introduced to somebody, or introducing yourself in a place where you're entitled to be. When you're barging in, 'Excuse me' is in order. So I added an 'Excuse me' and explained my interest, the Oliviers, Larry and Viv, and all the rest of it, and she turned back inside but held the door open for me to follow. What happened next was unbelievable: a sort of neo-Byzantine basilica, capped by a massively coffered ceiling, entirely swallowed me up. Ranged about this colossal hall were free-standing lanterns done in the baronial style, each as tall as a person. A broad staircase with barley-sugar banisters curved up from the main foyer, its back wall embossed with corybantic Greeks. Above the bottom of the staircase there hung a tasselled flag stitched with 'Mezzanine Lounge' in gold letters.

Pleased by my astonishment, almost smiling, the skinny one disappeared through paired doors on the left. Blackness, utter blackness beyond. 'Hang on, I'll find the lights,' she murmured from the dinge. As dozens of stained-glass lamps came on slowly, an auditorium glimmered cavernously into life. Ornate opera boxes bulged either side of the stage. The decor was even more ambiguous than before. Florentine Mediaeval? Venetian Renaissance? Jewelled and bloodthirsty Jacobean in pantomime mode? But the general effect was, well, Martian. After the shoddy takeaways of Queen Street, such an enormity was difficult to comprehend. What on earth was all this doing here? And how could such a vast declaration have been turned into such a vast secret?

My guide had the courtesy to let it sink in and it was more than half a minute before she said 'We hold raves here. So we took out the seats.'

'And above?'

'We left them in.'

'This is the stage on which Vivien Leigh and Laurence Olivier played.'

'I heard about that. I used to live in the house they rented in Parnell. It was divided into flats. It's been demolished now.'

'Do you own this theatre?'

'No, it's owned by a man. But he's not interested in it. He's a developer. We rent it from him. We're an entertainment company.'

'Can I walk on the stage?'

'Yes, of course. I'll turn on the backstage lights.'

Footsteps on dusty black boards resonate in the auditorium. After the age of ten I never had fantasies about being an actor and, even in this heavily pregnant atmosphere, experienced no desire to impose my strut upon the phantom throng. What I did feel was a terrible sense of waste.

'There's nothing much backstage,' she said. 'I thought there might be some old programmes from the great days but there was nothing much.'

'Can we go up to the Mezzanine Lounge?'

'Yes. Hang on. Let me turn on some more lights.'

We entered upon the stately rise of marble steps. Cornices of bronze filigree threw an apricot glow from concealed lamps up into the vault. It was more like an opium dream than a building.

'Are the opera boxes used?'

'They used to be. For shows. But there hasn't been live theatre here for years. When Queen Elizabeth and the Duke of Edinburgh came a long time ago, they sat them in one of the opera boxes and made special chairs for them. I've got one. I found it moth-eaten out the back and had it re-covered. Don't know what happened to the other one.'

At the top of the stairs she clacked off again, skinny hips moving like clockwork in their tight denim encasement, and flicked more switches: pillars with rich capitals of grotesque ornament; black ganymedes in stone niches holding torches aloft and lit lavender from behind. The entire Mezzanine Lounge throbbed in a deep orange and red light. It was pagan. Infernal. The hellish hue poured through the cornices and melted upwards, making a fiery furnace over our heads. Here was a space fit for Cleopatra's suicide.

I didn't speak for quite a while – it had been a long time since I'd been so affected by a decayed, forgotten palace, in this case a palace of entertainment – but when I did speak it was rather practical.

'Why doesn't the local council do something?'

'They're not interested. They were offered it for a dollar but turned it down and built that new thing opposite.'

'But it must be the most lavish piece of neglect in the city.'

She shrugs. 'When the theatre first opened there were terrible protests about those naked boys in the alcoves, so they had to put fig-leaves on them. But my favourite theatre was His Majesty's. They bulldozed it. There were demonstrations, people handcuffed themselves to the doors, that sort of thing. It was an absolute gem, not big like this, but so pretty, and a lovely old arcade of shops was attached to it. But the bulldozers went in overnight and flattened it.'

'Did the arcade go too?'

'Of course. Then the developer – a young man – went bust and so nothing was built there. For years it was a car park, for *years*.'

'What's there now?'

'I'm not sure. A big lump of nothing I expect. So much has been destroyed. Come and look at the urinals.'

A row of Shanks Vitreous China to breast height, dark wood-work and brass coat-hooks. One could envisage the uniformed attendant turning on a basin tap, hand-towel over forearm, ready with the brush across the shoulders, and receiving his coin. The Ladies Powder Room was nearby. A series of round mirrors along the wall, flanked by French wall-lights with shades, and glass shelves beneath, and matching stools. Look, this site is a major find, with all fittings intact, and I am an explorer in aqualung swimming through the sunken wreck of a luxury liner, or panting in an overgrown temple lost deep in the jungle of the Yucatan where creepers blot the sky and parokeets paint the air …

∾

Ferry to Devonport. The air is cool and the sun seems gentle, casting down a lemon light from a flatness of blue. A woman on the seat opposite is saying to her friend 'I do know how to use candles to change the atmosphere of a room …' In a few minutes we have crossed the channel and tap Devonport Wharf. The first thing to greet you on stepping ashore are the Edwardian flourishes of the Esplanade Hotel and the trees of the Windsor Reserve. These trees are enormous and have a fluid look, with their branches seeming to drip downwards into the soil like reptiles colonising the Earth from outer space. Many children and young adults are walking about barefooted.

I veer to the right because my eye has been caught by a row of cottages seen through the trees, and I find myself walking along King Edward Parade. The cottages overlook the water and some are quite large but all are in wood with carved verandahs, painted white, blue or cream, and set back in lush gardens of jacaranda, jasmine and climbing roses. Only the corrugated iron roofs make me uneasy. I am reminded of the tea-plantation bungalows in Ootacamund and Nuwara Eliya and know that it was a useful building material in the Empire, but for an Englishman no real building employs corrugated iron.

As I pass the Yacht Club and the pastry shop, my spirits continue to climb, until turning into Cheltenham Road I find myself in – it has to be – one of the great residential streets of the world. It is not simply the quality of the Edwardian houses, though that is very high, nor is it their size, because they are generally on a modest scale. It is that the perfection of the street itself is reinforced at the south end by Torpedo Bay and the Auckland skyline, and at the north end by Cheltenham Beach and the indolent Rangitoto volcano; a remarkable urban view and a no less remarkable natural one linked by a quiet neighbourhood street whose suburban serenity has something of science fiction about it.

And what has happened to my eyes? Have they been electronically boosted? The clarity of this land we have mentioned. But today an additional patina has been scraped off and all the intervening layers which normally come between us and the objects of our perception quite sponged away. There is a certain anxiety in being alone and perhaps for the first time in one's life finding the world, as it were, *nude*. It must have something to do not only with the light but also with the slow-motion, the quietness, the emptiness, the lack of dirt. I can't say what it really is.

Cheltenham Beach at lunchtime is vacant except for a solitary sunbather. Offshore Rangitoto casts, like all volcanoes, an occult mood, suggesting that its orifice leads if not to the underworld at least to profound regions of the soul. It lies on the blue water with its mouth upturned to the sky in pouting slumber. One would need days or maybe weeks to adjust to the richness of colour, the depth of the peace. In fact I don't think I could ever adjust to it. Anyway I want to move here. And perhaps live in Cheltenham

Road for ever. In such a street one would never know sadness because one could never have a past or a future. The tremulous perfection of the present would obliterate everything else.

They were very helpful at the Visitor's Centre in Victoria Road and told me that those freaky trees on the Windsor Reserve are unusually fine examples of the Moreton Bay Fig. On checking the lists they confirmed their hunch that there was never anything for rent in Cheltenham Road itself but came up with alternatives and before long I found myself ringing the doorbell of 15 Kerr Street, where I was shown round the flat on the lower floor by a very nice man called Mr Jinks who says I can move in on Friday. From the flat's wooden terrace out the back there is a view through the semi-tropical garden to the Auckland skyscrapers on the far side of the water. It will look sensational at night. Jinks. Never come across that name before.

~

The St James Theatre fills my mind like a macabre space station, abandoned and adrift in the black wastes between galaxies. The woman, whose name was Anne, said it was designed by a man called Henry Eli White and was built in 1910, but surely that's too soon – it feels more like the early 1920s. But who knows? Styles do funny things so far from their points of origin. Some of the ceilings were stippled and I don't think that came in before the Great War. A sitting-room in one of my parents' early houses had stippled walls and I remember as a boy of five or so wondering why an interior wall should be made so very unpleasant by covering it with thorns. One question I did put to Anne was 'Do you know someone called Shirley O'Connor?'

'No. Who is she?'

'Her husband used to put on shows in this very theatre.'

'Really? When was that?'

'Sixty, seventy years ago.'

'Jesus ...'

Dan O'Connor was the impresario who set up the Old Vic Tour of 1948 but he'd started doing that sort of thing before the Second World War. In England, the ancient troupers Michael Redington and Peter Hiley both informed me that Dan had married a lovely girl called Shirley during the tour, but both had wondered: was Shirley O'Connor still alive?

~

Put my card in the wall today and retrieved cash from my account in London. The last time I did this was a few days ago in Notting Hill. The elimination of distance by technology is paralysing. The awareness of having come so far is not an awareness of motion. It is as though I stayed in the same place while everything else switched around me: the world has revolved like a circus ball beneath my rapid feet. The local paper money is not pleasant, greasy to the touch, incorporating a plastic see-through hole and the Queen looking sick, and with it I went into a record shop in the Queen's Arcade and purchased A *Shropshire Lad: three song cycles to poems by A. E. Housman* (two by Ivor Gurney, one by Vaughan Williams). I'd been looking for this in London record shops but never found it and when finally I ordered it over the phone and got the manufacturer to post it to me, it was stolen by one of the many thieves working for the Royal Mail. But here, as far as it is possible to be from its birthplace, the music slips effortlessly into my hand.

Mr Lyndon Brown rang and asked 'Can we have dinner? But not fusion food.'

'I thought your country invented fusion food.'

'It did! I hate fusion food! It's a mess!'

Mr Lyndon Brown, who wrote to me in London having enjoyed

one of my books, is quite odd and I think he's talented but in what way it's not easy to tell because he's very big on silence, that's one of his talents, small explosions followed by large silences ... But I don't know anyone in this country. I have a few phone numbers, a Lutyens one, and a Todd one because an hour before I left London Mike Horowitz rang up and said give Jenny Todd my love, she lives on an island somewhere, here's her phone number.

≈

At last I've found a surviving remnant of the original harbour city, classical façades painted in dark colours to cancel their features, with fire-escapes zigzagging down the front, and everything neglected and covered with seagull droppings. At street level beneath the canopies are massage parlours, liquor shops, pool halls, gay bars, girl bars – all except the gay bars are run by Chinese. Despite its destroyed heart, Auckland can still on occasion evoke a distant trading post out of Conrad or Sax Rohmer. Dr Fu Manchu might wheel round the corner at any minute and say 'Shsh – if anyone asks, you haven't seen me.'

≈

Tall in shirt and slim-fit slacks, and with hair youthfully bobbed, Shirley O'Connor smiles across her sitting-room in Rota Place in the pretty suburb of Parnell. It's tea-time and the sun is slanting on to African sculpture. She isn't dead after all.

'I thought you might like to have that,' she says, indicating something on the table.

It's the souvenir programme of the Old Vic Tour, designed by Loudon Sainthill. Lions and unicorns, crowns and skulls and cherubs are printed on flat washes of red, yellow, mauve and grey. A pierrot in pompommed pumps holds aloft a placard naming the members of the cast, who are headed of course by our glamorous

couple, Larry and Viv. The large cartridge pages are interspersed
with black-and-white photographs. Here's a full-page one of
Olivier by Angus MacBean: a face of ideal proportions, the black
wavy hair Brylcreemed and combed back with a parting as straight
as the edge of a creased trouser, the line of the mouth cruel with
its upper lip much narrower than the lower, plus that great gift to
male sex appeal – a cleft chin. Olivier's dark eyes stare out in
relaxed concentration, assisted by a little mascara. The eyebrows
have been trimmed but not enough. They are still quite twiggy. I
have an extreme aversion to overgrown eyebrows. I look up from
the page. I am alone. I have received a beautiful present. I'm over
the moon.

Mrs O'Connor re-enters with a tray and says 'By the time the
Old Vic arrived, Dan was quite experienced at that sort of thing.
Before the war he brought the Vienna Boys Choir out to Australia
and at the outbreak of the war the boys were in Melbourne. He
wrote to their parents to ask if they would like them to be sent
home or remain where they were and every single parent requested
that their boy should remain. After the war he brought over the
Boyd Neel Orchestra – forgive me these hearty sandwiches, I'm
not good at afternoon tea, I'd rather cook dinner for thirty. Isn't
the bread a bit thick? Then Dan thought he'd like to bring over
the Ballet Rambert and the Old Vic Company.'

'To the St James Theatre.'

'That's right, which was owned by Kerridge Odeon, and Bob
Kerridge suggested Dan use it. Though it was built as a theatre, for
many years it had been used only as a cinema. However, it had an
orchestra pit, which was needed for the ballet . I hope you're going
to have another sandwich.'

'I am.'

'All the musicians for the ballet had to come out from England.
We had our National Symphony Orchestra but it was run like a

trades union. They'd look at their watches and stop in the middle of a movement unless they were paid more money. Actually they were part of the Plumbers' Union and there was a reason for that but I've forgotten what it was. The NSO couldn't sight-read well enough to play for the ballet, but in order to enforce union rights they sat themselves underneath the stage while the English musicians performed in the pit.'

'And were there musicians for the Old Vic performances too?'

'No, thank heavens. I remember the opening night. It was incredible. In Sydney the audience came to see two film stars and I could see that Larry was guying them a bit. But in Auckland the audience had come to see Shakespeare, and Larry immediately sensed this, and it was the real McCoy. The intensity – with all those people. The theatre held over two thousand, you know.

But backstage was awful. The Company loathed it. You see, the back of the stage was the back wall of the building. The dressing-rooms, which hadn't been used for years, were rat-ridden dungeons underneath.'

'I know. I was exploring it.'

'Really? I thought it had been shut for years.'

'Yes, but I managed to get in. It's simply incredible.'

'Oh, yes, that *is* the word!'

'Can you remember the Grand Hotel where the Oliviers stayed, up near the park?'

'Certainly I can remember it but I don't think they stayed in it, or if they did not for long. Vivien Leigh did – but later. They stayed in a house at the end of the road here called Roedean, a lovely house, part of the White Heron Hotel, which Bob Kerridge also owned. All now pulled down. Elsie Beyer, the travelling manager, came out from London to make sure the accommodation was all right. Dan took a *fantastic* place for the Oliviers on the beach at Sydney, but there were some open-air steps up from the house to the garage and Elsie said "No, no, the Oliviers can't possibly stay here. Vivien will get her dress wet when it rains, walking from the house to the car." Elsie was very fussy. She even brought out drawing-pins and paperclips from England thinking we wouldn't have such things! So Dan and I occupied the house ourselves and it was wonderful and it didn't rain at all – it was the dry season.'

'And the Grand Hotel?'

'It was owned by Ernie Davis, who had a great affair with Vivien when she came back with *an* Old Vic Company – without Olivier – he'd been sacked – Larry heard about his sacking while on the tour, which didn't help matters, though he hid his feelings about it. Ernie Davis was a scallywag. When Vivien Leigh's estate was wound up they found that the only asset she had left was 30,000 shares in Ernie's brewery. That was the Lion Brewery. It was very profitable and owned the Grand Hotel. We had early closing in those days, 6 p.m., which gave rise to what was called the six o'clock swill, all these drunken men pouring on to the streets at six, and no women in the bars of course, which was how the men liked it.'

Many new names – that's one of the rewarding things about going far away – a completely new set of characters – but I need Shirley to slow down a bit and fill me in, so she explains that Ernie Davis was Jewish and the Mayor of Auckland and that he died in the 1960s. 'During the war there was a brothel for naval officers just across the road here, in what used to be a large farmhouse. The residents of Parnell, which was founded by the Church of England, got fed up with all the noise and complained and the brothel was raided by the police. They found Ernie Davis the Mayor inside, so of course the police couldn't do anything.'

'You still haven't told me about the Grand Hotel.'

'Oh yes, the Grand Hotel – it was *plush*. Dinner was from six to seven, and at seven you had to be out because they closed the dining-room. A large oil painting of a nude woman hung in there and Ernie always dined at the table facing the picture. Lewis Casson was very anxious to meet Edmund Hillary, and Dan and I arranged that at the Grand.'

Meanwhile, back at the Old Vic Tour, Olivier developed a painful knee problem and had his leg operated on in Wellington.

'That's right. He was in agony a lot of the time but manfully waited until the end of the tour for the operation. Afterwards his leg was sticking out in plaster so he was winched aboard the ship by a crane. He adored that. Played it to the hilt. The photo went all over the world.'

Then the Old Vic had a month on the boat back to England. Were there no aeroplanes?

'Yes, but a company that size, with all the stuff, I suppose … Oh, it was great – you'd fly London to Cairo – Cairo to Singapore – Singapore to Christmas Island – Christmas Island to Auckland. On the old *Constellation*.'

I had a model of one when I was a little boy. It was made from lead and painted in a livery of pale green and cream. With four propellors.

'And a lounge-bar in its tail,' she adds. 'You could wander down, have a drink and talk to the other passengers. We had flying boats too, of course, between Sydney and Auckland.'

Shirley offers to drop me back at the Hilton. 'Look, that's where the brothel was, there in that lovely old house. They've built another house in front, on what used to be the tennis court … and that's where Roedean was over there.'

In Roedean's place is an icy essay in post-Corbusier.

'And this down here is Judge's Bay, a darling little bay, with Parnell Park up above. All that land used to belong to the Streets. Mrs Street was Edward Lear's sister.'

'The flame trees are beginning to come out over there.'

'You are not allowed to buy them now in any nurseries. They're dangerous,' she says ominously.

'Flame trees are dangerous?'

'The wood is soft and a big bough can suddenly come down and hit you on the head.'

She's driving fast. A circuitous flyover. Zipping over concrete towards the harbour.

'I feel very grateful,' she says languidly while swerving on to another flyover, 'that Dan and I saw Europe at its *peak*. Before it became overcrowded and dirty. We lived in Curzon Place at one time and used to go to that lovely tea-room in Curzon Street called … um …'

'Rumpelmeyer's?'

'No … wait a minute, it'll come to me … Gunter's!'

'By the way, how did you find the Oliviers?'

'Charming, charming. But they were putting up a good front. He had a great sense of humour. Although I say that, when many years later Dan and I visited Larry down in Brighton, it was just after he'd been made Lord Olivier – Dan said "How does it feel, being the Brighton Peer?" And Larry didn't get it.'

～

Morrin Rout, of Plains Radio in Christchurch, rang the hotel and asked me 'live on air' who I was and what I was doing here. Big questions, and I cannot recall what answers I gave. But I did afterwards ask her about Karl Popper. You see, I intend to visit Christchurch, not only because the Oliviers did, but also because it is where Popper, during the Second World War, wrote his landmark book, *The Open Society and its Enemies* – a work which anyone who wants to live in a sane society should take a look at. Popper fled Nazi Vienna and in 1937 turned up in Christchurch, where, inhaling a free and quiet air, he set about intellectually demolishing the whole notion of what Robert Conquest has called 'the ideomaniac state' which in Popper's day was terrorising most of Europe in the guises of Fascism and Communism and which in our own time has been resurgent in the Islamic world. Popper wanted to write his book in English. He refused to write or speak German again and thought that the English cultural and political model, all things considered, was the safest one available if you were hoping to combine prosperity with justice. But he had never published in English before and it was a young student called Margaret Dalziel who acted as his language assistant. Morrin Rout thought that Margaret Dalziel was still alive, and said she would help me track her down.

~

It's my last night at the Hilton. The boy who turns down my bed has turned into a girl. She is also an Indian from Fiji. 'It was the coup,' she explains matter-of-factly. 'There was an Indian prime minister. But the Army said there must be a Fijian prime minister. Indians formed the majority, but not now. Only the older generation stayed, and some farmers. There is no future for young Indians in Fiji. Lots came here.' Her arms are firm and her full breasts move creamily against each other as she rearranges the sheets.

'Will you stay in this country?' I enquire.

'Yes. I have a resident's permit.'

'I knew some Fijians in London but not Indian ones. Do you know what the population is of Britain?'

'No.'

'Sixty million.'

'Phew! I can't believe it.'

'Rats in an overcrowded cage.'

'So you came here to breathe,' she says, filling in the blank from that crepuscular dinner with Bunny a couple of months before she died. The girl bows herself out with a smile. She is happy. Yes, I'm

doing something which is very difficult to do in Britain. I'm
flowing outwards unhindered …

~

In searching for an old postcard of Auckland's Grand Hotel, I was
directed to a stamp shop on the second floor of a building in
Vulcan Lane. A young man with black curly hair and studious
spectacles rushed up behind the glass counter and leaned eagerly
across it towards me. 'Would that be the Grand Hotel,' he asked,
'which was built in 1886 and burnt down in 1901?'

'No, later than that. It was closed in 1966. Then demolished.'

'In Princes Street?'

'Yes.'

'There was a fire there in 1901. Whole place gutted. Have a
look in these boxes. And in these. I'm really an archaeologist. This
is just my day job.'

'Really? What do you do at night?'

'Not much. Sleep mostly. They kept the façade.'

He pronounces it 'fuck-ard', so it's a split second before I reply
'No, they kept only a bit of that.' I resist the inclination to use the
word 'façade' itself, not wishing to embarrass him. He hasn't heard
anyone pronounce the word 'façade' but he's studied a great deal,
read it many times in books, and knows a lot. His mispronuncia-
tion has a passion about it which is sexy.

'You should see what they did to the Clarendon Hotel in
Christchurch. Flattened it. But kept the fuck-ard. Attached this
orrible great building to it. That's where I'm from.
Christchurch.'

'I'm from London.'

'I'd like to go to London and do some archaeology. You dig down
just a few feet beneath a building and you find this layer of black
ash. From the fire of 1666.'

'I'm not having much luck in these boxes. What do you think is the prettiest little town in this country?'

'Um … Cambridge is nice. You mustn't miss Dunedin. That has the best old buildings.'

'I was thinking of smaller towns. Oamaru?'

'Yes, especially Thames Street. And Timaru. Most of the nice towns are in South Island. I would say that, because it's where I'm from, but it's true. Arrowtown. Geraldine.'

'How could a place called Geraldine be other than delightful?'

He gives me a funny look and adds 'There's also places you should avoid.'

'For example?'

'Northland.'

'But I want to go there next week.'

'The Bay of Islands is all right because it's touristy, but anywhere even a bit off the main track is not good, loads of very poor people up there, living in rusty old cars, drunk, things like that, and the whole of the East Coast of North Island, avoid it, more poor people, very crime-ridden. Excuse me, I must attend to this customer.'

~

To the Auckland Art Gallery. It was founded by Sir George Grey, who understood beauty, which no modern administrator does, although he didn't understand his wife. Grey was born in Lisbon in 1812. His first go at running the colony began in 1845 and was a success. He learned to speak Maori and was able to put down native rebellions while retaining the goodwill of the Maori chiefs. Grey's careful approach to Maori matters is clearly stated in the introduction to his book *Polynesian Mythology*, still a classic but one I'd never come across until, back in England the following year, it was presented to me by Jenny Skilbeck, a neighbour in Notting Hill.

Polynesian Mythology reflects a widespread attitude among British administrators overseas which I feel goes a long way to explaining British imperial success in general:

> I soon perceived that I could neither successfully govern, nor hope to conciliate, a numerous and turbulent people with whose language, manners, customs, religion, and modes of thought I was quite unacquainted. In order to redress their grievances, and apply remedies which would neither wound their feelings nor militate against their prejudices, it was necessary that I should be able thoroughly to understand their complaints; and to win their confidence and regard, it was also requisite that I should be able at all times and in all places patiently to listen to the tales of their wrongs or sufferings, and, even if I could not assist them, to give them a kind reply, couched in such terms as should leave no doubt on their minds that I clearly understood and felt for them, and was really well disposed towards them.

Lady Grey received less consideration. The couple's only child, a boy, died after five months, and subsequently Grey was unfaithful to his wife under her own roof. In an outburst of exasperation he had the poor woman put ashore at Rio de Janeiro while they happened one day to be sailing past it and, as an escape for himself, he purchased Kawau Island to the north of Auckland, beautifying the place with plantations of trees and a waterside house of tiered verandahs. Gifted and headstrong, Grey grew too independent for Whitehall and he was sacked from his second stint as Governor-General in 1868, although he carried on dabbling in the colony's affairs until almost the end of his life. At the very last he became reconciled with Lady Grey back in England. But there was no real home for him in the old country and he died in a London hotel in 1898 – I've been unable to discover which one. And I'd also quite

like to know which room (these are the sort of trigger details a
nostalgia buff gets hooked on) so that I might sit in it and suss the
vibes. A grateful nation buried him in St Paul's Cathedral.

Grey kicked off the collection at the Auckland Art Gallery by
donating fifty-three pictures, including works by Fuseli, Blake and
David Wilkie, but not in fact the work in front of which I have
presently halted. This is A *View in Dusky Bay* by William Hodges,
acquired by purchase in 1961. A Maori male, draped in animal
furs, stands in noble-savage mode in the foreground while in the
background the energy burst from a sun (which is either rising or
setting behind a mountain) has the violent attributes of a volcanic
eruption. Hodges was the official painter aboard the *Resolution* on
Captain Cook's second voyage of exploration, which sailed from
Plymouth in 1772. Ill-served in his lifetime and cruelly neglected
since, Hodges invented the romantic landscape of faraway places,
the progenitor of every travel poster you ever saw. His best pictures hang unobtrusively among the naval institutions at Greenwich in London. Before my departure for the Antipodes I read in
a newspaper that high quality copies of the major Hodges works
were sent out to New Zealand by the Admiralty in the 1960s as a
gift to the nation. I wouldn't mind taking a look at those copies.
Perhaps they are to be found in this very gallery. But my enquiries
are greeted with bemusement. None of the staff has an inkling.

But what really blows me away is not a painting at all but a
series of greetings cards in the gallery shop. They are modern sea-
scapes and landscapes, vividly coloured, and the artist has managed,
despite the heat coming off his images, to avoid the influence of
Gauguin which afflicts so many painters working in this part of
the world. (Gauguin, part Peruvian with Indian blood, spent his
childhood in Lima on the shore of the South Pacific.) Turning over
one of the greetings cards in its wrapper I see that the pictures are
by an artist called Tony Ogle and the cards have been printed by

the Flagstaff Gallery in Devonport. I shall call in there and ask about him.

~

Today I've moved to Devonport, into the flat at 15 Kerr Street, tucked beneath the Jinks's old wooden house but not overshadowed by it. The accommodation is immaculately white and I shiver. I need to turn up the heating in here. And I'm hungry.

While I am peeling vegetables in the kitchen, Mr Jinks pops down to see if there's anything I need. I need a scourer for the washing-up. He nods and apologises for not coming down sooner but he's been very busy helping his daughter who is spearheading the return to reusable nappies. Her business is really taking off. Earlier today they were at a nappy exhibition and it was *packed*. I ask him what the floor is made of and he says it's kauri wood. The planks are polished to a gloss which over the years has brought out fantastic variations of colour, pattern and texture; from pale hay to deep cinnamon with streaks of dark chocolate; and if you look closely into the grain you will see that it contains a cellulose sparkle. Outside, between the paddle-shaped leaves in the garden and across the water, the sun has gone down behind skyscrapers which come alive with neon-coloured lights and resemble the gigantic toys of a Cyclops. The Skytower, Auckland's chief prong, is floodlit lavender.

'Actually it's pink,' says Mr Jinks.

'Is it? It looks lavender.'

'They have different colours for different reasons.'

'So is this pink for Gay Liberation?'

'No, for Breast Cancer Week. I'll just pop up and get you that scourer.'

Later that night there are loud noises, harsh voices, crude words. I clamber out of bed and prise up one of the slats on the

Venetian blind. Young American males are drunk and rowdy on the upper floor next door. Every so often several of them spring out semi-clothed on to the balcony to wrestle or jive. 'Hey, look at that fuckin skyline, let's party!' Sound of smashing glass. Fuck this, friggin that, holy shit, ra-ra-rah. I hang on in case anyone decides to do a striptease or piss off the balcony into the garden, but they haven't got the quality for that sort of abandon so I return to bed and open *The Golden Bowl* by Henry James.

~

Saturday morning television at 7.40 a.m. I've been dreaming very heavily the last few nights, heavier than in years. It's as though a lid has been taken off my dreams. Last night I dreamed that a Chinese hairdresser in London squeezed a boil in my nose and the discharge went on and on like a string of spaghetti. I'm up early because I'm meeting Bob Campbell, the wine expert recommended by Margaret Harvey. The venue is the Stone Oven bakery at 9 a.m. Though Bob lives only a few doors away from me on Kerr Street and I loathe morning engagements, he's off to Singapore before lunch and it's the only chance I'll have of saying hullo. On break-fast television a woman called Kim Hill is interviewing Professor Bryan Sykes, whose great thing is that men are dying out. He's deduced this from an examination of the chromosome record. Kim Hill looks pretty delighted by the prospect.

The more I travel the more it does seem that the future belongs to girls because everywhere one looks boys are hitting the buffers, causing trouble, screwing up, sitting in dead ends being violent, pointless and stupid, not all boys, not most boys, only a minority, but too many boys, one sees this everywhere. Thomas Mann wrote 'England is the classical land of the boy and has the best boys' stories in the world.' But that is no longer true of England, where the boy has become the repository of great anxiety. It doesn't help that society has adopted a hands-off approach to them, since it is a law of nature that youngsters are unruly if not guided. I suppose that going for 'no discipline' is an attempt to compensate boys for having been pupped in hideous urban environments: crime, though destructive, is a sort of freedom. Perhaps New Zealand is the last free playground of the boy, though even here they often seem futile. Governments the world over are desperately trying to find jobs for all these boys, but there are too many and they are surplus to requirements. The reason is obvious. Masculinity has brought the planet to the brink of destruction. Evolution wants less of it. Nature isn't interested in human rights. She doesn't want them in jobs, marrying, bringing up large families of more redundant, murderous males. Dragging myself past the house next door, I see smashed bottles strewn across the pavement and road where last night those enraptured hoodlums defiled the street.

Bob Campbell is sitting stoutly under a canvas umbrella on the terrace of the bakery. He is not a boy, though he's streaked with boyishness of the playful, affable kind, the way a man's greying hair may jockey with its original colour. Assorted sweetmeats are arranged in front of him in a Bunteresque tableau.

'Did you hear that terrible noise last night?' I ask.

'Oh yes! An American bought that flat and it gets *used*. The police turned up and took some of them away.'

I order a cappuccino and an 'apricot scroll'.

'Why are you interested in rosé wine?' he asks.

'Because it needs help.'

'Here they don't plant grapes for rosé and nobody drinks rosé. No, I lie – there is *one* grower in Central Otago who is growing grapes especially for rosé but I can't think of his name.'

My coffee arrives in a soup bowl. The coffee is excellent but gives me an uncomfortable rush. I'm never good at this sort of thing – or any sort of thing – at 9 a.m. Bob is very good at 9 a.m.

and orders another coffee and says 'They say that ozone depletion and heavy ultraviolet is what gives our wine its rich, bright
features. So I decided to check it out with an expert, David
Jordan, who lives here in Devonport, and he said bollocks, if
anything it will cause problems by burning the grapes. A rosé
with real class is hard to find, even in the South of France, where
most of them are.'

'Our local rosé at La Croix Valmer is considered one of the best,'
I remark, 'and it often has no taste whatsoever. "Gris" the French
say. They seem very proud of that, to produce an *absolutely empty*
wine.'

The apricot scroll is like chewing carpet and I give up on it and
push it aside. I suppose what I'm really looking for is that rarest
wine in the world, a rosé with *soul*.

'Come back to the house and I'll give you a rosé print-out from
the computer.'

His house has polished kauri floors that reflect like still water,
and high tongue-and-groove ceilings.

'Where are you going after Devonport?' he asks.

'Northland. I thought I'd rent a car and drive up to Russell next
Saturday.'

'That's Labour Day weekend. You'll never get there. It'll be
bumper to bumper.'

Quick ponder. The stamp-boy's warning about drunks living in
rusty cars also cuts in, and I make a snap decision. 'Excellent. That
saves me a problem. I'll take the train straight down to Napier.'

'You'll have a job,' he observes nonchalantly.

'Why?'

'They abolished the train.'

Before dashing off to the airport, Bob slips a bottle of rosé into my
hand, saying 'Give this a go,' and I decide to walk over to the Naval
Museum. Though it's a chilly morning, the postgirl is making her

deliveries on a bicycle wearing only shorts and a T-shirt, pounding from house to pretty house with flushed, heavy-titted goodwill.

The national navy is based at Devonport. Three frigates are berthed on the water. I think that's about the extent of the fleet. The Naval Museum is set up in an old clapboard house just outside the base and displays many black-and-white photographs. Oh, the radiant joy and confidence on those faces from long ago! I'm particularly drawn to photographs of the 1931 Napier Earthquake and the cheerfulness of the sailors digging out the dead. In the affluent world, as physical death is increasingly delayed and kept away from our daily experience, how perplexed or disgusted or anguished are our faces round a car crash, for example, but these sailors are smoking, joking and laughing as they peg away at their task – death is not so freakish for them and, until their time comes, they're going to get the most out of life. When the earthquake struck, HMS *Veronica* was in port. A sailor on deck described how suddenly all the water was sucked out to sea and the ship was beached. Another photograph records the ceremony of Crossing the Line, which means crossing the Equator for the first time. I 'crossed the line' when I flew here, but there was no ceremony. Ours is not a ceremonial age.

As my nose almost touches the wall of photographs, a voice from behind says over my shoulder 'In the 1880s the Russians were threatening the outlying British colonies as part of the Great Game in India. That's why there's a Khyber Pass Road in Auckland. It was thought the Russians might sail down from Vladivostok, and so Devonport was reinforced with massive guns sent out from England.'

Turning round I see a portly fellow with a polished face. It's the Warden of the museum. I ask him if he's ever been to England and he says no but he's going next year, 'to Shropshire to work as a gilly on an estate called Pradoe.'

'Sounds Spanish.'

'It's near Oswestry and belongs to Colonel Hadley,' explains the Warden.

'And you're allowed to leave the navy?'

'I'm not in the navy. I used to be a schoolmaster.'

~

Mrs Jinks – Maria – came down to say hullo. I'd not met her before. She has big blonde hair with a big smile and said that their nappy idea was a huge success at the exhibition and Mothercare are interested. So I opened Bob Campbell's gift of a bottle of Ata Rangi rosé wine and asked her if she'd been born in Auckland.

'No, I'm South African Dutch but my family lived for many years in Indonesia and at the outbreak of the Second World War they were captured by the Japanese. My mother and her children were put into a concentration camp and my father was sent to Japan to work in the mines. My mother had two boys and a girl – I hadn't come along yet – and she told my sister "I'm going to tell them you're a boy. They will treat us better if I have three sons." What she meant was there was less chance of my sister being abused if she were a boy. So my sister was dressed and treated as a boy. But the war went on and on and my sister was growing up and my mother became increasingly anxious that the disguise would become obvious. But luckily the war ended just in time, when my sister was thirteen. Meanwhile my father was working in the mines which were underneath Nagasaki. One day the guards disappeared and the prisoners learned that a bomb had gone off. They came up three days later, looked about, and said "It must have been a very big bomb" because they'd no idea what had really happened. My father would never speak about all this but my mother told us a lot.'

The Ata Rangi rosé has balanced acidity and fruit but a slightly too confectionery nose and the colour is too red. The taste should be less serious, should have something scenty and frivolous about it. It has depth but not height.

~

A platoon of naval cadets jogging in shorts passed me on Oxford Terrace. None of them had hairy legs. Then I realised that half of them were women. They didn't have hairy legs either. There is something androgynous in the look of the Kiwis, and androgyny is a kind of innocence. There is an innocence to these people, which is their particular magic. Of course they've known hard times, fought in wars and all the rest of it, but the country itself is somehow innocent. And you don't see skinny people either. Hairlessness, chubbiness, androgynousness are also features of the Pacific Islanders, so maybe it has something to do with the geography, which gets to everyone eventually, regardless of genetic origins.

At Narrowneck Beach I became mildly disorientated. Further north was Takapuna and Torbay, where the modernist English writer Anna Kavan lived with her lover Ian Hamilton during the Second World War. In Anna's time the life there must have been of an extreme simplicity, so much so that she wrote that nowhere in the locality was 'there any place where alcohol can be bought, but as against this it must be recorded that the post office store provides soft drinks in a wondrous range of colours, as well as choc-bons and ice-creams ...' (Anna was using alcohol to try to get off heroin).

I fumbled with the map before asking a young man at a busstop where Seabreeze Road was. He didn't know, peered down at my map and said in a thick accent 'I think it is near where we are.'

'Ah, you're not from this country.'

'Of course I am! It's just the accent!' he snapped and glared.

'Is it Russian?'

'Polish! If you must know.'

This was the first nasty note since my arrival. In the prevailing softness, it struck me with extraordinary force, that delinquent snarl for no reason. It is so familiar to me from the youths and drivers of inner London, but here I felt physically slapped. On the other hand it roused me. It's time to move on. There's a whole new country to look at!

Violence, though shocking, can do this. In 1982 I was living in Hay-on-Wye but the reason for doing so (writing a book about the transsexual April Ashley) had come to an end. One evening two young men followed me into the loo of a pub in Clyro and tried to beat me up for no reason whatsoever; they afterwards claimed I was trying to pull them, which was a lie; even odder, they were complete strangers to me. Luckily I managed to escape with only a bust lip, but later a gang of teenagers laid siege to April's house with wooden staves, baying for my blood. I nipped over the back wall, so they smashed up my car instead. But it roused me from my torpor – I realised it was time to pull stumps and move back to London.

～

Unusual birdsong from the garden but no bird is visible. It is a sunny afternoon with triangles of blue water between the bushes. The verandah faces south and since it's early spring the sun hasn't yet reached it. The warm side is to the north. The word 'north' here has all the luscious connotations of the Englishman's 'south'. It's taken far longer than I thought it would for my metabolism to settle into a rhythm. Just acquiring an actual as opposed to theoretical sense of where I am at any particular moment, that has eluded me. But now at last my feet are beginning to connect properly with the ground – and they are itching to hit the road and move into the depths of this strange land. One of the gay men who live next door, beneath the Americans, says that the bird is a grey warbler and it is tiny.

∼

As I left my London home I threw into the hold-all a couple of novels, both by chance American: Edgar Allan Poe's *The Narrative of Arthur Gordon Pym of Nantucket* and James's *The Golden Bowl*. I glanced at the Poe only on arrival and discovered that, coincidentally, it is about a voyage to the South Seas. But I thought I'd begin the Henry James first, though for many days I was in no state to embark on any book, let alone on a novel I knew to be of highly refined character. When, however, I did begin the James book, I came across, a few pages into the first chapter, the following, even greater coincidence:

> He remembered to have read, as a boy, a wonderful tale by Allan Poe, his prospective wife's countryman – which was a thing to show, by the way, what imagination Americans could have: the story of the shipwrecked Gordon Pym, who, drifting in a small boat further toward the North Pole – or was it the South? – than anyone had ever done, found at a given moment before him a thickness of white air that was like a dazzling curtain of light …

∼

Television news bulletin. A report on a boy called Alice, detained in a lunatic asylum after experiencing paranoid delusions and murdering his father. The newscaster explains that 'he was obsessed by the German philosopher Friedrich Nietzsche and Doors singer Jim Morrison.'

Maria Jinks pops down to ask if everything's OK and I say yes it is, thanks for the scourer, but earlier today I saw a slate slide off the roof next door. It made a leafy splash into the undergrowth. The neighbouring house, on the side opposite from the Americans, is derelict and hidden in an overgrowth of jasmine and arum lilies. Its windows are dirty and broken, the doors hang off, chimneys are cracked, woodwork is rotting and unpainted. It looks uninhabitable, but after dark, through one of the windows covered by a dirty muslin sheet, there shines a feeble light. The place is always as silent as death and what sort of life is conducted within is beyond imagining. I ask Maria who, if anyone, lives in that ruin and she says 'I've only met her once, by chance, coming out of her front door, and the weirdest thing was she was *totally normal*. It really shook me how normal she was.'

'Is Alice a normal name for a boy here?'

'No. Why do you ask that?'

'This boy who murdered his father–'

'No, no. Ellis. Ellis. Alice is how they pronounce it.'

≈

The Velvet Underground are on the radio: *Run, run, run, run, run – take a drag or two, Chestnut Avenue, hey what d'you do?* The room is high on a hill and its walls are of glass. One wall looks out towards Bethell's Beach and fluffy lines of surf. Another looks over to the hills where a sand dune's giant tongue licks inland. In the foreground, yuccas make starbursts of spikes. They say that Bethell's Beach is wild but it doesn't seem so to me. Scenically it is grand but there are plenty of houses tucked into the vegetation and it isn't far from the city. This is the house of the artist Tony Ogle, whose greetings cards I went mad about at the Auckland Gallery, and he's left me alone in his big sitting-room while he goes surfing, which he was longing to do since before I arrived.

Tony Ogle thought I was coming at two o'clock. But we had

arranged three. But I turned up at four. His name curls and rolls like the waves along the distant beach; it derives, however, from Ogle in Northumberland, whose coast is far grimmer than this one. It is the perfect name for an artist addicted to surfing and who has the blond, blue-eyed looks of the archetypal surfer; he has to get in that water every day, he told me, and that's where he is now. Tony said that the Maori call the East Coast feminine and the West Coast masculine. Bethell's Beach is on the West Coast. Tony is into the West Coast these days.

Tony's work is very acid – he laughed aloud when I said so – he never took acid – but I did, and his pictures have the mobile vehemence of acid. He said I must be referring to what he calls the High Summer pictures which he did in the 1990s and which first put him on the map and that he could probably track down a puff of local grass if I wanted it, but I said no thanks, I was already tripping in a foreign land, it would throw me, I didn't want to trip over.

The radio has switched to hip-hop music. His brother-in-law was supposed to be coming to collect me and take me to the station – a light railway is the only way back to the city and I've now done what I came here to do, which was to meet Tony and buy some of his pictures. I can't phone for a taxi because I don't think there are any taxis this far out and anyway his phone looks too complicated and besides I couldn't walk out of the house leaving it unlocked and full of pictures, though that's London thinking, not Bethell's Beach thinking. But I've been sitting here alone for nearly two hours, flicking through art books on the leather sofa which makes a right-angle round a coffee table. His house is all chic modern right-angles, but Tony is very much in love with the old-fashioned holiday home, known as a 'bach' or 'crib', built from scavenged and salvaged materials. The word 'bach' derives from 'bachelor', because these honky-tonk dwellings were originally retreats for males wanting to go off alone, whether married or not. Though part of the national mythology, the genuine bach is quite rare since most of them have been replaced by identikit bungalettes.

A shadow is edging across the inland sand dune as the sun goes down and tea trees, cabbage trees and ponga ferns fade into dusk. I don't particularly want to stay here all night. The ponga is a fern that looks like a palm tree and is one of a genus of tree-ferns which are native to these islands and have more decorative value than any plants I can think of. They are so lighthearted, sending up slim trunks and unscrolling their sprays of tendrils like Ascot hats.

Still no brother-in-law. Still no Ogle. Where is he? I can't spot a single human fleck on the far-off waves. What else can I tell you while I'm waiting? The Bethell family, who gave their name to this beach and were originally from Wales, are still down there some-where, six generations later, buried in the trees, having dinner in their homestead. I'm hungry. I've eaten the banana I brought with me. Shall I pinch one of his? It's gone seven o'clock.

Did I tell you how I got here? Firstly the ferry from Devonport to Auckland city proper – then the train from the new Britomart station, which is all that's left since the abolition of the main railway; but architecturally Britomart is a marvel, a steel grotto with steaming gardens constructed in the basement of the old Central Post Office. This is a car-country in the extreme and the only people who use railways or buses are paupers, weirdos, back-packers, school kids and myself.

Graffiti covered every smashed-up, unmanned railway station we passed through, and all done in that universal graffito scrawl which has no individual expression. Litter and graffiti are the beginning of the criminal mind. Suddenly one saw the underbelly, that this nation too is *fucked* like every other, that the whole world has surrendered to the suppurating, copulating mob. At Boston

Road we passed Auckland Gaol, a noble edifice in black volcanic rock with parapets and castellations ... Mount Eden ... Morningside ... Avondale ... I counted them off on the map inside the carriage, because it was impossible to read platform signs since graffiti obscured them at every stop. But by the time I got to Swanson things were looking up. Which was fortunate since that's where I had to get out.

Swanson is an attractive little place set among velour hills feathered with ferns and pampas grass. Jenny Nagle was picking me up at the station and taking me on to Ogle's, and bang on time there she was, swooping into the forecourt, with a pair of cherubs in the back, the Winthrop Boys, her sons Lewis and Archie, seven and five years old. Though we were late for the artist, Jenny was keen to show me the beach, where the Winthrop Boys whipped off their clothes with an unstoppable instinct for freedom and ran away like rabbits straight past a sign reading *Danger! Quicksand!* I was aghast but Jenny said there was no quicksand.

... I wander into Tony Ogle's hall and look through the window. No sign of life in the drive. All events frozen. Tony Ogle's vision is lush and panoramic, but what clinches his appeal for me are the architectural features, evidence of the human, which creep into the pictures: a corner of a verandah, a distant hut, an oil drum against clapboard, a towel, sometimes a small figure itself. I give way and take one of the bananas from the fruit bowl, eating it quickly in case he comes in while I'm only half through it.

Tony's pictures are all screenprints. He pulled out drawersful and eventually I chose three: a view of Cheltenham Beach through an open door, one of – good Lord, here he is.

'I guess you're not feeling too friendly,' he proposes.

'I was beginning to think that ... '

'Fancy a beer?'

He is amiable but uneasy. He was uneasy when I arrived, too. Perhaps it's artistic tension. But it's OK by me. I'm comfortable with uneasiness if it's someone else's. Less OK is that Tony doesn't want to take me to the station. He wants that brother-in-law to do it. He sweeps the faraway beach with binoculars, hoping to find a clue to the brother-in-law's whereabouts.

The last train is at 9.05 p.m. It's getting close. And now I'm getting uneasy too and say to him 'What's your brother-in-law like? Mine's a ****.' Tony gets the point, surrenders and agrees to drive me to the Waitakere halt, which doesn't look as though it's a railway station. Strange to say Tony has never seen it before. He asks in the Dairy. Yes – this is the Waitakere halt. The train will arrive in a few minutes. He waits with me in the spidery gloom and we find ourselves chatting in a relaxed manner for the first time. We both agree that the world these days is on the side of the nomad, the vagrant, the dodger. The train when it arrives – a couple of carriages – is empty …

A few stops down the line a middle-aged woman got in. She was thin, agitated, with short red hair, a raffia rucksack, and shrugged her shoulders and flashed me sudden nervous grins. 'I saw my husband die,' she announced. 'I'm from a village.' These two statements jumped out of her on top of each other. Followed by a third. 'I'm a bit eccentric.' She's too frazzled to stay silent. 'We're all a bit eccentric in my village. We all like loud music – I suppose the emptiness takes it away.'

'Takes it away?'

'It doesn't drive people mad because it can drift away into the emptiness.'

Two rapid grins.

'Where is your village?' I ask.

She utters some Maori words, impossible to remember, a twitchy white woman with flicky pale eyes and these split-second grins. 'I

saw my husband die,' she repeats. 'Two years ago. But you don't
get over it. Terrible. Terrible. He died on the floor in front of me.
I read a lot of theosophy. Sanskrit has words to describe these
things. The beyond.'

'I don't believe in the beyond.'

'Don't you?'

'Not any more.'

'There's lots out there.'

'I believe in the here and now. That's mystery enough for me.'

'There's lots we don't know.'

'Oh yes. A big mystery out there. But I feel the beyond is all part
of the here and now.'

'You don't believe in the afterlife. I've placed my four children
in safe hands.' She is hugging her raffia rucksack. 'And now I'm off
to have an adventure. This is going to be my afterlife. For a little
while anyway. Be careful while you are here. This is a violent
country now.'

Quite apart from the physical disorientation of one's body and
brain and magnetic field brought about by the rapidity of international travel, it also takes time to get the practical hang of things
at the destination: to learn what a letterbox looks like, for example,
or what the taxis and buses look like, what the food shops look like,
how much is 'expensive', where the internet points are likely to be
for checking emails (I don't carry a mobile phone). And I always
acquire so many books and papers that, even though I regularly
post stuff home, luggage is a real drag on public transport, not to
mention the danger of my back *going*. When my back went last
time, my physiotherapist Pippa Warrell said 'Whenever you are
about to pick up anything heavy, *hiss*. This activates the muscular
corset about the midriff, thereby protecting the weakness at the
base of the spine.' So I've been hissing like crazy. But I've decided:
if my back does go on this expedition there will be none of this

do-this-do-that-and-it-should-be-better-in-two-weeks, no, no, I'll
have it injected *immediately*. I'm not a public transport person as
it happens. None of my family is. I'll have to rent a car before
long.

~

OK, sorry to keep you waiting, this morning we're off on the Auckland to Napier bus. Mr and Mrs Jinks have kindly offered to give
me a lift to the bus station in their Rover. Mr Jinks googled me and
discovered that once upon a time I worked with Can – they are
great Can lovers. 'Oh, we drove all round Europe in the Dormobile
when we were first married,' says Mrs Jinks, 'playing Can!' Her
sweet face has gone soggy behind the wheel. He doesn't drive.

I ask them why Maori names have so little variation and Paul
says that it's because they have only fifteen or so letters in their
alphabet; not that they had writing – that was given to them by a
Reverend somebody or other. But I love to see these bilingual
signs, in Maori and English, even if they aren't evocative for me
except in a general way, because – as in Wales – they enhance the
sense of place.

Thankfully the bus isn't full and I find a panoramic seat on the
top deck. It seems ages before the driver gets in and when we pull
away it's to join a crawl along a jammed motorway – over there is
Ellerslie racecourse – over here a placard announces that Wan-
ganui Collegiate will be celebrating its 150th anniversary this year
– the driver says we are forty-five minutes behind schedule and it
takes more than an hour to clear the Auckland conurbation – the
Bombay Hills … roadside caff: Whitebait and Devonshire teas –
Hamilton, a town of motels and car showrooms – jams in and out
of towns – the by-pass concept hasn't arrived here yet – stop start
jerk – Cambridge with its glamorous stud farms … phew … now
at last – *at last* – we are fully into their famous countryside, which

doesn't resemble any countryside that I've seen before, and between Cambridge and Tirau it attains to a spellbinding arcadian fruition. Low hills are bumpy and uneven, with lines of poplars or elms on their crests. Small crags pierce the tilted pasture, and cows, with tails docked, graze between scattered boulders. Oak trees and palm trees, ponga and jacaranda are disposed individually to make of the wilderness an informal, otherworldly park.

There is a Maori passenger who skips off at every stop to knock back a bottle of beer and have a cigarette (since these things are forbidden on board), repeatedly holding up our getaway. He is smelly with booze, tobacco and unwashedness, but cheerful and quite different from everyone else, so unfailingly charming in fact that the bus driver, who obviously wants to rebuke him, finds he is unable to do so. When we all disembarked for a long break the Maori passenger was the only person to fondle the ears of a blind man's dog and talk to both. He has that presumptive familiarity with strangers which white society finds so awkward – no, no, now I'm being silly – I should say 'urban' society, since I have noticed this easy familiarity in the rural populations of Herefordshire, Devon and Yorkshire.

A host of schoolboys fills up the bus and the countryside flows dreamily past the window, with cherry blossom and end-of-season camellias now added to its repertoire. But there are no old colonial cottages, nor even handmade baches, just modern bungalows and characterless sheds. A huge expanse of pine plantation in the oncoming distance provides a distant backdrop to the idyll, like a long and brooding bass chord in Wagner. At the next stop some dark boys by the road look up at the white boys on the top deck and jeer in oblique tones. They have adopted the hip-hop style from American records and films, the sullen swagger laced with little explosions of cursing which has become the international style for the underdog male. Aboard, the Maori drinker is this time sitting next to a Sikh in a purple turban, not by choice I think but it was the only seat left when the Maori got back on. There is a perceptible *froideur* between them and they exchange not a word and their bodies are angled apart.

The approach to Lake Taupo is ugly, with vast areas given over to pine forestry. Maria Jinks had said 'It's always cold round Lake Taupo.' The Maori and the Sikh disembark and go their separate ways, obviously relieved that the angle between them can now be extended to maximum, and another group of schoolchildren scrambles aboard. They are very spotty, doubtless from feasting on the poor Anglo-American diet (French and Italian teenagers have much better complexions). Taupo itself is a holiday encampment extending for miles and miles in a bleak, lunar suburbia. There is something repulsive too about the lake, which is harsh and steely. And beyond, hideous vistas of dust where they've harvested pine trees, an endless nuclear-blasted heath to the limits of the horizon.

We are now on the Thermal Explorer Highway and eventually the deathscape switches to a natural landscape of low trees with silver branches tipped green, and noisy streams hidden at the bottom of gulleys lined with patches of rust-red scrub. Darkness is falling at 8 p.m. Behind me Japanese girls are talking and giggling with a male compatriot. It seems that, for a Japanese girl, to talk is to giggle. It's raining. There's not a light to be seen through the window. The darkness outside is absolute. Nothing much has changed since Anna Kavan and Ian Hamilton drove on this very road through a rainy night in 1941 and Anna wrote: 'I turned round once and looked out of the back window and the darkness was like a hole in the universe.'

~

The bus drives slowly through the streets of Napier glossy with rain and stops on a parade-ground of cement from where I take a taxi to the Te Pania Hotel, the most expensive in town. It's a holiday weekend and all cheaper hotels were fully booked. The Te Pania is ultra-modern, its Parisian glass curve overlooking Marine Parade. This is the main promenade which runs along beside the ocean. Marine Parade is silent except for the crash of waves muffled in darkness. It is empty except for a coloured fountain which glows in the night like a shrine to the goddess of neon pleasure. Its plinth sweats a sharp peppermint-green light and from it spurt upward sprays of water through which illuminations play in cobalt-blue, blood-red, lavender, and citric orange.

Turning back into the room, I unpack and order a supper of rock oysters with salad and await its arrival lying flat out on the bed. The joy of rock oysters is not only the completely unfishy and gentle taste of the sea they have but also the beauty of the shells, craggy outside, pearl within, wholly irregular, pure rococo. I don't think one should drink while eating oysters, not even champagne, because the flavour is so subtle. Afterwards I have a finger of vodka, cold and neat. On the radio Clare Martin sings 'Get Out of Town'.

~

Napier is the second city in the world to greet the new day after Gisborne. I awake at 8 a.m. and push back the floor-length curtains for my first-ever view of the South Pacific. Mist. Drizzle. Under a grey sky. The sea is a quivering jade green and in the morning I go out walking through cold wind and rain. Napier is like Noto, rebuilt after an earthquake in a unified, jolly, rather gimcrack manner. It is billed as the world's only art deco town, but its central streets are named after the English writers who were contemporary with the development of the first town: Tennyson, Browning, Dickens, Thackeray. Further out are older writers:

Milton, Shakespeare, Herrick, even a Chaucer Road South. But if this is a holiday weekend and the hotels are full, where are all the people? It is possible that I still haven't grasped what it is to be in a country which has a very low population and which is not on the way to anywhere else.

So I decide that in the absence of people I shall look at things, because Napier has a small museum of quality. Its opening room affords my first encounter with Maori woodcarving. Such ferocious faces! Why are these primitives so grim? Did nobody ever smile in the Stone Age? Was smiling considered too unimportant and too human for primitive art? When did smiling come in in art? The art of the Buddha sometimes smiles of course and he died in 483 BC at the age of eighty. I once found a smile in the Cairo Museum, on the ground floor, in room 14, New Kingdom, a sandstone head of an unknown king which had been found at Luxor. The young king was smiling! Which could well be the first smile in recorded history, since the New Kingdom ended in 1100 BC.

The Maori carvings, in totra wood, are old but glow with nutty health and look as though they've been oiled quite recently. They are of naked males. The one closest to me has an erection and so I can't tell if he's circumcised. Ah, those over there are not erect, and it seems … yes, they are circumcised. Beyond the cocks is 'Paths of Conversion', the depressing story of missionary activity in the Pacific, and crossing to the photo-record I mourn the loss of innocent sensuality on seeing sunny limbs imprisoned in a parody of Victorian dress – here is the beginning of many a Freudian fuck-up.

A couple of rooms are devoted to the 1931 Napier Earthquake, and we learn that days before the earthquake on 3 February, cattle refused to go into their sheds and the sea threw up unnaturally large waves. After the two main shocks (7.8 on the Richter scale) subterranean explosions with resonant booms continued for a long time, which must indeed have been terrifying but at the same time magnificent, like finding oneself in a Greek myth. A non-stop documentary film called *Survivors' Stories* pieces together the events and I enter the loop as a woman with grey locks called Lauris Edmond reads a poem about her child-hood experience of the cataclysm. To my amazement it's a brilliant poem but my attempts to track down the text, either in the museum itself or in Napier bookshops, fail; and to this day, I've been unable to find it.

Nearly all those adolescent boys who crowded on to my bus had their underpanted bums hanging out over the waistband of their trousers, exposing buttock cleavage. On coming across a competition in the roller-pit on Marine Parade this afternoon, I realise that this is part of the uniform of rollerskaters and skateboarders. They need to wear loose clothes to perform the manoeuvres and this has now reached the point where they deliberately wear trousers below the bum while somehow keeping the cock covered in front. In animal language such ostentatious displays of the rear-end are a plea for anal penetration, though the boys appear in most cases not to realise it.

Not only is it Labour Day Weekend, it's also the centenary (or something like it) of the Hawke's Bay Show, while the larger global conjunctions include the Festival of Diwali on Saturday, the ending of British Summer Time on Sunday, and the First Day of Ramadan on Monday. So it's all happening. Towards the end of Marine Parade is the Bank Holiday Gypsy Fair, a travelling enterprise of hippy stuff, folk art, homemade clothes, tarot reading, pony rides, portraits painted, smell of patchouli and tinkle of chimes in the bitter breeze. It is desolate, with the cold drizzle hitting again, blowing up from the south. Lights come on along the esplanade beneath the Norfolk pines. Overheard above the squall: 'We've got the teats for you. A slow one, and one medium fast.'

∽

This art deco thing – they are not taking it seriously. They think conservation is a matter of printing brochures. Yesterday I saw an art deco shop completely smashed through, its interior of pale green pillars mangled into rubble. As for the iconic Gaiety de Luxe Cinema in Dickens Street, all that remains is the outdoor Moorish balcony with a round-headed window; the rest has been chopped up into a café, a model railway exhibition and a Two Dollar Shop.

~

Some kid-slobs walk by, bums hanging out of dirty clothes. They sneer and hiss at a boy sitting on a bench, calling him 'gay'. He is similarly dressed and ignores them. Soon after, I pass a bar called Neil's Place, which in displaying the following sign gives a thumb-nail of contemporary youth fashion:

NO!!!
Track pants @ all
Numbered shirts
Hooded tops
Caps/beanies/sunglasses
Leather pants
Jackets and vests
Jandals, workboots, scuffs
Dirty or holey sneakers
Gang insignias
Drugs
Offensive/bad attitudes
Dirty faded ripped T-shirts
Dirty faded ripped jeans

The *patron* has decided to put his foot down. A society terrorised by its own children is the sickest of all societies.

~

Try to sleep. Insomnia. I've had more room service, more oysters, but too late in the evening. The protein boost leaps in the blood and the amino acids make me very randy. Napier of course is a wasteland for casual sex, merely a few families quietly window-shopping. Just as the girls don't do cleavage, New Zealand males seem to have discovered the secret of the cockless crotch. As they walk about in shorts or trousers there is never any suggestion, not even with the faintest shadow, let alone a bulge, that they have anything between their legs. The only other place I've encountered this complete effacement of dong was Austria.

~

The National Aquarium on Marine Parade is where I see my first kiwi, symbol of this land. Being nocturnal, kiwis are kept in darkness and it takes a little time for one's eyes to adjust to the dark brown light and be capable of discerning the brown humpbacked birds which potter about like old men in a brown garden. Here a prod, there a prod, with their beaks which are yellow, long and slender. They are careful, shy, endearing creatures, unable to bear any form of crudeness, so that when a harsh voice sounds 'Bredley, wait!', the kiwis wobble and shuffle out of sight, and though I hang on they do not reappear. The other remarkable creature exhibited in the aquarium has, likewise, nothing to do with water. This is the tuatara, the lizard with a vestigial third eye, rare survivor from the age of the dinosaurs. I scan the glassy enclosure for something freakish but nothing is to be seen. It must have shot back into its burrow. I notice that the impatient Bradley is on his way out the other side.

~

The Golden Bowl employs a recurring use of architectural metaphor: people and situations are compared to buildings, rooms, gardens. Since I am fascinated by the relationship between buildings and people I was hooked from the outset. The novel is written in an exceedingly slow time signature, but is not necessarily leisurely, for the psychological tension produces stress and drama as well as reflection, and there is about the great significance accorded to the badminton of small gestures something which is addictive. The narrative proceeds via those fine gradations of thought between people which usually go unsaid and often undetected. James gives them dialogue and explication but the interactions are at the level of telepathy. His later novels are really novels of telepathy.

Ian Sharp advised me to read some Maori writers and suggested Patricia Grace. When I dipped into her novels in Dymocks Bookshop, I found the usual Plain Jane prose which is the only permissible style in modern fiction. Though the geographical territory of English has increased enormously, its expressive range has been much reduced by simplified grammar and shrunken emotional vocabulary. Who cares if it is Plain Jane prose about Maoris or Measles or Mayfair or the Modern Media, when there is no challenge of interest in the medium itself? Judging by her photograph, Patricia looks mixed race. These racial representatives often are (Malcolm X and Bob Marley for example). The double origin may make them obvious bridges but can also make them rejected by both sides and oblige them to jump deliberately one way or the other. What does make me uncomfortable is the current convention, particularly common in the left-wing press, of describing mixed-race people as black, as though everyone who isn't 100 per cent white is black. They aren't. The racing driver Lewis Hamilton is often described as the first black champion in Formula One. He isn't. His mum's white. It must be a great bore for him constantly to be lined up for some dreary racial crusade. And while we're on the subject I can still remember as though it were yesterday the boxer Mohammed Ali appearing on the *Parkinson* show years ago and saying how blacks should marry blacks and whites should marry whites coz anything else was unnatural. Parky nodded sagely, refusing to challenge him, while Ali ranted on about how sparrows didn't go with blue-tits, or some crap like that, and I thought what a horrible stupid bully and of all the mixed-race kids watching their hero on prime-time TV and being told they were freaks. Ali's own mother was mixed race. Someone told me that 'mixed race' is the fastest growing ethnic group, but they didn't specify where. In England? In Europe? In the world? The mixed-race predicament of 'having to choose' is passé in a twenty-first century which functions increasingly through multiple identities. Anyway, the world is so jumbled up these days that everyone on the planet is going through an identity crisis. As for multi-culturalism, you'd be forgiven for thinking all it's done is create an industry of taking offence. We're all in ghettoes now. Comment is prejudice if you're not in my ghetto. But which ghetto shall I inhabit this week? I belong to quite a few. To what shall I take offence today?

SOME WORDS AND PHRASES NEW TO ME
Nature spread
Fucken bewdy
Queen Anne turrets
Wopwops
High studs
Trolley! (expression of surprise, i.e. truly)

≈

Bluff Hill is a crag dividing the port from Marine Parade and is the smart place to live in Napier, its wooden mansions having survived the earthquake. The walk up is taxing, but it's a sunny day and the scent of hawthorn and dog roses and nasturtium is supportive. At the top I'm wheezing but the Lookout has the best view to be had of Hawke's Bay. Green hills in kittenish heaps, with serious mountain ranges behind them, describe a great arc lapped by the saucer of the Pacific whose ceaseless sucking at the shore renders the water too dangerous for swimming. The beach therefore is deserted, miles and miles of it curving round in bands of grey and lemon. The silence is profoundly thrilling. Up here atop the grassy citadel there is not even the sound of breeze. A morose teenager in studded leather collar is making silent gestures of elopement to his girl-friend. Sparrows hop at one's feet, expecting food. One day something will break the silence, something dreadful. But not yet.

≈

The Napier to Wellington bus. I'm at the back with three boisterous brothers – Luke, Josh, can't remember the third one's name. The youngest is in my window seat, his two siblings in the paired seat behind. They wrestle, fart, and make silly jokes with each other, and after half an hour of this I'm compelled to turn round to the two older ones and say 'Can't you calm down a bit?' That was all that was necessary. Afterwards they were good as gold and got off at Palmerston North. Writing can make one very *particular*, more and more wanting to control everything. Periodically one has to break away and be cleansed of fussiness by dumping oneself in the river of ordinary life. It does one good to be bundled up uncomfortably with strangers and hassled by kids on a bus. We stop at Levin, where the streets are named after English cathedral cities: Oxford, Bath, Durham, Salisbury … Roadside sign: *Facial Eczema Risk!* The weather is still cool. Horses in the fields are dressed in blankets. Arum lilies grow everywhere like spring daffodils. The hills loom ever closer until we are driving right under them along the seashore. The beach is of low unpleasant rock and the sea looks intimidating.

The approach to Wellington, the capital, is via inlets and sub-urban gorges fuzzy with pubic shrubbery, spattered with cabins. One more swoop and there's the metropolitan clutter round the bay which looks like a lake and the bus drops us down at the main railway station on Waterloo Quay. It's a massive building with giant Doric portico, but trainless and ghostly and made older still by the fact that cab drivers, wearing jackets and ties, queue up outside in readiness for the non-existent rail passengers. One of them takes me to the Cambridge Hotel, which is a squat classical building with preserved interiors. Another good omen is the statue of 'Victoria Regina et Imperatrix' outside it. But I was discon-certed by the intervening drive along the waterfront, which seemed strangely bereft of any sort of building one might associate with a capital city.

~

Bowl out on to the street after a bad night failing to sleep more than forty winks at a stretch – my room is above the bar, which becomes a disco around 11 p.m. – and say good morning to Queen Victoria. Why are the English so ashamed of their Empire? They build a global miracle with their bare hands and look blushingly at the ground and mumble 'Terribly sorry.' The grandeur and opti-mistic energy of the imperial adventure, the *sheer exhilaration* of it, as well as its deep competence, can still be felt in lands such as this, in the open look of the people in the streets, in the grace and effectiveness of the political and legal arrangements, in the probity of public life, felt like the faint echoes of the cosmic big bang picked up by a sensitive radio telescope, that underlying hiss of the English genius. But where has all the architecture gone? Let's find out.

~

OK, I've walked and walked and I've found out and I'm in a state of shock. Where to begin? At the end, at the conclusion: Wellington has been even more catastrophically demolished than Auckland. This is the capital city, so one was looking for *style*. Style is not achieved by wholesale clearance of the past. And keeping a façade isn't style, it's wrapping – that is, it is image, and image can have no style of itself since style is not surface but comes from within. The only central street with historical architecture more or less intact is Cuba Street, which isn't grand but it has a fruity liveliness, and they are hoping to put a motorway through it. The Town Hall was once very grand but only the truncated rump remains in Civic Square. This is Wellington's central piazza and has been created from three old buildings and three new ones jammed together and the pooled space fed by a flight of stairs at an odd angle. It's all completely wonky, nothing is aligned with anything else, but that's fine because wonkiness becomes the integrating idea. I sat in it on a Saturday night at eight o'clock in the evening with the lights sparkling in the trees and it was delightful. *But I was the only person there*. Everyone else was in Cuba Street.

The reason I was sitting in Civic Square was to recover from a particular shock. A building I was eager to locate was one I'd seen in old photographs. It occupied a prominent corner on Wellington's most prestigious thoroughfare, Lambton Quay. Tall arcaded windows ran up through half a dozen floors and were stopped at the roof by loggias with deep eaves redolent of Florentine palazzi. The corner, connecting the two façades, began with an entrance anchored by fat Babylonian pillars, and climaxed at the top with an umbrella pagoda flanked by urns, everything superbly accomplished to the very tip of its flagpole. I read into it Otto Wagner, Stravinsky, Diaghilev, Freud, Mahler, all that, and research later revealed that it had indeed been put up in 1917. It was equal to anything of its date anywhere, but that pagoda at the top seemed to say 'No, not Vienna, Paris, Berlin or London – this is the Pacific!' As I approached its location my hand went up to my mouth. I checked the street-map. My forehead prickled. I looked around. Something heavy weighed in my stomach. It wasn't there. In fact almost the whole of Lambton Quay wasn't there ... Lambton Quay, which was the glory of the city, the Champs Elysées of Australasia, the Piccadilly of the South Pacific, the nation's grandest boulevard. It is not straight but follows the old shoreline and moves with a rocking sinuosity. So its sumptuous parades would have unfolded ahead of you in shifting, swaying vistas. And now? Virtually nothing left. All junk to the sky.

Later I was to ascertain that my particular favourite was called the State Fire Insurance Building. It was owned by the Government, the Government destroyed it, and the Government replaced it with another governmental building called the Department of Internal Affairs, a very sullen thing. I'm not anti-modern. I'm anti-bad. I'm pro holding on to what's good. Who the hell is running this place? I couldn't bear it and turned off down a side street and there in front of me was another corner building, a dirty, pinkish, down-at-heel confection. It was the St George Hotel, where the Oliviers had stayed on their 1948 tour. I thought I'd go inside for some comfort, but turned back in disgust. The ground floor was terribly disfigured and had become a beer supermarket. The rest was a student hostel. Valéry considered architecture the supreme expression of repose, but here it has produced violence. We have been lulled by our prosperity and technology into thinking that civilisation is automatic. It isn't. It has to be worked for and guarded because, as history repeatedly reminds us, it collapses quite easily. I don't feel very well.

≈

My right knee is twingeing badly due to an excess of walking. Beneath my room the hotel bar is drilling bang-bang music up to me. Wellington is such a hard city. I'm not against hard cities per se. Soft cities can be just as self-destructive. Paris is a hard city and I love it, but only in cool weather. One must visit hard cities from time to time because certain things can only be achieved by being hard. New York is a hard city. Florence and Manchester are hard cities. Rome and London are soft cities. Edinburgh is hard, Glasgow is soft. Marseilles is very hard but Nice is soft, though it thinks it's hard. Los Angeles is soft. Calcutta is soft, Bombay is hard. Singapore, Hong Kong, Tokyo, all hard. Berlin is hard. Moscow is hard, St Petersburg soft. Mexico City funnily enough is hard. Rio is soft. Sydney is soft, apparently. Peking, I'm willing to bet, despite trying hard to be hard, is probably soft. Vienna, too, tries to be hard but is wonderfully soft. Budapest soft, Copenhagen hard, Amsterdam soft, Oslo soft, Stockholm hard, Madrid hard, Barcelona soft, Cairo soft, Istanbul soft, Tel Aviv soft, Riyadh hard, Tehran rock hard, Cape Town soft, Dublin soft, Brussels – amazingly – is soft, and certain things can only be achieved by being soft. I could only ever live in a soft city. All cities are becoming increasingly hard in their centres. All cities are harder in their centres than on their peripheries. Cities which still have unusually soft centres are London, Calcutta, Venice and Los Angeles.

~

Roger Lewis sent me a letter.

> I have a great-aunt out there, my grandfather's youngest sister (of thirteen siblings) – Aunt Nora, born 23 November 1913 and the very last link with my Monmouthshire Edwardian past. I believe she is still alive and she might just afford you a Henry James-ish half page. She lives near Wellington in a place called Eastbourne.

She was still in the phonebook and ninety years old this month. So I rang Aunt Nora, explained that I was a friend of Roger's and had just come right across the world and had news of him, that I'd be catching the ferry over to Eastbourne at the weekend, and would love to call on her for a cup of tea and say hullo if I may.

Her response was 'I'd rather not.'

～

The housekeeper at the Cambridge Hotel addressed a chamber-maid in querulous tones: 'Room 211 has gone through ten loo rolls in three days. Better keep an eye open.'

～

To the Botanical Gardens. The cab drivers read a lot here while they're waiting and mine was reading *1984* when I got in. He exclaimed passionately 'And it's still irrelevant today!' Well, thank God for that. Long may it remain so. I surrender to a sticky medi-tation on the precariousness of beauty, in a glasshouse in front of Sir Walter and Lady Norwood's lily pond, where I am transfixed by a vegetoid monster hanging over the syrupy water. Its fleshy leaves fan out from a shaggy lolling trunk strung up to a beam. The label identifies this shuddering horror as *Polypodiaceae Platyc-erium superbum*. It takes me ages before I read the last word correctly.

～

Call on Antrim House, the headquarters of the Historic Places Trust, to enquire about the lost State Fire Insurance Building but nobody there can recall anything.

'Nothing on our database,' says the man. Oh, for heaven's sake. Fuck your database, haven't you got eyes, a memory, a heart? I show him an old photograph. 'Doesn't ring a bell,' he responds limply. Another of them suggests I contact a man called Chris Cochran. 'He's a conservation architect. He knows a lot about old buildings.' Back at the Cambridge Hotel I do telephone him; and acquire an ally at last!

'To be honest I hardly remember it myself,' confesses Mr Cochran over the phone. 'I remember more the wonderful Moorish Midland Hotel, which must have been next to it on Lambton Quay.'

'Wasn't it loved, my building?'

'No, I don't think it was. It went without anyone much noticing. There was no outcry. No opposition was mounted.'

'Even more important that I should love it then. It was a building of international quality.'

'Buildings of that period – 1918, 1919 was it?–'

'1917. The year my father was born.'

'–just weren't appreciated. If I remember, a group of architectural students did save one of its front door pillars. I don't know what happened to that – oh – I do remember – there is a famous 1940 building next to it – still standing though mutilated – and set into the *pavement* outside there's a sort of sculpture made from bits of the 1940 and 1917 building. Look, how long are you in Wellington for? You must come over for a drink.'

'Thank-you, I'd like to. One other thing – you know the Old Vic Tour of 1948?'

'Certainly.'

'Well, do you remember which theatre they used in Wellington?'

'The St James.'

'You've got a St James Theatre too?'

'Yes.'

'Is it still standing?'

'Remarkably it is. They tried so hard to pull it down. Only a very

determined effort by conservationists saved it at the last minute
– and they used some words from Laurence Olivier in the
campaign.'

~

After a rigmarole at reception I've moved up a floor from the disco
bar banging beneath my bedroom. My new room has a view on to
the side street and is twice the size. Let's hope I can get some sleep
now … No – this hotel is jinxed. There's something outside my
window which makes a high-pitched screaming noise … I've popped
across to the Bay Plaza, who have given me a deal. $90 per night, a
few dollars cheaper than my room here. I'll move there. The Cambridge is sexy in the wrong way – lots of noise and no sex.

~

It was a very windy day. Walking upwards, away from the flatness
of waterside Wellington, I approached some bushes and, pushing
through, found myself at the foot of a broad flight of stone steps.
They were green with unuse and I took care not to slip as I found
myself rising, with astonishment, into a major piece of abandoned
cityscape. It wasn't visible from any of the main thoroughfares and
must have been shut out of the action on purpose.

A tall campanile with attached terraces fronted a massive pil-
lared temple, all strapped together with staircases and balustrades
into a masterpiece of 1930s heroic architecture. The main block,
in grey stone with pink stains, is ostensibly Greek but really it's
cubist, while flanking urns of enormous size give an Assyrian
touch. I'd been thinking it odd that the capital of a civilised nation
should have no national gallery, and as I read across the lintel the
conundrum was answered: the National Gallery and Dominion
Museum opened by Viscount Galway in 1936. They've closed it
down.

I looked about me – no cars – no people – nothing. The buffeting wind aggravated the desolation. But the building wasn't locked. I pushed open one of its giant metal doors and entered beneath a grille of bronze stars. The entrance hall was cube-shaped with galleries on square pillars and marbled in various fawns and meat-pinks. Staircases rose from left and right, with handrails supported by bronze kiwis on panels of fluted plasterwork. The glazings were of jazz-age geometry in lemon and pale pink glass, conferring a gentle light. Hexagonal lamps on chains of bronze dropped into the air. Another great hall beyond, and twice the size, was also empty. I was entirely alone. Ascending one of the flights, I found that the kiwi banisters continued round into the upper landing and ahead of me stood what must be the finest wooden doors in the southern hemisphere, two pairs of them, each door constructed from a dozen carved and recessed panels, forty-eight panels in all. These doors gave admission to what would have been the upstairs picture galleries, whose walls were now bare and cold.

The whole arrangement, with its receding spaces, was a marvel of co-ordination, and demonstrably the work of an architect who knew just about everything there is to know concerning volume, proportion, rhythm, design and harmony (a firm called Gummer & Ford, it turned out). They closed down the National Gallery because Viscount Galway had opened it and it bore the word 'dominion' on the front. Perhaps they are embarrassed by their heritage. It's too grand for them. They now prefer junk buildings the way they prefer sloppy clothes. From the terraces the view across the city was entire. The wind moaned and whined and sighed.

The tall campanile out front resembled an archaic electric generator or some other apparatus from Jules Verne. It seemed heathen, but on entering a door at its base I realised it was the most visible feature of something called the National War Memorial, whose chapel had been inserted into the hillside beneath. For many minutes I stood in the secret chapel. It was ablaze with martial insignia. Here, in the public sanctuary of the nation, there was no one, presumably because the whole complex and idea has been effectively shuffled out of sight by reallocation of routes so that no major roads or sightlines or tourist tracks go near it.

I jumped backwards as a caretaker popped out of a stone cubby-hole. 'Windy,' he observed in a slightly camp manner.

'Yes.'

'Thinking?'

'Yes.'

'It's nice, isn't it.'

'Yes. I like that red stone down there.'

'That's Hanmer marble, that is.'

'Have you got any postcards?'

'Somewhere. One or two. We don't get any call for them these days. Do you want to look at the bells?'

'Where are they?'

'Up there. At the top. They were made in Croydon.'

'Is there a lift?'

'Yes, there is,' he said.

'Because I've done my knee in.' It was true – the right knee was getting worse – I've been walking miles every day. The lift was the size of a vertical coffin. We both entered it and he shut us in. I thought he might grope me but he behaved like a gentleman. It was black as pitch in there. Then he had to open up again to admit sufficient light to find where the controls were and what to do to yank us upwards.

'I think I move this … ' He closed the grilles once more, fumbled at the wall and moved a lever. I couldn't see a single dot. I was absolutely petrified. 'I hope this is right,' he speculated with a giggle.

'Haven't you worked the lift before?'

'No.'

A tremor ran up from my ankles and blossomed in my knees, liquefying them. The crate moved aloft slowly, making random and hair-raising clicking noises – as did my heart. Every plummeting lift in every ciné noir film I've ever seen zipped through my head. Periodically our blackness was intercut by bands of whiteness as we passed floor openings. There were loads of them. We rose for a hideous eternity. More and longer blackness. Clunk. The top.

'Here we are,' he said, 'the clavier chamber.'

Honey-coloured floor and banks of thin cables – it looked like a loom in a Halifax carpet mill. The cables governed the playing of the bells, which were in gantries above. A little ladder ran up to them.

'Do you want to go up there?'

'No! … I'll look from here.'

'It's got seventy-four. One of the biggest carillons in the world.'

'Do you know what the art of bell-ringing is called?'

'I don't.'

'Campanology.'

'Is it?' He frowned and laughed at the same time.

'Are you the campanologist?'

'Me? Never. Anyway, we say carillonist.'

'Perhaps it's different. Perhaps campanology is hanging from a rope. It's terrifying up here.'

'It is, isn't it,' he concurred.

'But you're the caretaker.'

'That doesn't mean it isn't terrifying. Look out here. It's a long way down.'

'No. Yes. I know it is.'

'Go on, look at the view,' he urged.

'I'm not going near the view.' Besides, there were banging noises coming from outside. The wind did not howl around the tower but bumped it, like something in boxing gloves trying to get in. The tower, constructed from reinforced concrete in the 1930s, was a rigid structure. It didn't sway, or give, so much as respond abruptly to being bumped.

'What if there's an earthquake?'

'Then we'd be in the wrong place,' he replied phlegmatically.

'Can we go down now?' My legs were feeling distinctly watery again, and I knew we'd have to be reburied alive in the vertical coffin, shoulder to shoulder, breath to breath, and I sort of wanted to get on with all that, put it behind me rather than have it ahead of me.

He plucked at some of the cables with a nonchalant hand. 'We've got an American carillonist at the moment. He's very good. But doesn't do it on Saturdays.' The American had a large box of Quality Street on the go in one of the corners. 'He came down in quite a sweat once, saying this bloody thing's moving in the wind, I can't stay up there a second longer. He doesn't like doing it in a high wind. Now … let me see … if I pull this the other way, maybe it will take us down.'

Once again he clanged the folding grilles, pulled back the lever, and the floor gave way. Down. Slowly, clickingly, but − strange to say − satisfyingly, as every second deleted more and more the abnormality and brought us closer to normality, a descent into life. By the time we'd stepped out on to the lower platform and nipped down the stairs into the chapel entrance, we were both euphoric.

'Where are you going next?' he asked.

'Invercargill.'

He laughed. 'You're not, are you?'

'Why does everyone laugh when I say Invercargill?'

'My brother lives there. They can talk about anything down

there. They'll look at a drawing pin and go on and on about it – for ages.'

~

The hellish noise in my bedroom is, I discover, some ventilation device on the roof above my room. It turns when the wind blows, making a squealing noise, and of course the wind blows most of the time in Wellington. It was blowing when I arrived in this room and has been blowing ever since. I turn on the television and find that it is a third of the way through *Mulholland Drive*, the most haunting American film in years, a dream film about the failure of dreams and wholly unAmerican in its refusal to *explain*. People forget that failure is as important to evolution as success.

~

Te Papa is the new national museum on the waterfront, designed in a colourful irrational style, with an admired natural history department and important Maori rooms; but when I visit I discover that the European collection is kept locked in dungeons and the fact that we're in a Western English-speaking democracy has been eliminated from what the museum has on display. They don't even exhibit the famous portrait of their most celebrated author, Katherine Mansfield. In fact the receptionists aren't aware of this picture's existence, so they summon a curator called Tony Mackle. He's very on the ball and takes me below, apologising all the while for current museum policy; and through locked metal doors to the secret bunker where the European art is sequestered from public gaze as though it were an obscenity. In silence he pulls out from the racks Anne Rice's portrait of Katherine Mansfield.

It's a very strong painting, gaudy but not garish, intense but not sullen, done in Cornwall in 1918. The scarlet shape of the sitter's dress knocks you back at first. Then you adjust, drawn in by the power of the eyes. The head is posed slightly forward and the facial expression is concentrated, pushing out of the picture at an angle of forty-five degrees, indifferent to the viewer. The candour and aggression of the eyes are issuing a challenge: 'I don't lie to you so don't you dare lie to me.' How often I've wanted to say the very same thing to people and held back, because that attitude doesn't win you friends. But I'm getting better. I'm learning to say it more – as I've suffered more from liars. You give honesty and discover you've been given counterfeit in return. It's the most painful thing of all in personal relationships.

There is a fracture in Mansfield's deportment. The head is perfectly balanced on the neck but the body is slumped and on a tilt. The red dress has slipped slightly over to one side. The scoop of the neck is off-centre. And the small breasts are flattened into squares. The painter has caught the mix of petulance and sensuality in Mansfield's mouth which, judging from photographs, always looked as though it was in the aftermath of a slightly disappointing snog. Tony Mackle, with a shrug of hopelessness, slides the picture back into its annihilating slit.

I look around the morgue. Hundreds of canvases shut away in upright drawers. A pair of huge Frank Brangwyn murals, scenes of Venetian life, are pinned against a wall.

'There were six of these altogether,' he says.

'Where are the other four?'

'Dunedin.'

'Are they shown?'

'Not when I was last there.'

It's claustrophobic down here, tense with the pressure of incarceration. 'Show me – let us say – two more prisoners,' I suggest.

'Anything in particular?'

'I want you to choose.'

He pulls out a lustrous William Nicholson, *Zinnias,* and an

S. J. Peploe, *Still Life*, just as good. We stare at them speechlessly. 'That's the strength of the collection,' he says. 'British art from the first half of the twentieth century. But we're not allowed to show it.'

I explain the story of the William Hodges copies sent out from England and ask 'Do you think they could be somewhere down here?'

'Oh no. Everything is meticulously accounted for. To tell the truth I've never heard of any Hodges copies. Perhaps they were sent but never arrived and are languishing somewhere. We lent the Mansfield portrait to Edinburgh once. Afterwards they crated it up and dispatched it back to us. But it never arrived. We asked "Where's our picture?" They said "Hasn't it arrived yet? We sent it ages ago." Mass panic. They'd addressed it to the National Gallery, Wellington. But we don't have a national gallery any more. It was found sitting in the gallery at Wellington … in I think it was Illinois.'

I need air and thank Tony but, inspired by the three colourful life-enhancing pictures I have seen, I move on to Courtenay Place in order to gain admission to the St James Theatre, which is sited there. I wish to maintain the flow of high culture – which is the European in me. The St James Theatre has an impressive classical façade on to the street but its heavy doors are bolted shut and it is some time before I work out that admission is gained through a restored art deco building next door, to which it is now married.

As with the St James Theatre in Auckland, this one was designed by Henry Eli White. I found out something about him from Chris Cochran, who's a great admirer of his work. Born in Dunedin in 1877, White had his own building business while still in his teens. He designed over a hundred theatres around Australasia and most of them seem to have been called St James or His Majesty's. When no more theatres were required he switched to mining dolomite for lightbulbs and ended his days sailing a yacht round Sydney Harbour from one waterside cocktail-party to another. He died in 1952. The Wellington St James was opened in 1912 and it's less momentously weird than the Auckland one, its interior fitted up in a restrained and Frenchified style enlivened with gilt cherubs. But by the time the Old Vic Company arrived it was already doubling as a cinema. Where the Oliviers blazed, Ralph Richardson and Sybil Thorndike were to follow. Later Winifred Atwell, Vera Lynn, the Leningrad Ballet and Dave Brubeck were brought here by Sir Robert Kerridge, but by the time Kerridge Odeon sold the theatre to a developer in the mid-1980s it had reverted to showing films and was drawing in only a few dozen patrons. In the subsequent drawn-out battle to save it Laurence Olivier's words were heard once again: 'Don't let any theatres be pulled down. The building of theatres seems to be an art we have lost.'

~

Katherine Mansfield's Birthplace is perched above a roaring motorway which, after the passing in 1967 of a Parliamentary Act, the authorities were able to drive straight through Wellington's most venerable quarter. What should have been the city's bay-villa Belgravia overhung by thick woods, and which is still somehow the embassy district, was sliced in half and destroyed for ever. The motorway passed through the heart of Bolton Street Cemetery, the colony's historic burial ground, causing 3,693 disinterments. Does it have to be true that the less people have, the more they throw it away?

There's no one else viewing the Birthplace at present and I potter unimpeded through this shrine to the modest good sense of middle class colonialism, passing from one small room to another, each filled with objéts of comfort and ingenuity, each the venue long ago for carefully managed social interactions. Oh, middle-classes of the world, unite – you have nothing to lose but your thugs! While I'm scrutinising a copper kettle with elaborate heating arrangements under its base, a little visage in specs leans across me and says 'There's a video upstairs, you know.'

It's the assistant curator, Miss Jill Mathews.

'Is there? What's it of?'

'Her.'

I'd better go up there then. In a bedroom, arranged with viewing chairs instead of a bed, I switch on the official film of the author's life and settle down for a wallow: to retreat into the past is such a delicious temptation because really it's the only place where one is safe. At first I can hardly hear anything above the pulsing roar of the motorway outside, but such is the interest of the story – the melancholy tale of a young girl becoming the first New Woman and getting it heroically wrong – that my attention in due course blocks out the filthy noise.

There was something seriously inane at work in Mansfield's erotic life. Here at the shrine I thought they might pull their punches on that account, but they don't. She came to live in London in 1908 at the age of nineteen and by the end of the following year she'd got pregnant by one man, married a second (the marriage lasted one night), had a miscarriage, and contracted gonorrhoea from a third. Her dithering and ongoing bisexuality, the death of her brother in the Great War, the second husband, John Middleton Murry, and her early death from tuberculosis at Gurdjieff's commune are further lurid themes. There's no more pitiful sight than a woman grovelling to a creep who's unworthy of her, and Middleton Murry was vain and morose. He had 'a faculty of estranging you by a manner which suggests that you are in a stage of development from which he has just emerged ... ' (William Gerhardie).

Mansfield's brief and productive happiness at Menton in

1920–21 was illustrated, in my recollection of the video, by grainy footage of figures larking for the camera under grey palm trees and parasols, with someone doing a silly dance in a striped bathing costume among flickering sunlight. But I'm pretty sure there were no home movies in this video, just contemporary photographs, so that these capers are a trick of the memory and most of what follows is a film of my own.

The official video did not explore the gonorrhoea question. It was mentioned in a throwaway line towards the end, but in fact Katherine contracted it early on, from a Polish boyfriend in 1909. The disease was untreated, maybe undiagnosed for many years, and as a result of it, her TB when it came was exceptionally virulent and did not respond to care. She was an oddly infernal, Baudelairean girl, altogether stranger and stronger than her reputation, which is that of the writer of wistful short stories (her writing is stronger than that too). As a New Woman she did have something of H. G. Wells's *Ann Veronica* (1909); in that novel one may read 'If individuality means anything it means breaking bounds – adventure. Will you be moral and your species, or immoral and yourself? We've decided to be immoral.' But she was of course far more original and colourful than that: a disciple of Oscar Wilde and Gurdjieff; mistress of ceremonies at Madame Strindberg's cabaret-nightclub, the Cave of the Golden Calf off Regent Street. Katherine's first book, *In a German Pension* (1911), was amazingly advanced, anticipating by many years the streamlining in modern fiction usually credited to Ronald Firbank and Ernest Hemingway. With her archetypal antipodean yearning to see the world, the shy sinning, the head-need to sin even if the body didn't want it, she had transferred from a country which had female suffrage to a country which did not and one which defeated her as a woman though it did not break her. The offspring she never had are born in her stories, which are teeming with children.

It was her father who recommended Menton in 1919 on one of his motor tours. Katherine's first choice had been San Remo, the seaside resort which had been so kind to the epileptic, rheumatic and homosexual Edward Lear for the last seventeen years of his life. But the Italians had lately taken robust measures against tuberculosis and the hotel in San Remo, on divining her condition, said she would have to leave and pay for the fumigation of her apartment there. So she moved to a private villa in the hideously named resort of Ospedaletti nearby.

Ever since her first haemorrhage, at the Hotel Beau Rivage in Bandol in 1918, Katherine had been shifting about, looking for the ideal climate. Her husband remained in London and her letters to him are upsetting in their attempts to maintain the illusion of love. The arrival of her rich father in a deluxe motor cheered her no end. In a letter to Middleton Murry she wrote that bowling along the roads 'was *thrilling* for me. I didn't dare to speak hardly because it was so wonderful & people laughing & silly Papa talking Maori down the whistle to the chauffeur ... They were horrified by the cold. Pa said at Menton they have had *none* of this bitter wind. They said Menton was warm, with really exquisite walks, sheltered. I said I'd consider going there in the spring. But I won't.' But she did.

Menton was never fashionable – Edward VII, who was the arbiter of these things during the *belle époque*, never visited it – and it still doesn't have a first-class hotel. But with the mildest climate in France, it became second home to the tubercular English, who formed the largest colony by far. It was subsequently established, some time in the 1930s, that a warm climate doesn't make much difference to the progress of the disease and anyway medicine was able to eradicate it in Europe (until globalisation started to bring it back in recent years).

Clinically beneficial or not, most people would prefer to die where there's a sparkle in the air and so those remittance invalids were wheeled out in cots on to the terraces and coughed their last in serried ranks looking south, their baskets of bloodied handker-chiefs subsequently incinerated because tuberculosis is a conta-gion. An air of malaise always overhung the town's wedding-cake charm, but today this malaise (crutches, neck braces and wheel-chairs still bedeck the promenades) has been rendered somewhat acrid by the modern flats put up recklessly in old operatic streets.

When I revisited Menton recently, after a gap of twenty years or more, I booked into the Prince de Galles on the promenade du Soleil. The hotel used to be barracks for the guard of the Palais Carnolès, which lies behind it. Built by one of the Monégasque princes in the seventeenth century, the pink and white palais is now the municipal art gallery and on a fresh spring morning, creaking across wooden floors from saloon to saloon, I discover that the one really striking picture it contains is an oil by an artist previously unknown to me, a man called Maurice Hensel. Painted in 1914, *Portrait de femme buvant l'absinthe* is a quintessential rep-resentation of the Katherine Mansfield/Sally Bowles/Robin Hyde/ Delmira Agustini type. It's all there in black and phlegm green and muddy purple: the bohemian adventure, the stylish shabbiness, the courage. And in the hollow eyes – I was going to say 'disillu-sion', but looking more carefully I see that's not true. What makes this picture so memorable is that in those green eyes hope, pleas-ure, love of life and a predatory eroticism still shine, and this is reinforced symbolically by the dark pink flower in the beret. They always forget that, don't they, the puritans; that though the pleas-ures of life can exact a high price, without them life is odious and drab and not worth living. No, this *femme buvant* is not to be pitied, not to be patronised, not to be written off. Who was she? Impossible to discover. As for the artist Hensel, he is hardly better known. Born in Paris in 1890 or 1891, he specialised in depicting women of easy virtue. In 1918 he left for Algeria and by the 1930s was in the Pacific, doing gouaches and aquarelles of young Tahitians. Where and when he died is a mystery, one which has faded on some distant shore of white sand and blue waves and eternal sunshine.

Quite a few of the 1890s people ended their days in Menton. Aubrey Beardsley, Richard Le Gallienne , Robert de Montesquiou. It remains a town of ghosts, and Katherine Mansfield had a dream there of meeting Oscar Wilde and wrote it down in a letter to her husband:

> In a café. Gertler met me. 'Katherine you must come to my table. I've got Oscar Wilde there. He's the most marvellous man I ever met. He's splendid!' Gertler was flushed. When he spoke of Wilde he began to cry – tears hung on his lashes but he smiled. Oscar Wilde was very shabby. He wore a green overcoat. He kept tossing & tossing back his long greasy hair with the whitest hand. When he met me he said: 'Oh *Katherine!*' – very affected. But I did find him a fascinating talker. So much so I asked him to come to my home. He said would 12.30 tonight do? When I arrived home it seemed madness to have asked him. Father & Mother were in bed. What if Father came down & found that chap Wilde in one of the chintz armchairs? Too late now. I waited by the door. He came with Lady Ottoline. I saw he was disgustingly pleased to have brought her. Dear *Lady* Ottoline & Ottoline in a red hat on her rust hair ... He said 'Katherine's hand – the same gentle hand!' as he took mine. But again when we sat down – I couldn't help it. He *was* attractive – as a curiosity. He was fatuous & brilliant!

I think Wilde, or his milieu at least, reappears in Mansfield's homosexual story 'Je ne parle pas français' ... Not long ago Francis King came round to my flat in London for lunch and he told me he'd been very much involved in the Katherine Mansfield Prize funded by the municipality of Menton. Why were you involved, Francis?

'Because I won it once.'

'Oh, when was that?'

'I can't remember. Yes I can. It was … 1965. It was established by the Mayor of Menton, who was in those days a very cultivated man. Actually there were two prizes, one for a French short story and another for one in English. I won it with "A Corner of a Foreign Field", which was about Japan, so I went out to Menton and we had this weekend in a lovely hotel and there was a ceremony at that house.'

'The villa where Katherine had lived?'

'Yes, the Villa Isola Bella.'

Which sounds idyllic but it's right on the railway line by the Garavan station. Maybe people didn't mind it in those days, as the railway also runs along the beach at San Remo, and at La Napoule, and Taormina, and lots of other places. But all that smoke – and Katherine's poor lungs like rotten lace!

'The Mayor made a speech,' continues Francis, 'and I was presented with the money and I had to make a speech and then somebody else made a speech and I met Lauris Edmond. She was staying in the flat at the villa on a six-month scholarship and we got on extremely well. We had a correspondence for quite a while afterwards.'

'Like me you originally thought oh this nice–'

'Yes, this nice housewife.'

After seeing her read her poem in the earthquake film at the Napier Museum I had checked Lauris out and so was able to say 'She had six children, you know, Francis, and published her first volume at the age of fifty-one, almost as late as Herrick. After a lifetime's service to others she escaped into the solitude of writing,

like a swallow uncaged. She did a great poem about the word
"yes".'

'I'd like to read that. What's it called?'

'"The Subject in Hand".'

'I'll look it up, because she sent me copies of her books and then
I realised just how good she was. The next time the Mansfield
Prize was handed out – I think it was every two years it was given
– I was invited back to be one of the judges. Then I was invited to
be a judge *again* because I got on very well with the Mayor whose
name I've forgotten. This steak's very good.'

'It's fillet. I got it at Kingsland's round the corner. More veg?
Who were the judges when you won it?'

'Raleigh Trevelyan was one I remember and I think Olivia
Manning. Yes, more veg please. Poor Olivia Manning didn't win it
because the year she was up for it Rayner Heppenstall was one of
the judges and he said "We want to have a pleasant weekend and
we know perfectly well that if Olivia Manning wins there are obviously going to be problems because you know how quarrelsome and
difficult she is, so we don't want to give it to her." So they gave it to
that Scottish writer – what's he called – George Mackay Brown.
Because they thought he would be easier to get on with, more
amenable, because we all had to travel out together and so on.'

'I didn't know Olivia Manning was a nightmare.'

'She wasn't to me. She was one of my closest friends. But she
was a great complainer and was known as Olivia Moaning. Olivia
was full of gossip, most of it totally inaccurate. What was rather
interesting was that on one of these occasions when we were celebrating on the terrace outside the villa – it was some sort of anniversary of Katherine Mansfield's brother's death in the First World
War, the beloved brother – this strange figure in his early twenties
suddenly appeared, carrying a rucksack and wearing shorts with
these very sunburnt legs and very outdoor-looking and very

handsome. He'd tramped, you see, over the mountains and come down into Menton, and we all looked at this person who hadn't been invited, who'd just walked on to the terrace and stood a little way off staring at us and not speaking, oh, he was the most beautiful young man, and we all agreed that it was just like the ghost of Katherine Mansfield's brother. Even his clothes might have been of that period. It was a very ghostly feeling. Then he vanished. He was gone. Later I saw him in the town and went up and spoke to him and he said yes, he'd always admired Katherine Mansfield, he was a New Zealander, and, well, er, you see, he then came to stay with me in London. Now he is married with wife and children.'

'Did you have him?'

'Well, I thought I can't make a pass at my age so I didn't.'

'Might you have got somewhere had you'd tried?'

'Well, the awful thing was I had a friend called David Turley, who's dead now, who was *far* from attractive, he was a very sweet man though, and he was very bold and made the pass and they started a relationship.'

'This is the secret.'

'Yes, one must be bold.'

'Because otherwise they just stand there.'

'And expect one to do something.'

'Yes, I did in my youth,' I say, 'stood there making myself available and hoping someone would just start on me, because at that age one doesn't have the confidence to take the initiative with someone of an older generation and one was longing to be sort of … *dishevelled*, often not because you fancied the other person as such, but because you wanted to connect with the wider world and any form of connection was valid. But now it's the other way round it's sometimes disconcerting – that they just stand there giving not the slightest hint even with body language. I'm prepared to take the initiative but one does need some kind of hint that it's OK, I mean I'm not a rapist. The problem, especially with the straight ones, is that they're saying – I'm making myself available to you but I can't say so and you must take all the responsibility. But it's amazing what you can do to people if you keep telling them they're beautiful. Do you still enjoy sex, Francis?'

'Yes, I do.'

'But you said you didn't make a pass at that man because you were afraid he'd think you too old.'

'That was when I was considerably younger. It's only since I became really old that I've realised how many gerontophiles there are.'

I refill Francis's glass.

'Mmm, pink champagne, lovely, refreshing, *very* good,' he says in the buoyant convivial tone which survived unimpared a recent mugging and stroke. 'Harold Nicolson always gave me pink champagne when he dined me at the Travellers'. The funny thing is, when having sex, I seem never to suffer the breathlessness that assails me when I have to go upstairs for the handkerchief that I have yet again forgotten.'

'What about Viagra?'

'Never used it. Never had to. I have no problems with erections but my cock seems to have shrunk. Old people often find that this happens. I've never gone in for anal sex. I prefer manual and oral. Perhaps that helps.'

I'm getting lots of useful tips for my own old age, and pursue this with 'As I grow older I find that sex becomes less genitally fixated and sort of spreads out in space and in the mind and is more free. One wants to eat everything but more slowly.'

'Yes, it's more contemplative and dreamy, like when I take a walk these days – no striding out, a slow pace, and so I observe and experience more. When I lived in Greece in my twenties, I had it at least once a day. Now it's once a week or so.'

'What I'd say is that though sex improves with age, falling in love never changes – if you fall in love at fifty it's exactly like falling in love as a teenager.'

The conversation moved on to another gifted female author, Anna Kavan, and I tell Francis that she lived in New Zealand during the Second World War.

'Did she? How extraordinary. I used to meet her in Brunswick Square. At Herman Schrijver's. He was an interior decorator and alcoholic, a Dutch Jew whose parents were killed in the concentration camps, and a great friend of Ivy Compton-Burnett and Nancy Cunard. He did up Fort Belvedere for, you know, who became Edward VIII. Herman gave dinner parties only ever for four because any more he said wrecks general conversation, people split into groups, and he never invited couples because he said they paralyse each other. Olivia Manning was always furious because he'd never invite her husband. Rebecca West I first met at his flat – and Anna Kavan too. She was in her sixties when I knew her and very elegant but in a cold way, and I was always a bit nervous of her because you never knew what she might come out with. She might snap at you and say "That's a stupid remark." What was very disconcerting too was that at about 10 p.m. she'd suddenly leave the table without an explanation and disappear for a bit and when she came back, having been awkward before, she was quite in the swim. As we now know she disappeared to the bathroom to inject herself with heroin. My other connection with her was that my Aunt Evelyn had been in the same asylum as Anna Kavan in Switzerland. When Anna came out she wrote *Asylum Piece*, but when my aunt came out she had another attack of paranoia and committed suicide.'

'And what's happened to the Mansfield Prize by the way? Is it still going?'

'I'm afraid it isn't. On my third visit A. L. Barker won and we

met this new mayor who was a retired general and he'd already
made up his mind that it was going to be the final prize; all this
money on air fares, hotels, entertainment, for one short story, he
didn't see the point.'

In her Lawrentian way, Mansfield went off Menton and wrote
to Ottoline Morrell in February 1921 'I mean to leave the Riviera
as soon as possible. I've turned frightfully against it and the
French. Life seems to me ignoble here. It all turns on money.' But
I don't think this was an absolute judgement. Anyone who's had
to do with French society blows hot and cold about it. In 1923
Katherine Mansfield died at the Prieuré, Gurdjieff's establishment near Fontainebleau.

The video flickers to its end and the zooming traffic noise surges
back into my ears. At the bottom of the staircase, as I turn to
examine the postcards, Miss Jill Mathews, the assistant curator, is
at the ready and asks 'Did you enjoy the film?'

'Very much.'

She hovers a bit before stepping forward with another question.

'May I ask where you're from?'

'London.'

'Which part?'

'Notting Hill.'

Her whole being lights up. 'I lived in Notting Hill in the 1960s!
Pembridge Villas!'

And most unexpectedly we're off on another tack.

'Have you heard of Giles Romilly?' she asks.

I think for a moment and come up with 'Was he something to
do with Esmond Romilly, who eloped with Jessica Mitford?'

'Yes, Esmond's elder brother. He had a big thing about his
mother. She was sister-in-law to Winston Churchill. I must say
Giles Romilly was a very odd man. Very odd indeed. It upsets me
to think about it,' says Jill sadly. 'I was working as a private nurse

and he had a house in Pimlico with a kitchen in the basement but he spent most of his time in his bedroom on the second floor. There were Rolling Stones posters on the wall, though he was about fifty years old, and I remember his bed had no sheets on it and was full of stuffed toys, teddy bears and so on. The house was filthy and he was uncooperative and rather puffed because of having to go up and down the stairs. His ex-wife was sometimes there and she also found the stairs a problem because she had asthma. I didn't last long. After a few days his doctor said to me "I don't think you're suitable for a psychiatric case such as this". I believe he'd been imprisoned in Colditz and it had affected him.'

'Do you know what happened to him eventually?'

'Not really. I think I heard he died from an overdose in America.'

On leaving Katherine Mansfield's Birthplace I walk further along Tinakori Road, past the official residence of the Prime Minister, which is not a large house but is set in a succulent garden rising up a bank to woods, a garden not of flowers but of green shrubs and trees all overflowing and interlaced, with the subtle pink of rhododendron blossoms showing through in deft touches, and the house itself only half peeping out, if indeed that, rather just a group of windows here, a portion of cornice or glassed verandah there, and painted in a variety of greens too, the whole thing a Mozartian symphony of greens – no dictator could live here. It is a measure of Katherine Mansfield's social position that when she left for England for the second and final time in 1908, the Prime Minister's wife gave her a farewell party at the official residence. Katherine's father was a banker, Harold Beauchamp. Mansfield was her middle name and her real Christian name was Kathleen. He was knighted a week before her death and took as his motto *Verité sans peur* and built a memorial to her that was typically practical, a tram shelter with twin pavilions at the end of Fitzherbert Terrace. Of course it's been demolished.

~

Virginia Abernethy rang from the Wakefield Hospital. This is the place where Laurence Olivier went for his operation in 1948. 'You could come and look round,' she said, 'and although it's changed its name a few times, the building is much as it was when Olivier was here.'

~

Who told me about Professor Munz? Yes – it was Deb Nation from Plains Radio in Christchurch, and she emailed me his details. He's coming to tea on Thursday. The professor was a student of Karl Popper's at Christchurch, and is now retired as Professor of History at Victoria University. He's well worth meeting, so stick around.

~

A taxi to the Wakefield Hospital in Newtown takes me past Government House, home to the Governors-General. The gates have lanterns on the piers and are smart with crests. Beside them a flag flaps on its pole; beyond them a drive curves away between shrubbery. Of the house itself nothing can be seen.

Newtown is the medical district and its high street is well preserved, with old gables strung together by covered verandahs. The hospital, which is adjacent to Athletic Park, once the home of the All Blacks (and now being covered in retirement homes), was established by a nursing order called the Little Company of Mary, founded by Mary Potter. At first glance it looks new, but closer inspection reveals the pre-war quality of its long main building, which has generous balconies attached to each room. These had to be glassed in, soon after the opening in 1929, because patients underwent difficulties during high winds.

The hallway is restful and woody and from it the wide stairs lead up to a lawn-like landing on the first floor, beyond which is the office of Virginia Abernethy. She is young and pretty, with black hair and blue eyes, and says 'Look, I found this in the nun's log.' The nuns kept a daily record of their doings. The entry for 10 October 1948 reads:

Sir Laurence Olivier injured his knee when playing *Richard III* in Dunedin. On arrival in Wellington he was sent in for operation by Doctor Kennedy Elliott. It was great excitement for the Sisters seeing his wife, Vivien Leigh, coming to visit him. Sister Wilfrid, who was not of this world, one day brought her up in the lift to the top floor where Sir Laurence was in Room 49. All the Sisters were agog at Sister Wilfrid's luck, and questioned her on all sides about the encounter. Sister Wilfrid was not interested at all, then she said 'Oh, do you mean that poor consumptive looking little thing? I thought she looked so miserable.' I don't think that was one of the compliments usually accorded Vivien Leigh, considered one of the greatest artists and loveliest women of her time. Before his departure, Sir Laurence broadcast from his room to the people of New Zealand. His was a corner room and as one of Wellington's fiercest northerly winds was blowing, on the radio one could hear the howling of the wind.

Virginia urges me to telephone Sister Ray, one of the few survivors from the community of that era, and a colleague of Virginia's asks 'Have you told him about Archbishop Redwood's leg?'

'You tell him.'

'Archbishop Redwood was in his nineties and had attended the opening of the hospital. Later he was admitted for treatment and had to have a leg amputated. The nuns had never been in this situation before and went to the Mother Superior and asked "What do we do with the Archbishop's leg?" The Mother Superior thought for a bit and then her face cleared. "Bury it in the garden."'

~

Professor Munz turns up punctually for tea in my room at the Bay Plaza. He is small, tanned, dapper, and lively. One recognises immediately that droll twinkle of old Europe. I wonder where he's from.

'If people ask if I'm a New Zealander, I have to say no. But I'm not really German either, though I still have a German accent. In Germany they think I'm from this country. But I had my childhood in Italy.'

His family, who had friends with connections to Timaru on the South Island, fled Fascist Italy in 1940.

'So you were in this country when the Old Vic came in 1948.'

'Yes! I saw all the plays, all three. They were fabulous. But the strange thing is that although I can remember the experience in general, I cannot recall anything particular about it.'

'What do you think of this?' I hand him Bryan Magee's little book on Karl Popper, a tea-stained copy which I bought under the flyover in Portobello Road, and he smiles.

'Popper said Magee's book was the best ever written on him. Do you know why? Because it is completely uncritical. Popper had a very authoritarian personality, you know. It was often said that *The Open Society* was written by one of its enemies.'

The boy brings tea into the room and I ask the professor to describe his first encounter with Popper.

'I'm an historian really. Philosophy is a sideline. I was a student in Christchurch and Popper had given a lecture there in which he blamed Plato for Fascism. Having grown up in Italy with a classical education, I thought this was heresy. I wrote an article in a student magazine, "Don't Blame Plato". Two or three days later in the library, this little man beckoned to me and said "I hear it was you who wrote this article." I was terrified, being just twenty or so. "Do you want to find out why you are wrong?" he asked. "Yes." "Then come to my room at three o'clock tomorrow." When I turned up he told me that I was wrong because Plato had this idea that it was possible to find out what everybody *deserves* – and it's not possible to find that out! Why not? Because people are too mysterious and changeable and creative. And it was a total revelation for me to hear this. I suddenly saw exactly what he meant. He was very friendly and calm in the way he explained it to me and it completely changed my view of the world. It was like Saul on the road to Damascus. I said to him "I'm enrolled in History but could I attend your lectures?" And we became great friends. He said "It's no use my telling you things. You must ask questions and I'll try to answer them."'

'But this was Plato's method, the Socratic method.'

'Precisely so. But he relented a bit on that aspect of Plato. Since we'd fled Fascism in Italy, I was a sort of Marxist at the time. What was right in Popper was that he identified what was dangerous in both Marx and Plato.'

'And what about Popper's third strand, the anti-Hegel strand?'

'He got Hegel totally wrong! Hegel worshipped the enlightened state of Prussia in his own time, but Popper assumed that that meant worshipping *any* state. His writing on Hegel is mostly vituperative. No sugar, thank-you. And just a touch of milk. *Half* a teaspoon of milk.'

I've never had that request before, half a teaspoon of milk.

'Tell me, what sort of figure did Popper cut?'

'The people of this country are not intellectual, they don't recognise those sorts of problems, so he was a fish out of water. But he believed that the only honest men were natural scientists. So the science professors at Christchurch were absolutely *devoted* to him. He was born in 1904 and had married but didn't have children. His wife was a hopeless housekeeper – typical Viennese intellectual Jewish background and couldn't cook. So at home he was always drinking warm milk, complaining of a stomach ailment, but really to avoid his wife's cooking, because whenever eating at a restaurant or at someone else's house he had an *enormous* appetite. Even though he was quite well paid and his life was comfortable, he was desperate to get away because he was very ambitious to be recognised. He wrote letters saying how hard his life was and hoping as a result to be offered something in America or England.'

'In his autobiography he said that he was very happy here and would've been quite happy to stay except that he was offered a job in London.'

'Yes, he wrote that and it wasn't true at all. He worked very hard to get appointed to the London School of Economics.'

'Would you have liked to work elsewhere too?'

'I have done.'

'But you were never regretful that your connection was with Timaru and you came here?'

'Never at all, no. Because of that I am the only person in the world who was a student of both Popper and Wittgenstein. I was a student of Wittgenstein's at Cambridge and it began to dawn on me that Popper and Wittgenstein were both barking up the same tree.'

'Won't you have a biscuit?'

'No, thank-you. But both being Viennese Jewish intellectuals they'd never have admitted it. There was something prophet-like about Wittgenstein. Whenever he came into the room everyone stopped talking, even if he never said anything. The whole room went silent – and stayed that way if he didn't speak!'

'Wittgenstein had this tortured homosexual quality.'

'Yes, his homosexuality was part of his exotic power. That film by Derek Jarman with all the leather and whips got it *totally* wrong.'

'Derek wasn't an intellectual.'

'Wittgenstein never acted on his homosexuality.'

'A great mistake – suicide almost inevitable. Is he the greater figure?'

'No. It's just that Popper was socially inept, with little charisma.'

'Did Wittgenstein have a sense of humour?'

'Absolutely none. Which is very strange for a Jew.'

'And Popper?'

'He did. He could be whimsical. Though I can't think of an example at present.'

'Did he go and see Laurence Olivier and Vivien Leigh?'

'He'd left the country by then, but no, of course not, he wouldn't go near the theatre! He felt it was an unphilosophical waste of time. He was keen on pure music however. I remember I managed to obtain some tickets for *The Marriage of Figaro* and invited him to go along with me but he just laughed and refused.'

'And the last time you saw him was—'

'In London in the early 1990s. He was nearly ninety. Whenever we saw each other we spoke English. Like many refugees from Nazism and Fascism, we rejected any opportunity to speak German. My mother stopped speaking German and to this day my sister refuses to speak German. Suddenly in London at the end of his life he lapsed into German and I responded in German and we used the German "du", which was perhaps unusual, the informal, since people of his generation used the more formal form of "you".

It was like when I was at Cambridge, the most intimate form of address you would have with another man was to use the family name plain. When I said to Popper "We are speaking in our mother tongue" he became very embarrassed and said "Do you know why? Because I don't want the cook to know what we're talking about." The cook? We were talking about Julius Caesar and mediaeval history!'

Professor Munz refuses a second cup of tea. He is very measured in what he takes into his body. It's because he wants to keep his figure and is careful about looking smart, being spry. I love it that he is still a sexual being in his eighties, as I love it in Francis King. After tea he offered to drive me to the house of the conservation architect Chris Cochran where I have an evening appointment and whom I shall finally meet. The professor's car was small and deeply dented. There was a large piece of driftwood in the back and a baby chair. I tell him I'm hoping to meet Margaret Dalziel in Dunedin and he confirms that 'though she was very young at the time, she went through the whole of *The Open Society* correcting Popper's English.'

≈

To Chris Cochran's wooden house in Thorndon I have brought a sheaf of pictures. They are photocopies of old photographs which I unearthed in the Alexander Turnbull Library.

'Look,' I say, 'there's the St George Hotel in its heyday when the Oliviers stayed there.'

'It was still in its heyday when the Beatles came. I remember they came out on to that balcony *there* to mass adulation.'

'They told me at the Wakefield Hospital that you're right on the main earthquake fault here in Thorndon.'

'That's right.' We both look out of the window and he moves his finger across it. 'It runs straight along there. I'm sorry you were in hospital.'

'I was only visiting.'

'Oh, visiting can be quite fun. As a reminder that one is well.'

'Like funerals. They remind you you're alive. Do you ever get earthquakes?'

'Yes, quite often. But sometimes you hardly notice the tremors. You may think "I felt a bit dizzy there." The last one? About a month ago. Things shook quite rapidly. All the cups clattered.'

I guide him to a photo of a stretch of Lambton Quay in 1977. Most of the major buildings are still *in situ*, including my wonderful State Fire Insurance Building.

'And there's the old Midland Hotel,' he observes ruefully, 'in the Moorish style, an absolute masterpiece by Henry Eli White, demolished in … not so long ago. In the 1980s, Wellington, you know, had a very aggressive mayor called Michael Fowler who cited the threat of earthquake risk to pull everything down. I'm willing to bet your SFI building was steel-framed with stone cladding. In which case the earthquake argument wouldn't stick. Hang on, I'll look it up.'

He crosses to the bookcase in his study and I look out of the window at pretty rooftops beneath a wooded crag and two questions slither through my mind. The first is How long can civilisation cling on? which is quickly followed by Where can I get some sex in this town? Somebody once asked me to define civilisation and I said that in the twenty-first century the test for a civilised person or society is whether or not it accepts gay rights. I'm not being militant about this. I'm not a militant person. You don't even have to espouse such rights to use the test. But you'll find it's infallible.

'Yes, here we are,' says Chris, turning back into the room. 'Hoggard & Prouse. They were joined by William Gummer in 1913. Their three main buildings in Wellington have all been demolished. Yes – I thought so – they were influenced by the steel-framed stone-cladding techniques used in San Francisco after the earthquake. Gummer later set up Gummer & Ford, who became our premier architects of the early twentieth century, based in Auckland.'

'My God, they did that National Gallery complex up the hill! Gummer is a genius! The Lutyens of your country. Is Michael Fowler still alive?'

'Yes, I think so. He left office very proud that most of downtown Wellington had been wiped off the map and said his only regret was that he didn't manage to pull down the remainder.'

The psychological as well as physical damage inflicted on the place is everywhere palpable. Wellington is a sick town. The only major earthquakes here have been human ones. Suddenly wearied by all the needless destruction of fine things by blind, philistine men, Chris asks 'Are you going to the South Island?'

'Yes, I want to go to St Bathan's.'

'Good Lord. How on earth have you heard of St Bathan's?'

'I explored the map and it looks like the remotest village you've got, so I want to go there. I like remote.'

'Look at these.' He spreads some architectural drawings on the desk. He did them for the restoration of the church at St Bathan's. It was a gold-mining settlement and the tin church had been sent out in kit-form from England. Several years ago one woman took it upon herself to organise its restoration and she contacted Chris. He asks me, if I manage to get there, to let him know how matters are proceeding.

His wife turns up and almost her first question is 'Have you met any Maoris yet?'

'Not properly. I want it to happen but I don't want to pay twenty dollars to sit with a coach party for the Maori Experience.'

'I got into terrible trouble the other day because I had a Maori bag which I used for shopping and somebody thought I wasn't paying it enough respect.'

As I leave, Chris hands me a bottle of wine called Ramblin' Rosé, produced by a friend of his.

~

The bracing Kim Hill interviewed me on National Radio and said 'Please be kind to us. We are very sensitive.'

'I haven't come here to draw blood. But I haven't come here to pretend either.'

'Reading your two other travel books, I see you were embraced in Russia, you were embraced in Sicily, you obviously like going round being embraced – so why come here? We are not good at embracing. We got that from the British.'

'The British are a bit better at embracing now.'

I added that I wanted to come to a place less culturally loaded up than St Petersburg or Palermo. I wanted somewhere spacier and more low key. I wanted my book to be quieter and more open to the elements and kind of, well, horizontal. So if you don't like my book, that's probably why. It's open to the elements. It will get more horizontal when I rent a car. Why haven't I done that yet? In England I drive everywhere, even to the bathroom.

~

When I said to Peter Munz 'I find it difficult getting behind the cheerfulness of the people, of the men in particular,' he replied 'That's because there isn't anything behind it. They don't have an intellectual life in that sense.'

'I wasn't thinking intellectually. I don't care about that really. I was thinking emotionally. Their cheerfulness is somehow a trap – for them. A way of avoiding emotion or masking it.'

'Yes. That can be a problem. The amount of domestic violence – these inevitable explosions when emotions are repressed – is extraordinarily great here.'

Looking out of the window I see a ship, long and black and glossy, slide slowly into the vulva of the dock.

~

Guy Fawkes. November the Fifth. I draw the cork of the Ramblin' Rosé and settle into my window seat on the seventh floor of the Bay Plaza for a sip and an ogle. The wine has the prettiest pink of all the rosés so far. Smells blossomy – good – with a hint of elder-flower. Taste is light – and the first hit is quite sweet but almost at once goes into a more delicate manoeuvre with a touch of astrin-gency at the end. Alcohol 12.5 per cent. Oh, if you don't mind that dash of sweetness at the beginning, this is a *charming* wine. Cer-tainly the best rosé so far and I'm not just saying that because it's made by Chris Cochran's friend. But you can't buy it, alas. For sale only in Tim Coney's Café, Dry River Road, Martinborough.

At dusk this broken city shimmers with more appeal than at any other hour. The bay bleeds darkly off the page to the right. Crowds are walking towards the waterfront, and cars throng the centre in weaving lines of headlights. From the amphitheatre of hills, numerous small firework displays take to the air where ordinary families in their back gardens are celebrating an event which took place very far away at the beginning of the seventeenth century. And while I'm standing in the window, tasting a glass of rosé, all the November the Fifths I've ever known succeed each other in rapid pictures, my whole life indeed starts running before me – I wish it wouldn't – I don't want to go that corny, upsetting route – but it does because I've always adored fireworks – and the film runs backwards to my early childhood and my first recollection of Guy Fawkes Night, a tube of golden rain lit by my father and flaring up thrillingly on the back terrace. But the attention doesn't rest there – soon it is off again – backwards and forwards in leaps and jerks – whole decades missed out. The result of this, however, is eventually to nudge me beyond being emotional about it all to being quite quiet inside, as though the shuffle of chronologies has resolved itself into a larger, rounder sense of self, because space has been made for a great deal more consciousness of the past than is customary.

An unseen helicopter is dragging across the sky a big firework in the form of a crown of red flares spewing golden rain. This heralds the main display, which is fired from barges in the bay. Most of it is aerial but there are striking close-to-water effects using reflections. Lattices of golden rain linger as they descend in overlapping veils. Coloured stars crackle, scream and hiss. Bombing noises shake windows and set off car alarms and one day surely, if the Wellingtonians keep spending their money like this, they will trigger a major earthquake.

Pink Verandah

The Ascot Park Hotel, Invercargill, is adjacent to the race-course and much further out of town than it looks on the map. This is because the town is so spread out. The hotel is very spread out too. My bedroom is very spread out. And now I'm spread out, lying on my back and staring at the ceiling. You see, I decided that I couldn't stand Wellington's devastating atmosphere any longer and what I had to do was jump on a plane and make an immediate swoop to the very bottom of South Island, a wise decision as it turned out, because the moment I exited Invercargill's mini-airport I felt a cleansing, better air. Wellington is a city in psychosis, floundering between feebleness and icono-clasm, a city which doesn't know what it is. But down here I am in a tranquillity of reasonableness and good health. Down here every-thing is on the level.

The hotel only has a ground floor and when I arrived its recep-tion area was chirpy with well-made women in blouses drinking Kiwi shampers. Cosmetics, clothes, even several small cars were arranged in the huge, low foyer for them to view. The locals speak with an almost Devonian burr and the receptionist said 'Excuse us. We're having a wee function.' You know the type – they pay their bills promptly. As I do (now).

Having unpacked and taken a shower, I ordered from room service blue cod & chips with mushy peas. The girl who brought it to me was very shy and beat a hasty retreat after I'd signed. Adjusting my bath-towel, I sat down to the best fish & chips I've ever had – and now writing about it so long afterwards, that sense of rarefied pleasure comes back to me, the spacious freedom and cleanliness and nourishment, the perfect and obvious simplicity of it all, though having stamped out these words I somehow haven't quite hit it, so maybe I'll return to this passage and rewrite it, but if I don't, it is because words fail me and I cannot exactly convey the beautiful *relief* in finding myself precisely here.

～

In the hotel sauna a big blond sportsman from Queenstown said 'Do you know what the South Islanders call the North Island?'
    'No.'
    'Pig Island.'
    'Why?'
    'Because it's a mess.'
    'And what do North Islanders call the South Island?'
    'The Mainland. Everyone calls it that. There's a Maori legend that their god sat on the South Island and fished up the other one.'

He had a sluggish passive sexiness and sloped off into the shower, where he was soon soaping genitalia halfway to his knees.

What time is breakfast? Really, the timing in these hotels is impossible. Breakfast ends at 9 a.m!

～

Apparently there was a violent thunderstorm last night but I only registered one clap of thunder, so I must have slept well. This morning a blue sky is pranked with cloudlets and I take the hotel's transit van to the Southland Museum, which is housed in what they call the largest pyramid in the southern hemisphere (I haven't checked out the veracity of that). Its great attraction is the tuatarium, which is the thing they keep the tuataras in. So I march straight through the pyramid to its rear, where these prehistoric relics live in their glass abode.

Tuataras are on a time register different from the rest of us, one that is closer to stones and bark. They are about ten inches long and completely still, so much so that it does occur to me that this is all a bit of a confidence trick, that they are in fact models, and after a while of nothing whatsoever happening you do decide you might as well leave, at which point a tiny pulse appears and disappears in the throat of one of the creatures, or if you are lucky – and I was because a keeper slammed a door – there might be more decisive activity, in this case an eye blinking. Generally they breathe about once a minute. And they look completely different from other creatures, even from crocodiles and chameleons, despite superficial resemblances.

Of the several here detained, the most beautiful is Henry, who was hatched in 1880. It is Henry who has at last blinked. He is the green of lichen on a Cotswold wall, his flanks ridged and his back spiked. The tuatara is nocturnal and since it enjoys eating its young, Nature in her wisdom has made the babies diurnal. Should it survive its parents, a tuatara requires twenty years to reach sexual maturity. Courtship is even more elaborate than among humans, involving endless amounts of farting about. Eventually the female will choose the male. He responds to her invitation by aggressively biting her neck, which stuns the poor woman, allowing her to be flipped on to her back. Since the male has no copulatory connective, the idea behind his attack is to bring about a propinquity of their bodies so that when the male does ooze his juice it is likely to enter the female aperture. If fertilisation should ensue from this ramshackle business, the female will lay some eggs under the earth, where they may incubate for well over a year. When the young ones hatch out and break surface their one objective is to escape any ravenous parents roaming about, and they skuttle off to hide under rocks or up trees. Fortunately they are much quicker than the adults. Much is made, as Bunny had noted, of the tuatara being the only living thing with a remnant of the third eye. The remnant is slightly light-sensitive, but useless. The far wall of the glass tank is also glass and gives on to Queen's Park, which is now being drenched by an unexpected downpour.

I'm upstairs now, in a chamber for the extinct and the nearly extinct. Three stuffed kakapo, for example, waving good-bye. They have abnormally large gripping claws. But it is their faces which are so arresting: really dumb-looking, frowning, down-turning faces like bulbous mutant babies ashamed of themselves. *The kakapo is heavily built and cannot fly. Very agile, it climbs with ease and is able to glide on outstretched wings for short distances*. A stuffed Laughing Owl, *believed* extinct … Skeleton of a moa, giant ostrich-like flightless birds, hunted to extinction by the Maoris, and beyond it a large, as yet unemployed space for future extinctions. In years to come this will no doubt contain effigies of boys and men.

Upstairs the recorded cry of an albatross follows one every-where. It is a despairing, descending scream. Once you've seen the bird, stuffed, once you've heard it, the cry follows you everywhere, imploring, plaintive, round the upper floors of the pyramid, raising the ghost of Coleridge's *Rime of the Ancient Mariner*, with the albatross hung about the mariner's neck. The poem was written in the year of William Hodges' death and is said to have been inspired by the second voyage of Captain Cook, which took in not only New

Zealand and the Pacific but also the Antarctic. Cook, the son of a Yorkshire farm labourer, volunteered for the Royal Navy in 1755 and from the outset displayed outstanding navigational skills. He made three expeditions to the Pacific and was murdered by natives in Hawaii on St Valentine's Day, 1779. His wife survived him by fifty-six years.

On my way out of the pyramid – hang on – surely – yes – here is a William Hodges painting, a real one, only my second of the trip. It's a recent acquisition and quite small, entitled *A Maori Before a Waterfall in Dusky Bay*. Again Dusky Bay, as in the Auckland Hodges. There are some wonderful names in this country: Mount Aspiring, Mount Difficulty, Doubtful Sound, Poverty Bay, the Bay of Plenty; they breathe the very spirit of endeavour. This picture is full of gush and billow and has the Hodges trademark, the silhouetting of figures and trees. I think it must be a study for the larger picture at Greenwich, where, coincidentally upon my return from the southern hemisphere, they at last gave William Hodges his first ever big show, at the Queen's House there. Some art critics attacked the painter's work as 'imperialist'. It's quite extraordinary coming across such catchphrasing now – the Pol Pot school of art criticism – as though artists are not permitted to seek inspiration in foreign places. Poor Hodges, forgotten since the eighteenth century and then crudely mugged on his first outing in the twenty-first. I've never seen the merit in Edward Said's 'Orientalist' argument, which sneers at Europeans who have sought inspiration in the Middle East because they got it 'wrong'. Said introduced racism into the cultural discourse, a racism which failed to grasp that Europe does itself no special favours in these matters and is as ruthless in self-analysis as in foreign analysis, a racism which says that one culture must not use material from another culture, a puritan nonsense in practice and really in his case just an expression of resentment that European art has powers of absorption which the arts of the Middle East do not. An artist may use whatever raw material he chooses and his whole art is in its transformation. Is Rimsky-Korsakov's *Sheherazade* to be denigrated because Arab music isn't like that? Is the whole of European gothic architecture to be considered invalid because the gothic arch is Saracenic in origin? It is part of the greatness of European culture that it has developed an intellectual capacity which can turn anything to its purposes. Besides, the general effect of European artists employing outlandish material has been not to belittle the sources but to aggrandise them. Polynesia is more sublime in Hodges than it ever is in its own art. The score of *Sheherazade* is more intellectually complex than anything found in Arab music. These are not moral judgements but critical observations. In other words the view which can absorb and transform must be greater than the view which cannot. Said's cultural puritanism is a dead end, for everything with a history can be pulled apart and its origins analysed; everything is a synthesis. What is crucial to bear in mind is that these artists could not have done their paintings or written their music had they not loved the sources of their inspiration. These are not works of subjugation but of adoration. Indeed I can think of no work of art that was inspired by contempt or hate. Milton tried in *Paradise Lost* to have us despise Satan but he failed utterly, and Mario Puzo sees in Milton's Satan the origin of that most beloved of species, the doomed Romantic hero (though most other people see his origin in Hamlet).

Hodges wrote in his *Travels in India* (1793) 'Everything has a peculiar character and it is the finding out of the real and natural character which is required; should a painter be possessed of the talents of a Raphael and were he to represent a Chinese with the beauty of a Grecian character and form, however excellent his work might be, it would still have no pretensions to reputation as characteristical of that nation.' In other words *look at what you're looking at*. This isn't always easy when, like Hodges, you are looking at things you've never before seen. He was classically trained and bound to use the parameters of eighteenth-century painting as a framework for his vision, but to suggest that he wasn't fully aware of this is, as the above quotation demonstrates, naive. It says much for Hodges' approach to art that his portrait of Captain Cook is the most direct and convincing we have, the least straightened by the decorum of contemporary portraiture. But it was not his job to record in the camera sense. He was not there to make a scientific portfolio of plants, birds, geologies and anthropologies; there were other draughtsmen on board to do that. Nor has he, say, the Pre-Raphaelite obsession for rendering every blade of grass, every cotton thread. His landscapes are suffused with notions of the Arcadian and have very often an airy gladness of execution which we associate with the art of a much later era. But there's more – for they convey too their original mood of wonder, including that apprehension which suggests that paradise is about to be destroyed by the very act of recording it.

The gracefulness of Hodges' pictures echoes what we know to have been the gracefulness of Cook's behaviour towards the natives. These voyages were not high-handed in the way, for example, the Spaniards had been in the New World. There was always debate, both private and public, unofficial and official, about the dangers of intruding upon alien societies. George Foster, in his *Voyage Round the World* of 1777, lamented that 'the voyages of Europeans cannot be performed without being fatal to the nations whom they visit.' The intrusion of the English crew into the seductive world of Tahitian eroticism brought gonorrhoea and syphilis with very destructive effects, but of course the Europeans had acquired these diseases several centuries before from the Indians of the New World. And so it goes on.

Whether sketches, watercolours or oils, whether done spontaneously at the time or worked up when he returned home, all Hodges' depictions from the Pacific are characterised by the peculiar effects of sunlight in this part of the world. Most of his New Zealand paintings are apocalyptic, dominated by cataracts, waterspouts and storms. These are not baroque or romantic exaggerations. Sea voyages in the age of sail were extremely perilous and filled with drama. As the ships moved on from New Zealand the light-effects in his pictures become more obviously tropical, climaxing in his resplendent scenes of the Society Islands, receding in shimmering chiffons of rose-pink, magenta-blue, lavender, yellow and coppery orange. Usually the horizon is low with vast expanses of sky, the frame is rectangular, the proportions cinematic. This is his Rodgers & Hammerstein Cinerama mode. Being in the service of the Admiralty, he could not keep any of this material, and after the initial splash it lay forgotten for 150 years in the vaults.

Hodges' subsequent career was far from plain sailing. He painted India for Warren Hastings and was caught up in the proceedings against Hastings, whose side he took. In May of 1792 Hodges went to St Petersburg for three months at the request of Catherine the Great with pictures he had painted at her command. This was noted by the *Morning Chronicle*. At that time another forgotten British genius, Charles Cameron, born the same year as Hodges in 1744, was in the full flood of his astounding schemes for the Tsaritsa's palaces. Cameron likewise deserves a major exhibition in London and I've been plaguing the Hermitage Rooms at Somerset House about it for years, but it seems that art institutions are impervious to outside suggestion. If they haven't thought up the idea themselves they are not interested, being terrified of losing control, losing influence and credit, losing the driver's seat in directing the zeitgeist. Did Hodges meet Cameron? He must have done. But all my attempts to uncover more about that Hodges summer stay in St Petersburg have failed. It would be a choice subject for a small book.

In 1794 he exhibited two pictures at a London exhibition, *The Effects of Peace* and *The Consequences of War*. At the time Britain was at war with revolutionary France and as George III's son, the Duke of York, looked at the paired paintings he made a derogatory remark to the effect that pacifism was inappropriate at a time like this. At once the pictures were whisked away. Hodges was damned, his career stalled, he stopped painting and, of all things, started up a bank. The bank went bust and in 1797 he committed suicide. To this day the two offending canvases have not been located.

I'm writing this down on a Friday evening. The wild weather has been blowing up again across the South Sea from Antarctica. You could see it roaring in on a huge sky over the sculpted clumps and spinneys of the Ascot Hotel grounds. And now it is dark, the wind is surging, and rain is crackling on the windowpanes.

$\sim$

Been ringing nuns. Sister Ray, it transpires, should be spelt Sister Rae. When I managed to get through to her she turned out to be a gentle soul who put me on to a slightly less gentle soul, Sister Camilla, who suggested I rang an even more gentle soul, Sister Aquinas, who is the oldest survivor of the community of nuns who nursed Olivier. It was evening-time in Sister Aquinas's retreat and in a tiny clear voice she explained 'I arrived at the Lewisham Hospital, as it was then called, on the First of December 1948 at the age of twenty-six. I am sorry to tell you that it was just *after* Laurence Olivier had been there. But they were still full of it. Everyone said that they were the essence of kindness, both of them were. Vivien Leigh came to visit every day. When her husband left she gifted all the staff who had looked after him, even the people in the kitchen, even the ones who cleaned the floors. The sister who nursed him was Sister Francesca.'

'Is Sister Francesca still alive?'

'She isn't, sir. She passed on only four or five years ago. She said he was the nicest person in the world to look after. Both he and his wife made an enormous impression and it was genuine. It was talked about for a long time after, they were so highly thought of by everyone. Doctor Kennedy Elliott operated on him and he passed on quite a long time ago.'

And what of Mary Potter, who founded the order?

'She was born in Nottingham, sir, and buried in Rome. A few years ago, in 1998, she returned to Nottingham Cathedral. Her tomb is now there, and all the memorabilia. She is a Venerable, which is the first step towards becoming a saint. She started the order in a disused hosiery factory in Nottingham, an order of nursing sisters, because you see it was so needed.'

How matters moved from Nottingham to Sydney was explained to me, though I didn't quite catch the gist, but Sister Aquinas emphasised that 'We were all properly trained and had to be registered nurses,' just in case one thought there was something amateurish about the set-up. It was a sad day when the sisters had to sell the hospital in Wellington.

'Yes, it was, sir. There just were not enough of us any more. But our hospice work is going very well, palliative care, helping people in pain, especially with cancer. It makes such a difference. It is very important to carry on. We have sisters in Korea and in Tunisia and in Albania. We had to leave Albania years ago but now we've gone back. All Mary Potter places. I'm semi-retired now. I've loved my life and I'd have it all over again if I could. Nursing is a wonderful profession.'

'Thank-you so much for talking to me. I hope I haven't interrupted your dinner.'

'No, no, sir. We've been watching television. And now we're going downstairs to say the rosary and to pray.'

'What will you pray for?'

'For peace in the world.'

~

Finally I've rented a car, a small white Toyota to transport me up the South Island in a serpentine route. I was nervous at first of driving. Not sure why – the roads were quiet, they drive on the left, and I've been knocking about the roads of continental Europe for years. But there was something about the newness of the land which was disconcerting – like starting a new school.

My first outing is to the Anderson Park estate a few miles outside Invercargill. The house resembles a neo-Georgian mansion in Surrey or Massachusetts, with bottle-green shutters at its windows and the slates on its roof from Lord Penrhyn's quarries in North Wales. These days it's run as a public art gallery and my eye is taken by a watercolour of 1873 in which, against empyrean recessions of light and cloud, a Maori is guiding a European party through the wilderness. Hodges again? No. This picture is by a name which is new to me: Nicholas Chevalier. The caption says that he was born in Russia and painted a survey of the Southern Alps before joining Queen Victoria's son, the Duke of Edinburgh, for a trip round the world. Another of those forgotten vagabond artists I seem to be collecting. Perhaps I'm one myself.

Attached to the estate is a small chunk of native forest traversed by chipstone paths for easy access. I haven't been in native forest yet – there's hardly any outside the national parks – so I dive into a mulching world of high trees, moss, rotten logs and clambering undergrowth. The trees are strange. One kind has brown bark coming away in vertical strips, another a trunk pitted with what

look like hammer blows. Oh … it's over … Bursting out of native
rainforest without warning on to the lawn of a Surrey mansion is
a very antipodean experience. In the olden days the lawns of
Anderson Park were cut by horse-drawn mowers, the horses
wearing leather overshoes to protect the turf.

≈

The migration from Great Britain to this land is the longest in
human history and that to Invercargill is the longest of all. The
town is the furthest flung of the Empire and it has held on to its
frontier spirit. This afternoon I felt so happy walking the open-
hearted streets in blasts of wind and rain. Dee Street in particular
has long runs of original commercial buildings with iron verandahs. Only the horses and wagons are missing. I've never seen a
street quite like this before, and its originality lies in its width. It
is mostly sky. Europe's grandest boulevards would be airless in
comparison. In the middle of my promenade the weather turned
particularly nasty, with stinging wind-blown hail, so I retreated
inside the town's department store where to my consternation I
found tinsel draped everywhere and Christmas carols playing over
the loudspeakers. It's only November the 8th.

≈

Have a go, give it a whirl. So I showered, washed my hair, put on
clean clothes, popped in contact lenses, and set off at 9 p.m. on a
Saturday night for Invercargill's one and only gay bar. It had closed
down.

≈

Mindful of what Peter Munz said concerning violent outbursts,
I've discovered that several people who I thought liked me do not
like me. They were to all appearances friendly, and then – unawares

– I crossed some invisible line and triggered unexpected displays of resentment or sullen silence: this has happened in three cases. I don't want to go into the details but in each case the behaviour was irrational, not specifically related to any misdemeanour on my part, or absurdly out of proportion to it. Also what Peter said about their being a non-intellectual people: this has given rise to certain other problems. Since laid-back cheerfulness is the way they try to deal with everything, they lack the necessary verbal repertoire for dealing with inevitable complexities. So when confronted by any sort of complexity – including perhaps, if you'll forgive me, meeting a person such as myself from another country – they tolerate it with a smile, suffering a build-up of negativity which then bursts at a trigger moment to which it is not quite related. In other words, a diet of underreaction must necessarily be punctuated by flashes of overreaction.

Another thing is the way the constant reiteration of this being God's own country, or how lucky they are to live here, or how they never take their good fortune for granted, eventually begins to convey the opposite impression, that there is lurking in the back of their minds the feeling that maybe it isn't so, that they live close to the void and are uncertain, even terrified, of the abyss. The narrow emotional ledge on which the nation squats does indeed have a grand view, but its population must suspect that it's possible not merely to squat but to launch oneself into space, to spread one's wings and fly. But that quiet, friendly, hard-working, protestant modesty holds them fast. Peter Munz said that though almost every young New Zealander of any education or affluence or ambition goes travelling to see the world, they are not transformed by the experience, and return home and carry on with the addition only of a set of foreign photographs.

～

Look down the room-service menu. *Grilled ostrich infused with an African rub served on an apricot and almond couscous, drizzled with a chargrilled capsicum, mint and yoghurt sauce.* Um, I don't think so.

～

We're heading for the Catlins. Couldn't do it without the car, and the girl at Budgetcar warned me about gravel roads in the Catlins area. Either side of the road are flat farms for a while, veiled in misty drizzle, but a little before Fortrose the vista shoots out wide and wet to the coast and bad weather is left behind. A patch of native forest to the right – high dark canopy supported on a criss-cross of upward branching trunks – one would hardly be surprised to hear a blood-curdling roar and to see the forest quake and part, as a mastodon comes stomping out. But nothing stirs except the air either side of the windscreen, zipping in through the top slits of the side windows.

Skim over muddy flats on long stilted bridges and make a turn to the right with cool breeze driving up the nostrils and into the lungs, after which I hit a stretch of gravel road that is not nearly as coarse as expected. The car hardly judders at all. Stop and get out. Lilting motets of birdsong map the sylvan depths and seem far older than the baa-baa-ing of sheep which mingles with them. Hill farms fade into forest bathed in pearly light. The farms are evidence that people do exist, and yet there's not a human to be seen anywhere; it's like a landscape version of the *Marie Celeste*, as though all the people have been sucked out by an incomprehensible mystery ... Hay ... Buckingham ... Jenks ... Todd ... The names on the postboxes at the end of farmers' drives flip past the window while the gravel road hums sweetly beneath the wheels. A gravel road has its own joy, and if ever it is sealed so will be the fate of this district because the tourist buses will simply charge in.

Slide towards the sea and stop at the little church of Waikawa, now a café. An old woman in cardigan and trousers mans the counter. Pies are on offer. Venison, mince, beef & cheese, steak & mushroom. I choose the last and order a cup of tea too. She says 'We don't see the wildlife like we used to. The dolphins don't come in any more. Too many people trying to play with them. They've moved off. And who can blame them? Would you want to be interfered with all the time?'

I don't answer that question and ask 'What's the weather forecast?'

'Same as usual. Cold, wet, windy, sunny. Our weather is worse than Invercargill's because we're further south.'

When after polishing off the pie I return the tray to the counter, she says 'Good on ya', and when I buy some postcards she says it again. 'Good on ya' is the local phrase for 'thank-you'.

The gravel road is now cutting through thick rainforest, which hereabouts looks like Borneo on best behaviour, and somewhere beyond the flow of trees lies the coast. I stop the car on a shoulder of shingle. A noticeboard says Lake Wilkie is nearby and so I take the narrow path. Forest sweeps cloak-like all around me and invisible birds call to each other in unearthly bell-like tones and ferns trace the air with the delicacy of Adam interiors. It is not sinister; there is no feeling that snakes might at any moment swing down across one's face or carnivores growl from an adjacent clump. It is more likely one will come across a tea party out of Lewis Carroll or Fellini. This country grants that rarest of gifts: to be free without being vulnerable.

As I continue along the path, the jungle to the right dips sharply away and there is Lake Wilkie – a vision from Conrad – Conrad again – a small lake settled motionlessly into its saucer, a silky gleaming volume so entirely still that one feels one is a corrupting influence merely for looking at it. Yet though without animation, the lake in no way suggests death but communicates some hermetic tang and looks extraordinarily alive and of life. If there are birds I can't hear them any longer because all I can hear is a roar, surely quite close, and it's like the roar of a gas ring on the hob turned up fully. It must be the sea pounding in, but it can't be seen and I am held, ferns brushing my face, by the lonely lake of petrol-coloured water, fringed with bullrushes, and yellow irises about to burst, the forest rising in protective banks around it, and that is all I can do, stand there with the strong undeviating roar in my ears, knowing that I shall never pass this way again, drinking at the ticking seconds …

The gravel road climbs up and up and the lake is lost and the forest slips off one's back and we are on the clifftop of Florence Hill, and before me is a second revelation, for it is the picture I dreamed of when first I thought of coming to this country, the conjured image which appeared in my head and has waited to be verified, and here it is, the beach with native forest extending right down to the sand's edge exactly as in my imagination except that it is vaster – much vaster – Tautuku Bay – a cosmic sweep of sand and surf – and the mood is not at all carefree. The perplexing thing is that you cannot objectify this view. Instead you are *taken* by it, taken by the implacable gentleness of the waves coming in and breaking into surf. The in-sliding movement defines the view and yet the relationship between water and land never alters. Why does the water not keep on coming in and cover the land? Viewed from up here, the motionlessness of sea and land combining with the constant in-sliding motion present a defiance of visual logic. One is in the grip of primaeval forces, prior to logic. The very existence of the universe is prior to logic and defies logic. Big bang? Steady state? The origin of matter? String theory? Just whistling in the dark.

Dead Horse Road … Old Coach Track … Rotten Row … the

romance of old roads and the landscape either side switching capriciously between wilderness and order – steep hills, parklike bush, grazing herds – stretches of high forest – yes – no – gone – large estuary – lonely cry of wading bird – Surat Bay. Every beauty spot has its crustacea of shacks. The road is no longer gravel. Shame. I love the gravel roads. They slow you down, that's all ... Kaka Point Motel. I'm in a 'unit' with a 'deck' and two windows looking the length of the beach. It was sunny when I arrived so I've booked for three days. But the weather seems to have regressed a season. I'm cold and use the electric blanket. The wife of the motel owner said 'We think anything above cold is a heatwave. A warm day in summer and we're all dying from it, gasping and melting.'

~

The following morning, as I look out of the window down the beach and feel through the glass the sun almost warm on my face, I sense that dangerous thing, *self-satisfaction*, and quietly prepare a simple breakfast: Fruity Bix mixed with Skippy Cornflakes, drenched in Trim low-fat Meadow Fresh milk out of a bottle which had a green and silver top. The toaster goes pop. Yank out two hot squares of Holson's Original Swiss Superthick Bread and put on plate. Take knife and smear on side of plate a large pat of Semi-Soft Mainland Butter with Canola Oil, along with a generous splodge of quivering Craig's Boysenberry Jam: break toast and apply.

North of Kaka Point the Catlins come to an end, but south, taking a road marked Sandy Bay, one is among switchback scenic changes covered with an antique detritus of forest clearance. Dead stumps, supine among boulders and turf, are bleached like the bones of dinosaurs by the wind and salt, sun and rain. Where grazing has been abandoned, the vegetation regenerates not with native forest but with gorse.

There is no Sandy Bay that I can find, but the road does deposit me at another – Cannibal Bay, which lies between rocky headlands and is backed by dunes. Three sea-lions are lolling on the beach. They are known as Hooker's sea-lions and resemble Roman emperors stupefied after the orgy, overweight and underexcited. A fourth, huge, waddles out of the sea and dumps down on the first gloss of sand, a giant black slug. Followed by another – this one rolls over on to his back, flippers akimbo. The three snoozing further up resemble sandy chunks of wood and, as you walk by, a flipper may lift or a querulous eye briefly fix you, nothing more. The charm of the faces belies an irascible temper, and one has been warned to keep well clear. Those higher up are noticeably smaller than the huge pair nearer the sea and are presumably females.

Sir James Hector, whose famous wildlife library has been dispersed through ineptitude, gave Cannibal Bay its name because he found human bones here, but couldn't they have been the result of a sea-lion attack? If approached more than they would like, the sea-lions rear up and shake themselves so that you get the message. But what can these massive creatures do to frighten off a car? A young man is driving his girlfriend up and down the beach past the sea-lions, revving the engine, making sand swerves. In the dunes behind, a backpacker has pitched his silver tent. A tourist levels a camera at me before realising I'm human and dropping it at his side. In the centre of a wreath of motorbike tracks a message has been drawn in the sand with a stick: 'Thomas was here! Love you all!' How much longer will these leisured, whiskered aristocrats put up with it before they find another place to call home?

I plunge through dunes clotted with lupin and agave, and this brings me from Cannibal Bay to Surat Bay's grand curve, where layer upon layer of surf, like shallow plates one upon the other, edge forward in arcs. The scale is immense, distantly guarded by rank upon rank of blue hills, blue hills again and again. No car can get here and my only companions are a charming couple, stout and black on pink skinny legs. They move about in synchronised tandem like ballroom dancers, squawking pleasantly from pink beaks which colour has in it the orange tinge I have vainly sought in the nation's rosé wines. They are oyster-catchers.

The temperature is comfortable, the sky is mottled with cloud, and the light doesn't have the glare which I experienced in North Island – or is it that I'm getting used to it? I sit on a knot of tussock to eat my sandwiches, the inevitable ham and cheese from the Dairy. Tautuku Bay was primaeval because the ancient forest came right down to the beach. The view of it from Florence Hill was from before Adam and Eve, before mankind ate the fruit of the tree of knowledge. That beach is indifferent to us; it can include us but we cannot include it; and it spoke of mysteries which were sealed from prying eyes long before mankind came on the scene. But Surat Bay, just as vast, is more companionable, has something of the munificent beaches of our childhood, spilling gold all around us. The sandwiches are very good.

∼

Along the beach below my motel room there is not a single boat, and not a single boat has passed on the sea, either close to shore or on the horizon. A limitless boatless ocean. I mentioned this to the owner of the motel and he said 'I saw a boat on the horizon a few days ago,' as though this made it a hive of activity.

∼

National Radio is a good station on which people really talk. The interviews and discussions can go on for an hour or more, which gives meaning the chance to emerge. Today they are discussing the malaise among boys. This is turning into a bit of a theme. Boys only want to do enough to get by, they say. They don't work at school and want to live on benefits afterwards. Universities have become parking places before going into the benefit system. These days nobody is allowed to love boys, I say. If you love them you arouse suspicion. In Britain the Government estimates that one in four boys between the ages of fourteen and seventeen is a serious or regular offender and that one in ten has carried a gun at some time. The owner of the motel tells me that all the sea-lions at Cannibal Bay are males. The smaller ones are boys. They've been kicked off Campbell Island further out by the females because they attack the pups. Campbell Island is the most southerly of the Sub-antarctic Islands and a World Heritage Site. The males have only been resident at Cannibal Bay for twenty-five years, and James Hector was right of course – the bones discovered by him were the result of inter-tribal warfare. But were they the result of cannibal-ism? Did they betray evidence of having been stewed in a pot?

At Cannibal Bay this morning there is only one other car. About a dozen seals occupy the far end. I wade along the ridge of the dunes for a better view, but the going gets tough after the path dribbles away and the thick scrub takes over. Eventually I drag myself on to a peak to observe a group of six boys dominated by a huge avuncular bull. The boys frolic gleefully and are very amorous with each other. Every so often a pair will form a rippling pyramid by raising up their heads and necks and rubbing their noses together. Two of them near the water are dancing until one col-lapses abruptly on to the sand. His companion looks about bemused before waddling away up the beach while the prone one, left behind, raises his head in disappointment as though to say 'I thought we were playing.' He rights himself and edges into the waves for a spot of lunch. Are they lovers or just good friends? I'm sure this animal world is rather more relaxed than that, and doesn't make such hard distinctions. The Hooker's sea-lions are very free.

Sometimes they snooze singly but at other times in mounds of three or four, periodically carressing each other. No noise has been made by any of these creatures. It is silent play, backed only by the whispers of breeze sifting long grasses, the faint clack of agave fronds against each other, and the quiet drone of surf. An offshore breeze picks off the waves' foamy tops and blows them into feathered crests.

∼

Said goodbye to the owners of the Kaka Point Motel. They asked me where I was heading. I'll drive up to Clyde to look at the vineyards around Bannockburn, mooch on to Gladstone beside Lake Hawea, and thence to St Bathan's. He asked 'Why Gladstone?' and I said 'I admire the Prime Minister.' He said 'We have a holiday cottage at Gladstone. I'd let you have the key but we had some trouble and now we've got a rule: strictly family. My mother bought a piece of land there. In those days land cost almost nothing.'

Fill up with petrol at Balclutha, buy sandwiches. There was rain in the night and the air is sulky. At Clydevale turn left for Beaumont with the Clutha on the right and the Beaumont Forest and Blue Mountains on the left. The Clutha is a frightening river of pale green milk whose movement suggests pure muscle. Matted rocks loom above its romping current. It must be getting a lot warmer already because the wet road is steamy. I insert a Hutch CD which I've imported and the power of the man's charm turns even these ominous crags into a cabaret.

Take a left for Roxburgh and the Clutha disappears from view. The hills fold upwards in gruff pelts, bristling with yellow broom and white hawthorn. At the roadside I see the first trickle of blue lupins – in the Catlins they were all yellow. In a gap in the hills above the car bonnet, a distant mountain range, white with snow, prises apart the sky.

At the Bridge Tavern I pause for refreshment. A middle-aged man sits at the bar staring fixedly into a half-pint of beer while an advertisement for Viagra runs on the television above his head. Another man nods and I ask 'May I have a cup of tea and a piece of cake?' A row of fruit machines is illuminated at the ready. To my left an archway is closed by a white lace curtain, and a pink boudoir can be detected beyond it. After about five minutes a grey-haired woman barges through the lace curtain with a tray and confidently addresses the air: 'Who wants a cup of tea and a sandwich?'

'I asked for a cup of tea and a piece of cake.'

'I heard tea and sandwich.'

'But a sandwich is fine.'

She dumps it at my table and walks past me. Gamely I work my way through a thin tasteless square of lino-ham while she natters to the two men at the bar about the heavy snow they've had recently and someone's wedding. On the way back to the kitchen she gives me a saucy look. 'Sammies OK?'

'Delicious, thanks.'

She doesn't trust me.

Bowl through Roxburgh. You can't do otherwise: it's such a fresh fruity town. The orchards which began at Miller's Flat are now plentiful but the stony hills are never far away. They suddenly close in either side of the Clutha River, which looks horrific now, deprived of all vegetation, a remorseless drowning machine scouring the crevice between steep stone banks. Almost at once a hydro-electric plant wrecks the scene, not so much the installation itself, its monumental grey being in the spirit of the place, but because pylon lines extend untidily from it in several directions.

The Clutha Valley is truly menacing and is to our English notion of a river valley what a battleship is to a poodle. The whole region has become harsh, brown and grey, and grows more messy as we approach the raggle-taggle of Alexandra. The town has a beflagged, big-sky look with golf-course and other sporting amenities, but uncontrolled development blemishes its setting. The map suggested a high degree of remoteness, but there is nothing remotely off-the-map about Alexandra and in fact I am learning that I shall not find remoteness in so-called remote places. The plenty of the good life and the closed-circuit camera of civilisation are everywhere.

At Clyde I'm shocked to find another bloody dam – really, it's too much – but at least the Antique Lodge Motel is a bargain, a collection of simple chalets at the end of an old-world high street. My unit has a large sitting-room and kitchen, bathroom and two bedrooms, everything spotless and in perfect order. There is a bottle of milk waiting in the fridge and a wooden bench on the gravel outside my front door. $75 per night (£30). I'm avoiding in my travels what the locals call boutique accommodation; it is over-priced and twee and one is never out of the glare of the owners.

It's hot. Yes. Pure and hot. I sit on the bench in the sunshine and try to adjust to the dam and the pylons and the dour fascination of the district. When and wherever I stop in this land, it's always eerie. Only motion may briefly dispel it. Eeriness is in everything and is ineradicable. This I must accept, that the vividness of the colour, the blinding clarity of vision, is shot through with a profound ghostliness, a hyper-reality which is a virtual reality, as though the world ended many centuries ago and one is living in a digital reconstruction. This eeriness, in the very molecules of the place, is so unlike anywhere else that I think William Hodges must have felt something similar when he went to the limit and tried to paint what he found.

∿

There's a new wine shop in Alexandra called The Grape, specialising in local makers. The owner, Tim, sells me a Rippon Gamay and I ask 'What about the dam at Clyde? I didn't expect that.'

'They filled it about '95 or so but they had a lot of problems beforehand. First the water company were told they didn't officially have water rights so Prime Minister Muldoon had to pass a law saying they did. Then they discovered that they were building it on a fault line, so it had to be redesigned. In fact it's two dams with a sixty-foot-high wedge jammed between them. The idea is that in an earthquake it can move without cracking up. They say even if it collapsed the water would miss Clyde because the gorge is so deep there, but I'm not sure. I live in Clyde myself and I didn't know whether to jump in the car with the kids three months ago because we had a really bad quake in the early hours of the morning. I went to get the kids and couldn't walk properly along the corridor – but the dam held. If you're here Friday morning we've got a really beautiful rosé from Auckland coming in. I said to the rep, aw, I've gotta have that.'

~

Open the Rippon Gamay Rosé, mid-pink, 12 per cent, pour a glass and put my feet up. Ah … sickly smell of boiled sweets followed by a sudden tart taste of extraordinary brutality. Long bitter finish … very long, very bitter … It's not off. It's oral rape. People sometimes use the word 'rape' when they mean 'ravish'. 'He ravished me' they should say, in reference to a man whose animal adoration came with a rush. 'Ravishing' is still the highest term of praise. It is more active than 'sublime'. Sublimity comes after ravishment. But this wine is not ravishing. Pour the rest down the sink. Switch on the electric blanket and settle down to several cosy hours finishing off *The Golden Bowl*.

James knew Europe at the height of its greatness and evokes it more fully than anyone else. Proust is provincial in comparison. James's milieu is the upper classes of London, New England and Paris. He takes you right *in*to it. And he did it from London, which

he described as 'on the whole the best point of view in the world.'
You either delight in the probing tendrils of his pussyfooting,
which climax at least once a page – at least! – in an orgasmic puff
of unique adroitness, or you don't. Like Mahler, like Proust, like
Musil, he was both the grand finale of romanticism and the herald
of modernism, exemplar of Byzantine engrossment and precursor
of a narrow Freudian narcissism. Why do we love him now?
Because we can retreat into his large and turbid enclosures and
close the door on everything else. We can glory in the circumscrip-
tion of a great wide world ruled from a Mayfair drawing-room. We
can be magnificent again in our wing collars and trailing cloaks
without feeling arcane. We can be stroked by high language, that
almost forbidden pleasure.

Henry James's stories are highly dramatic but his presentation
of them is oblique. *The Golden Bowl* is an endless taunt and moves
slowly by barely perceptible notional shifts – he was obviously on
tuatara time when he wrote it. Every line holds out the promise
that we might actually be told, quite soon, what we really want to
know, and this cock-teasing holds us to the very end when there
is … no ejaculation. We never know. The ongoing disquiet which
has held our attention is never quietened. It simply moves away
from us, still murmuring. The later work in particular – and it is
the later work that is of real interest – embodies a rejection of
commitment, as though commitment is death, as though *saying
anything definite* is to lie. All is contingent and relative. So I can
quite understand Cyril Connolly's inability to return to James. He
is delectable to read, but perhaps not to reread because one knows
it's a hopeless case – there is no catharsis. Henry James cowers in
his fabulous fog, terrified of direct observation, terrified of the
Evil Eye.

~

I'm not feeling sex around me. I'm quite good at finding sex in unlikely places but you have to get some sense of it first – it's not possible to make bricks without any straw at all and if you try you could be arrested. When travelling in a realm where sex has been suppressed beneath layers of seemliness, one has to stop awhile and linger at a tangent, this in order to decipher the super-subtle signalling and to curry sex out of an apparent void; but I've been driving on and on and on. Outside, in front of my cabin, there is utter silence. I can hear only the blood in my ears. The sky is the blackest sky I've seen – no Riviera navy-blue or African purple – so black indeed that there is almost a suggestion of brown in it. But it's only a suggestion and comes from the blood flowing red through one's eyes. There are plenty of stars to deepen the black and not masses of stars to lighten the sky and no stars that I recognise.

∼

On a sunny and very cold day I drive to Bannockburn, the Margaux of the Antipodes, past Champagne Gully, Italian Creek, Dead Man's Creek. Bannockburn is surrounded by arid peaks, with the cloudy liquid of the Clutha showing itself from time to time in a gruesome ravine. One cannot tell what is lake, what is dammed river, what is river proper, because everything's been messed up. Before all this interference, the ashen landscape must have had an extreme asceticism bordering on the divine. Now it looks like a megalithic builder's yard.

Visit the Akarua estate and buy, without tasting, a half dozen of their red Pinot Noir, which has just won the Wine of the Year prize. The main pylon cables run over the Akarua vines and maybe this gives the produce an extra voomph. Couldn't get talking to the woman running it, though. They are very businesslike round here and have learned to smell money and obviously didn't smell it on me. I asked her if I could drink the Akarua now. 'Drinking well now but with a cellar life of five to ten years.' And she was on to another job.

Take the road up the eastern side of Lake Dunstan ... John Bull Burn ... Devil's Burn ... Crippleton Burn ... layer upon layer of landscape, each layer entirely different from the others, receding to a high solid line iced with snow and smudged with cloud. Turn off to Bendigo on to a very rough track. Bendigo is a forgotten gold station, very little there now, they said, merely a couple of crumbling houses. WRONG. The most extensive vineyard installations in Central Otago are going on here, but the site remains far more lyrical than slashed Bannockburn. Bendigo Wines flying your way soon! I'm not sure this was the right thing to do – the car is going through hell on lumpy rubble. A burst tyre I don't need in the middle of nowhere under a corrosive, ice-sharp sun. While juddering along I look out of the window at the camel-coated uplands, then suddenly catch my first view of the Southern Alps. They are jagged and new, like the northern ones, and immaculately covered with snow. They yodel *health*. Men wave cheerfully from distant bulldozers.

Rejoining the main road without mishap, I realise the small of my back is wet with sweat. I must have been more anxious than I realised jerking over those stones. The landscape grows softer, greener, wider, lovelier, more human. This is a heavenly stretch of road. Turn left towards Wanaka and the road follows the upper Clutha Valley. We must be getting quite high because to my astonishment it starts to snow. Ah, there's the road to Gladstone – but it's another gravel road and I decide it's wiser not to take it with the snow coming down. Finally I roll to a stop at the Esplanade Reserve beside Lake Hawea. A glassy surface of no particular colour in today's light surrounded by interlocking triangles out of Cézanne, while straight ahead green mountains rise to a powdery slate-blue topped with crinkles of snow. A bellbird – or is it a tui? – sings welcome from a nearby eucalyptus tree.

But reverie is not possible; there is loud aggressive hammering. I have to tell you that the approach I made to the lakeside was through parcelled-out land where holiday homes are going up at a ferocious rate. As I leave by another road I see that development has been going on for quite a while and these settlements, though low key, have a mean look, as in other beauty spots, because even the luxury homes are little more than glorified cabins with tin roofs surrounded by all the scarring entailed in the provision of garages, driveways, gardens, sports amenities, supermarkets. The quality of the development is not good enough for the location. The great myth about this country is that it's empty, but it isn't. Four million inhabitants and sixteen million shacks. Another myth, perpetrated by North Islanders, is that on South Island you can drive for hours without seeing another car. In fact you hardly drive a minute without seeing another car. Even on gravel roads there are constant cars. In this land nothing can happen without a car. Small lumps of ice fall from the sky, not snow but hail. Dear me – on the way out I'm greeted by yet another dam. I hate dams! They are unnatural and send a deep shudder of horror through a landscape. They have a look of dread, of malign power. They always threaten inundation. They speak only of death by drowning.

~

Friday morning: I packed, left the Antique Lodge Motel, and called again at The Grape before hitting the Central Otago road. The wine-dealer Tim says 'I thought you'd like to try this rosé first – before the other one I promised you.'

He proffers a Gibbston Valley, blanc de Pinot Noir. 12.5 per cent, pale pink, not quite salmon or peach pink but the best pink I've come across. *Not* pale red. Some of the rosés I've seen have been *brown*. Its bouquet is bliss, like being invited to a picnic by Watteau or Fragonard. This wine is operating at an entirely new level.

Tim: 'Cabernet Sauvignony? Rieslingy? And I thought – cut grass.'

Thank God he's not going to continue with grape types. They mean very little to me. I'm used to thinking of wines by French region.

Me: 'Cut grass?'

Tim: 'Yeah, it had a real cut grass smell when we opened it last night.'

Me: 'I don't smell cut grass.'

Tim: 'Very slight now. More like … uncut grass.'

This vini-game of mutual suggestion, advancing an idea, half withdrawing it, proposing an alternative, groping for a parallel, a simile, an elucidation of … a smell, a taste, a savour, is all part of the fun, and yes, in this case the bouquet suggests the overture to a ballet with pastel Japonaiserie parasols and perhaps a kind of pre-pubescent flirtatiousness, not that I'm suggesting it's a twirly girlie rose-cheeked flutter-eyed molestation-type experience, because the molestation hasn't happened yet, we've only *sniffed*, and let's sniff again. Ah! Nostrils quiver above the tantalising surface and young geishas disrobe among blossom, a brook babbles through an apple orchard, and distant laughter – blond and pinktipped – passes over a daisy field … Time to sip. A tiny shout – even a rasp – but a winsome rasp – a waltz which carousels out of a pavilion among blue and lemon vistas as, turning in mid-air, the flavour unrolls along a meandering avenue to springtime, definite but delicate and its definition fading in curling reverberations of operetta under a slaking sky scattered with forget-me-nots and mignonette and lobelia. In other words, the best rosé yet. A real wine experience.

Tim opens the second wine. If we hadn't had the Gibbston first we'd be impressed by the Lincoln Heritage. It is similar but in mono rather than stereo, in black and white not colour. The Gibbston wins hands down. I'll take a case. No? I can't buy any? Tim doesn't have any in stock. He produced the bottle as a favour. He says it's expensive. All wine from this country is expensive. In France I'd get a rosé of this quality for £5. This, I believe, is over £10. But it's futile comparing prices. They depend on so many things. Anyway I couldn't exactly buy this wine anywhere else. Good wines are always *sui generis*.

~

Hit the State highway 85 going north of Alexandra into deepest Otago. I thought it would be bleak, this road, but it isn't. It's oddly verdant with deciduous trees in spinneys, and mountains which grow an ever deeper purple as they retreat. Nor is this bungalow territory. Every so often a venerable homestead triggers a sense of timeless peace, however fast one drives. I'm not driving fast. The locals are overtaking me. Drybread Road ... Brown Road ... Vinegar Hill Road ... roads which are really tracks leading off into secretive hillsides, and to what tortuous stories and bitter family feuds and inescapable sexual obsessions and slowly gratified hopes or gruelling eternities of frustration? Trees along streams, untrammelled pastures ... lovely, lovely ... Turn off left at a signpost to St Bathan's – gulp – sudden appearance of conifer plantations in long strips. More and more of them. This is criminal in such a landscape. Fortunately the conifers give way to real trees as, after a shorter drive than expected, we roll up to St Bathan's itself. And it's enchanting. Surviving from the nineteenth-century gold rush and set among groves on a sharply ascending lane, it coheres like an English hamlet. It has that mellow and concentrated cosiness. The Vulcan Hotel, where I want to stay for a night or two, is pungent with the past, not overdone, its historicism accruing naturally to it. The front bar has photos, thirty thighs apiece, of the local rugby team going back year after year. Damnation, it's fully booked. But with only four bedrooms I'm not surprised.

The Post Office is replete with souvenirs which politely I finger before asking about the church restoration that Chris Cochran was involved in. 'It's finished!' the postmistress yelps. 'Go and have a look! We had snow up on the mountain last night. Someone asked me what the noise was and it was branches snapping under the weight of the snow. We're in full leaf now, you see. Do you want any fudge? We've got great fudge.'

The church, further along the road and set on a grassy bank, is the size of a suitcase, and white with a green roof and red-painted wooden trim. What I thought was a well-head beside it is in fact a free-standing campaniletto, its bell breast-high. Oddly the church is called St Alban's. I know who St Alban was, the first Christian martyr in an England ruled by the Romans. As for St Bathan, the most known about him is that he has been associated with the Shetland Islands. The restoration, a plaque proclaims, was the personal achievement of Gillian McKnight. Chris said she campaigned like crazy. Gillian died on 25 September 2002, only in her mid-sixties but presumably fulfilled. Inside, the church is as fresh and tidy as a newly made bed.

≈

Back on the road, conifers recur, not the graceful native conifers like podocarp and kauri but the introduced pointy ones. This waxing coniferousness climaxes at Naseby which hides in its very own Black Forest, initially planted a hundred years ago. The atmosphere is murderous. Conifers block everything off with black walls. Conifers are like buying books by the yard and claiming you have a library. Conifers look so *cheap*. I enter a phonebox opposite the village green in order to book a room at Cargill's Hotel in Dunedin.

The receptionist tells me that I can have no more than two nights – the Ministry of Fisheries is having a conference in Dunedin next week and has booked out the whole town. On the subject of conifers I'll allow the mighty cedars and Lawson cypresses along the village green which I can see from this phonebox; they are awesome, like manic depression on a colossal scale.

Just as in Mazzano, Italy, I was served the worst spaghetti I've ever had in my life, so in Naseby I'm served the very worst lamb. The restaurant was inviting, with sofas and wood-burning stove. On my table was a sprig of lilac whose scent was so voluptuous that at 2,000 feet (Naseby is the country's highest town) it worked on me like opium; and the lamb when it arrived looked mouthwatering, with boiled potatoes and asparagus. But it was saddleleather end to end. I toiled valiantly but gave up. I should've sent it back but something about the innocence of the establishment oppressed me, made me unable to act.

My accommodation tonight is at the Ancient Briton Hotel in a shoddy annexe. Oh gawd. Two rowdy lesbians – mighty walkers by the glimpse of them – have moved into the room next door. All the other rooms are empty. So they've stuck 'em next door to me. The walls of course offer no more insulation than cardboard. While the girls knock each other about, with gushes of high whinnying laughter, I finish Poe's *Gordon Pym* – whose fancies hold one's attention even though they are implausible. Until, that is, about halfway through, at which point the book collapses into fatuity and becomes a trudge. In the end Pym perishes, though he has all the while been presenting us with his subsequent narrative. On the basis of such absurdities, Poe became a hero of Baudelaire and the Decadents and later the Surrealists. In Magritte's portrait of Edward James, called *La Reproduction Interdite* – you know, the one with the man looking into a mirror at the back of his own head – the book lying on the mantel-shelf is *Gordon Pym*.

~

After Ranfurly I take the road to Patearoa through farming country of quiet fields and copses against a backdrop of distant lethal hills. What I love most about this land are these soft, lonely farming areas, away from the tourist track, tenderly self-sufficient, uninvaded by the jumble of the world. The one I'm driving through now really is a secret Eden, the sort of place where one imagines that if the car broke down and I met a true pair of eyes I could never leave – no eyes in such a place could deceive – dishonesty and lies and cheating have no purpose in Eden – but it's also a mistake. I've taken the wrong road, and I have to backtrack otherwise I'll go awry and not make it to Dunedin. I loathe backtracking. It's a waste.

After the Kyeburn turn-off for Middlemarch I stop the car and take some photographs. Yes, I know it's futile, these mechanical attempts to ensnare such nuanced glory. But the pics will be reminders that it wasn't a dream. Along the Taieri River are groups of willows like fountains of green water. The plains heave in slow breathing, streaked with purple heather and splashes of yellow gorse, traversed by stony streams. Distant crags rear up like castles. Crystal air ascends into a blue sky without the quaver of the burning days to come. It's not hot but this landscape knows heat. Not a house in sight. Was that a car? No, it wasn't. I was wrong – sometimes there are no cars … And it is a moving thing to chance upon tiny settlements whose only memorials are those put up in honour of the two world wars. Here's one at Hyde now, a great name but just a few houses with two midget churches and a large lorry depot in the middle of nowhere, and this fine stone cross proud above the flying road. This was a land of few people, and requiring much labour to build the nation; yet how without a moment's hesitation they gave their men and came to the defence of the mother country.

~

Coming off the stark hills, the descent is magical to Middlemarch laid out in its shallow basin of farms with horses prancing across paddocks. Cared for but not fussed up, neither old-fashioned nor modern, Middlemarch is simply itself, with nothing 'wrong' grafted on to it, a perfect rural township. The main through-road is dead straight and very long, with a line of telegraph poles like retreating crucifixes, and it disappears in a bluish blur at the centre of one's vison. The lady behind the counter of the General Store nodded hullo. I ordered a cup of tea and read a notice about the local museum. The lady said they'd phone Dawn to open it up for me – but Dawn wasn't in.

'We can try again later.'

'Don't worry,' I said.

'It's no trouble. There are interesting things in it. An old cannon for example.'

I took myself off down a side street plotted with wooden cottages. A couple of the gardens corralled ponies, as though the whole town just paused here yesterday to rest and graze the horses and repair the wagons before drifting on again. I came into a large piazza-like space with a few Wild West huts on its edge. A solitary pick-up truck was parked beside one of them but there were no other vehicles to be seen and nobody was about. Along the far side a series of railway buildings were newly painted in white, pale green and terracotta. One door was painted scarlet with startling effect since it was the only piece of aggression for many miles around. The station was unattended and probably had been for years. Pairs of rails swung across each other making sidings overgrown with grass. Several pieces of rolling stock were parked picturesquely, tickling up against the buffers. Maybe once in a blue moon a bank holiday excursion organised by enthusiasts would bring to life those lonely platforms, but for the time being the station was as still as a photograph.

∿

Driving into Dunedin, fourth city of the nation, I glimpse Edwardian mansions in the hills, red-tiled or slated, turreted and balconied, brick not wood, sunk in rhododendron gardens, and down by the port a true whiff of the old shipping grandeur. Cargill's Hotel tell me that I can stay for five nights. So what was all that about being booked out by the Ministry of Fisheries?

Racism talk on my room radio while I'm unpacking. I'm not a racist – I know a heap of shit can come in any colour. A woman is saying whites are privileged in this country and that it's a problem which must be addressed. The use of the word 'privileged' is misleading in that it implies unfair advantages in a unified society. This is not exactly the case. The Maoris wish to adhere to their own way of going on. Fine. But that means they are less equipped to function in an advanced Western democracy, which is what this place is. So the problem to be addressed is: to what extent can the Maoris enjoy the fruits of prosperity while standing aloof from it? This is the problem of all third-world peoples living in developed societies. In Europe we have it most obviously with Muslim immigrants, many of whom want to import the very attitudes which have rendered their own societies moribund and places to be escaped from. Prosperity is not an accident. It is the result of a certain outlook on life. It should be distinguished from progress. Stalin achieved progress but never prosperity.

∿

Tried out Dunedin's gay sauna. A few scowling men with pot bellies shuffle at funereal pace from one damp cavern to another. Individually they slump to a halt in front of a television set showing pornographic films, where their expressions set like cement. Don't think I'll find any larry here. Then into the empty, simmering sauna cabin comes a human being, a jolly fellow who's just done four years in prison for having sex with a fifteen-year-old. It's wrong to contravene the age of consent – I want to say that before the turds start coming through the letterbox – but even Oscar Wilde only got two years at the height of the Victorian sexual neurosis and I think one of his lads was fifteen. The jolly fellow fills me in – the fifteen-year-old looked older and was working as an escort at the time and went to the police out of malice some years later when the jolly fellow wouldn't submit to blackmail. The boy apparently is still working as an escort. I think the jolly fellow thought that because the boy was working as an escort it made the boy less of an innocent, but doesn't the law view under-age prostitution as a worse offence than simple under-age sex? Bring on identity cards so that everyone knows everyone else's age.

Do you recall Chuck Berry's 'Almost Grown' and 'Sweet Little Sixteen'? Or America's sweetheart Doris Day singing 'Teacher's Pet', or Maurice Chevalier singing 'Thank Heaven for Little Girls'? That was from *Gigi* in 1958 and it was a global hit. Or Fred Astaire in *Funny Face* in 1957? Fred was nearly sixty and Audrey Hepburn looked eighteen. *Funny Face* is a celebration of transgenerational sex. It was thought touching at the time, not verging on the criminal. I suppose what has happened is that the spread of free love and AIDS has demonised transgenerational sex into that of predator and victim, especially in the Anglosphere whose current paedophilia obsession is fed by its angst about sex in general. Our so-called sexual liberation is a very odd affair and new forms of demonisation are spreading into all kinds of relationships, so that anyone taking any sexual initiative whatsoever runs the risk of being called a pervert. A recent television programme about the

comedian Frankie Howerd portrayed his propositioning of men as
a sickness, whereas he obviously just enjoyed sex.

The fellow who's recently come out of prison used to be a
barman at the Champion Pub in Notting Hill, and also in a
Dunedin seamen's bar in the 1970s. He said 'You could always
have the deck lads and cabin boys, whether they were from England
or from Kenya. Those were the days!' Yes, before being gay became
a vocation, an exclusive lifestyle, a business. I caught the tail end
of it, all those easy-going bisexual lads in London and Rome and
Istanbul. Why is everyone in a category now? It's confusing – the
movements for racial equality and sexual liberation have been
among the top stories of my times, and at the end of it what
happens? You have to tick a box defining your ethnicity and sexual
orientation.

So what am I saying? That I want to go back to the furtive,
guilty, nasty days when the penalties, in Britain especially, were
barbaric? To return to before Kinsey and his revolutionary *Sexual
Behavior in the Human Male*? No, of course not. Modern Jamaica,
with its gangsta cum Christian cruelty, shows us what that's like.
The old pleasure-loving Islam showed how it could be – well, for
men anyway (sorry, girls). In my youth the Islamic world was where
you went to escape the uptightness of the west, to smoke dope and
release your sexuality; from Morocco to Turkey, Afghanistan to
Indonesia, it was gay and hippy havens all the way. But that has
disappeared entirely with the spread of neo-primitivism among
Muslims.

Kinsey, working in the spirit of free enquiry, discovered that
most routes to sexual fulfilment are so widespread that they have
to be considered normal, and millions had the crushing burden of
shame lifted from their shoulders. But vested interests, especially
the religions, were outraged that their chief weapon – sin – had
been rendered useless. Kinsey's essential message is: don't live in

ignorance, don't live in fear. But what's happened is that in lifting the taboo on talking about sexual relations, we have obliged people to choose the label they can live with publicly: gay, straight or bisexual. Most people aren't that confident or that polarised. But I've noticed an escape category has come in, spearheaded by youth websites. This is 'open-minded', and masses of teenagers are opting for it when asked to click the sexuality box. Which strikes an optimistic note.

∼

Rang the English Department at the University of Otago who tell me that Margaret Dalziel, Popper's assistant in the early 1940s, died several months ago. I'm managing to catch most of them before they slip over the horizon, but not Miss Dalziel. 'Her female companion is still alive,' added the secretary, 'and I'm sure she'd be happy to tell you about Margaret.' But I think that's stretching it a bit.

∼

A Pre-Raphaelite exhibition, on in the centre of town, exposes the suffocating mouldy mediaevalism of these painters much more clearly than in London where they are simply part of the furniture. Rossetti's notable achievement was his bizarre series of paintings of women which grows stranger and greater with the passing years, represented here by two examples: *Proserpine*, with its representation of the vagina as a bitten fig, and *Monna Vanna* coiled in brocades and ready for a major orgy. They should look silly these women – well, they *do* look silly – but the genius of them is that the disturbing power comes through nonetheless.

Monna Vanna, a meddler in the affairs of fifteenth-century Pisa, is orientalised in tigerish colours, her hands tensely entangled in ropes of coral. She has a knowing feline viciousness whereas

Proserpine is poisonous despite herself. Proserpine's eyes are tender and deep; but all the rest of her is in reptilian writhe as, bare-backed, she sloughs off the skin of a silken blue shift, which forms an eddying vortex at the picture's base. She is in fact a portrait of William Morris's wife, Jane, with whom Rossetti had a long and claustrophobic affair in his later years under the influence of chloral washed down with whisky.

There is nothing 'before Raphael' about these female portraits of Rossetti's. Like Michelangelo's male nudes on the Sistine ceiling, they border on the grotesque, even on the comic, but the laughter is uneasy because these women hover dangerously between sadness and cruelty. Laden with symbols, sullen with eroticism, they are perverse romantic goddesses on the verge of an implacable, avenging arousal, and should they ever give birth, it would simply be the by-product of their relentless powers of absorption.

∾

A man called Roy Colbert, who runs a secondhand record shop, suggested I telephone his old schoolfriend Peter Entwisle, who's an architecture buff. When I got through to Peter he was very quick off the mark and proposed he come to Cargill's Hotel in half an hour's time at one o'clock. This is the only country I know where non-lunch appointments are arranged for 1 p.m. Perhaps they lunch at noon. It's a fascinating topic, the times which various societies and epochs keep. In Trollope's *Barchester Towers*, published in 1857, Bishop Proudie and his wife hold an evening party: *People were to arrive at ten, supper was to last from twelve till one, and at half-past one everybody was to be gone.* Talleyrand would get up between 11 a.m. and noon and usually had dinner at 5 p.m.

Peter Entwisle's alacrity was to solve a puzzle for me. All the travel promo for Dunedin uses idyllic photographs of the gothic-revival university building. But I couldn't locate it anywhere. Judging from the brochure, it should dominate the place, so where was it?

'You won't find it!' Peter snaps. 'It's been buried in a brutalist graveyard.' A fevered grin flashes across his face. 'Look, every single major Dunedin building has at some time been earmarked for demolition, including the railway station, the law courts, the old university buildings you're on about, and the town hall.' He puffs. He's very jittery and speedy. 'And only constant battles, *constant* battles, have saved them, and it's still going on, and I'm fed up with it! Constant battles!'

He allows himself a deep sigh and glances round Cargill's lounge area on the off-chance there might be something in it for him to admire. I don't think there is. His eyebrows bristle thickly above intense grey eyes. His mouth is very wide, thin-lipped, and sardonic, as though it could easily swallow saucers. Suddenly he appears haggard, like a choirboy who's shot from fifteen to fifty, and looks hungrily towards the door, eager to drag me outside. Next thing we are walking rapidly towards an anonymous block behind the hotel.

'That's the university.'

'But it's not gothic.'

'It's hideous. Keep walking.'

We enter the, er – I was going to say university precincts but the most elementary aspects of organisation and landscaping have never been considered. The departmental buildings are mostly debased modern hulks and parked at random. This lack of any intelligence at work in disposing the halls of academia, well, it's chilling. And finally, by contrast over there, beyond a stream, is the famous building of the travel poster, a gothic range in the Franco-Scottish manner.

Peter pauses in respectful silence, allowing himself to be soothed

by something decent. 'The University of Otago tried for years to
pull it down.'

'Why?'

'Why do you think? Because they're brain-dead. They said it
was old-fashioned.'

The range is long and prettily turreted, like one of Rossetti's
Pre-Raphaelite women lying horizontally in a nineteenth-century
fantasy of the Middle Ages. To the left there is a delightful spot,
with an old iron footbridge over the stream and roses and lawn, a
tiny surviving particle of what one thought the whole campus
would be like.

'Indeed,' says Peter with a thin high cackle, 'and they want to
demolish the bridge and drive a large road over the river and lawn
so that the professors can have easy access with their cars. They
want to eliminate the one picturesque corner which has by accident arisen on the campus. It's my latest fight, to stop them.' Peter
jerks his face at me and pushes back a dead straight cowlick of grey
hair. We squeeze through a chicken-wire fence. Next thing we are
driving along Royal Terrace in his jalopy, with rapid patter.

'This was where the nobs lived. That was the house where
Frances Hodgkins grew up.' He points to a mansion of the suburban type circa 1900. 'And that's where Charles Brasch lived. He
was an important cultural figure here.'

'Do you think he entertained the Oliviers when they came?'

'His boyfriend would've done. That was Rodney Kennedy, who
had a sort of studio in Bath Street where he had terrific parties.
He'd've thrown a party there for the Oliviers without a doubt.
Rodney was Dunedin's arbiter of taste.'

'Is he still alive?'

Deep inhalation before tumbling forward. 'No. Neither of them
is. Rodney Kennedy died in 1989. He was gay, a dwarf, not rich
and very rude. He took up with Charles Brasch who was also gay

but very rich and very polite. They could not have been more different. Rodney liked sex in toilets, Charles wouldn't've dreamt of it. Rodney was poor South Otago Irish. Charles was rich Jewish Dunedin who went to Oxford. His father took the "c" out of the name but Charles put it back in. His family owned chains of shops. The Jews were without doubt the principal benefactors of Dunedin's cultural life – the Hallensteins, Theomins, de Beers, Fels. Mostly of German origin. They don't have any identity now. Even their beautiful synagogue has been demolished and a multi-storey car park put there.'

We are zipping up a hill and his car shrieks to a halt. A driver honks furiously from behind – smell of burning rubber – but Peter is already bowling out on to a main road without looking – horn blares – not his. This combination of peril and information is very invigorating. We plunge almost vertically down. I'm pressing the floor with my feet.

'I know what this is,' I gamely volunteer. 'I've seen it in the brochures. It's the steepest street in the world.'

'Wrong! It's the second steepest street in the world. The steepest street in the world is about five minutes away. Do you want to go there?'

'No!'

'Look at that! Now, the man who lived there was a child molester. He had–'

But I'm not listening. 'Are we on the right side of the road?'

Zoooom – shaved by a van. Seconds later his arm shoots across my face. 'That's where the City Hotel was. Lovely building. Where the Oliviers stayed when they came. Demolished. If you're interested in the Oliviers you should contact Des Smith. He was a great friend of Rodney Kennedy's and I bet Des was at any party Rodney gave for them.'

The motor revs and rattles and I'm pressed against the door as

Peter takes a corner in a straight line. A contorted pedestrian jerks backwards on to the pavement. As we fly along the road between the Leviathan Hotel and the Otago Settlers Museum I point to a huge hole in the townscape. Peter looks bitter. 'There was a superb range of classical buildings there, including that of the *Otago Daily Times*. The owner flattened them, hoping to attract the attentions of a Japanese hotel chain. Of course the Japanese weren't interested. So we've been stuck with the hole for years.'

In the centre of town there are holes everywhere.

'This is a city of holes!' he cries. 'All the holes were once wonderful Victorian buildings. The owner demolishes a building and turns it into a car park while he tries to sell the site for a new project. But the sad thing is our country didn't *have* to demolish anything of quality. We have the space.'

'Is it the same in Australia?'

'More or less. Australia is like our elder brother and Britain is our parentage. That's why it felt so strange when Britain joined the Common Market. The parents left home. It's supposed to be the children who leave home but in our case it was like the parents walked out of the house, leaving the children behind. So we suddenly felt much more isolated than we already were. We still haven't quite understood it. All our trade agreements with Britain, the major prop of our economy, disappeared overnight. It triggered an economic depression to match the psychological one we suffered.'

'Do you think the wound of rejection went so deep that the architectural clearance was an attempt to remove the visual legacy of England?'

'Of course. To reinvent ourselves as a new Pacific Rim nation. What I think should happen now,' he says with a sidelong leer, 'is that Australia and ourselves should apply for membership of the European Union. We're more European than Turkey.'

'That's a brilliant idea. But I warn you: EU corruption is breathtaking. I know this from personal experience. Which is why they aren't worried by Turkish corruption.'

'How corrupt is Turkey?'

'Ankara produced its own report on the economy. It said that 25 per cent of the Turkish GNP was controlled by organised crime.'

He gives out a low whistle. 'Perhaps we're better off out of it.' He's grinding up the loops of Signal Hill to a war memorial. Another one. As war memorials go, this is very big. It's supported by heroic figures of native cast overlooking the whole city. Beneath us the South Pacific does an excellent impersonation of the North Sea.

'I think the most beautiful Maori faces have a slightly oriental look,' I remark. 'They remind me of the faces I saw in Thailand on thickset wrestlers.'

'A lot of them are very racially mixed now,' he says, 'but the basic Polynesian strain is Mongoloid, whereas the basic Melanesian strain is Australoid. Our Maoris look down on the Australian aborigines. Are you interested in the Maoris?'

'Not much.'

'You should be.' His lips go wide and tight. 'They have a very interesting architecture related to that of South China.'

'I'm not very interested in China either.'

≈

Got a parking ticket today for an offence I never knew existed: *Facing the wrong way*. And I've developed a nasty pain in the small of my back. Please God it doesn't go into spasm.

≈

Crikey, I've fallen for the hotel barman. He's cuddly and muscly with a hint of naughtiness. I make a slight reference to one of my adventures in Sicily, so he may deduce my orientation – I'm not a

flaunter but I don't like to deceive either. On returning to my room
I find that I've taken his pen. Printed on the side are the words
Rim Shot Frenzy. I get a hard-on immediately.

∽

Des Smith, that member of the Kennedy–Brasch circle, is cautious
on the phone and I can tell he doesn't want to meet me, so I don't
push it. But he says 'Socially I was exposed to the Oliviers for
about ten minutes. I was a student and went to *The School for
Scandal* which was at His Majesty's Theatre on Crawford Street.
The building has had its front ripped off but the auditorium is still
there, now a sort of nightclub called Sammy's. What I remember
about the production was the setting. The interiors were all painted
on cloth in sepia tones and all brought out from England of course.
In those days Dunedin was very conservative – they applauded
with their gloves on – but the response to the Old Vic Tour was
quite different. Booking was heavy, every ticket sold, and the audience really responded physically. This was of a different order to
anything we'd seen before.'

'You suddenly felt part of the greater world.'

'Well, you see, Vivien Leigh was *Gone with the Wind* and Laurence Olivier was *Rebecca* and *Wuthering Heights*. This wasn't
alien. It was our own culture – at its most brilliant.'

'What about Rodney Kennedy?'

The veil of caution descends again. 'Rodney Kennedy didn't
have any education but he acquired great knowledge.' I'm obviously going to get nothing on sex in toilets. 'And his Bath Street
premises were an artist's studio. Strange people used to turn up
there, painters, actors, musicians. It was in a terrace of fine colonial houses.'

'Could I visit it?'

'All demolished I'm afraid.'

~

The barman wasn't in the bar tonight – some overweight scruff instead – but the pain in my lower back has vanished. The Dunedin climate is tough, so perhaps it was a chill in the kidneys. I was all for calling Harley Street and setting up a cortizone injection down here. The disappearance of the pain must, I think, have something to do with my sexual arousal. I probably don't have a chance in hell with that barman, but you have to try, don't you. Proceed discreetly.

~

Fockin bejaysus – he wasn't in the bar *again*. He only works three nights a week they tell me and I'm moving on tomorrow, so I left him a letter at reception with my email address on it, went back to my room and tossed off in irritation.

Sprawling disconsolately across the bed, I open a book of poems by Ivor Gurney which I bought earlier today in a secondhand bookshop (along with a copy of *Pickwick Papers*, which I've also never read). There's an erratic beauty in some of these poems, brilliant phrases, several lines which stick, occasionally almost an entire poem, but they are vague and sexless. I think the poetry, and the music too, which he wrote after he lost his grip on the world is more original, more modern, than his saner work; it conveys the sense of an art pushing at the boundaries, daring to move outward. I believe he wrote over three hundred songs. During his final period of insanity Gurney was very creative and many of the later songs are unfinished or unrevised. I am fascinated by unfinished art. It is the opposite of a ruin: it's on the way up rather than on the way down. I'd love someone to bring out a Gurney album called *Unfinished Songs*. Apart from Katherine Mansfield, he is the only other writer or artist I can think of who died from TB complicated by gonorrhoea. Born in 1890, two years after her, Gurney was committed to a mental home in 1922 and stayed there until his miserable death in 1937.

∾

Drive northwards, hugging a complexity of small coves and beaches. My strong attraction to the barman seems to have eroticised this land, or at least peeled some membrane off me, so that I can detect more readily those realms of emotion and desire extending behind their jovial courtesies. The high suicide rate among their young men at least proves they are romantics underneath. Only romantics commit suicide. Hutch is playing now.

> Up among the stars we'll find
> A harmony of life to a lovely tune
> East of the sun and west of the moon

Stop at Fleur's Place for banana cake and coffee. Baghdad Creek … Big Kuri Creek … Break Neck Road … I've just told you about Gurney and now I'm going to tell you about Hutch. He was a bisexual from Grenada in the Caribbean who had a great success in the Mayfair of the 1930s as a cabaret pianist and singer wearing white tie & tails. Hutch was tall, handsome and charming, with an enormous penis, all of which proved irresistible to Tallulah Bankhead, Cole Porter, Edwina Mountbatten, Prince George and Princess Marina of Kent, Merle Oberon, Ivor Novello and many more. But his success didn't really survive the Second World War. In the 1960s he performed quite often at the White Hart, Sonning-on-Thames, where I saw him because it was one of the places where our parents took us to eat when we were young; that old black gent in the corner tinkling the ivories – it was Hutch, though I didn't realise it then. He died in 1969 largely forgotten and is buried in

Highgate cemetery. Lord Mountbatten rang the undertakers and offered to pay for the grave, so presumably Hutch had been there too.

Driving through Palmerston – nothing to detain us except the fine statue of Zealandia, one of those powerfully chinned figures like Britannia or the Statue of Liberty who are not only suggestive of ancient Greece and Rome but also kindred to those palpitating bisons of Rossetti. Zealandia, lifted above mere mortals on a massive plinth, holds a bouquet of stone flowers down by her side but her other arm is upraised and you wouldn't want to bump into her on a dark night. Caught something phantasmal, strange, sad on the radio which at first I thought might be Ligeti, Penderecki, Silvestrov – turns out to be 'Music for Jonny' by Ross Harris.

≈

The sentinel of Oamaru is the Junction Hotel. Its opulent silhouette, appearing out of farmland, announces one's arrival in the town of palaces. The Junction Hotel is abandoned and in unstable condition, its urns and balustrades toppling, but the descent to the town is full of style, and on Thames Street a sequence of Palladian temples in cream stone is etched against a sky of seaside blue. Corinthian pillars and deeply gouged pediments stand timelessly as though transplanted from an Italian town or an English hillside. At the defunct harbour, several whole streets have been salvaged, their edifices richly ornamented. This must be one of the most majestic small towns south of the Equator. They don't have the interiors of course – there are lavish salons in Latin America – but they don't have the crime and squalor either. Oamaru turns its back on the ocean and protects itself with a sea wall of piled-up rocks. The ocean, a motley of blues, looks extremely threatening as it takes deep firm tugs at the shore.

Michael O'Brien, a book-binder who wears Victorian clothes,

advised me to book into the Criterion Hotel a few doors along from his shop, and I'm jotting these notes in its upstairs sitting room. Beneath my feet a blues guitarist is entertaining the public bar. I feel I should go below and join them. But they are all a bit old down there and in couples and I'd soon have the empty feeling. Periodically they break into community-singsong of old Rolling Stones numbers. 'You Can't Always Get What You Want' is especially full-throated. What do I want? A Kiwi in his early twenties, the years of the height of sexual beauty, that would be nice. 'Late teens' has the taut bloom of that which is still burgeoning; 'early twenties' is the moment of equipoise before the rot begins. What do I adore in life? Dancing with the one I love. When did I last do that? Two years ago.

~

I'm driving through an uncorrupted landscape. Perfection. I didn't think I'd find perfection. I was about to say 'And I'm not looking for it' but of course one always is, and this journey like all journeys is the quest for perfection, for legends that are true. When I was young I was always obsessed with what was over the hill, round the corner, and walked off from the rest of the family leaving them sitting on the beach, walked off for hours looking, exploring, going up secret tracks, and when I returned they'd ask 'Where have you been?' but not in an inquisitorial or worried way, they knew I'd just gone off on one of my wanders, and I'd say 'Were you sitting here all the time?' and my mother would say 'Yes. Peter and Daddy are playing cricket on the sand.' And my sister would be sunbathing in dark glasses. In those days perfection had nothing to do with it, I was driven by sheer curiosity, a yearning to annihilate the mystery of distance. It was in early middle age that the terrible dream of perfection also took hold. I try to shake it off because it can so easily turn into rage. But I do dream of finding the perfect spot; and I have found a few, most of them since defiled. It's the greatest feeling when you find one, a slow drug-like intoxication. It begins with a general sense of absolute rightness, followed by the eyes scanning everywhere with high intensity, searching out any imperfection. Blots, however small, can always be detected by a ruthless eye – but with the ongoing failure to find any imperfection, euphoria mounts. Perfection is not so much a finished state as a living state in which imperfection has failed to assert itself.

Well, this is happening now. I've driven a few miles north of Oamaru and turned left on to the State Highway 83, turned inland, turned west, and am now pootling up a wide valley with, on its floor, horizontal farms divided by windbreaks of poplar trees. The buildings are mostly traditional and gabled, the hills either side are moss-green, while directly ahead snowy peaks crunch upwards. To my right, flowing through vegetation of almost tropical lushness, is the multi-channelled Waitaki River, a kind of Alpine Amazon, something never before seen. At a glance it is swamp-like, difficult to determine since the level of the road is scarcely higher than that of the river. But occasionally, where the road lifts up, the lace-like pattern of its flow among countless low mounds, pebbly and flowered, becomes so attractive that I run a risk of driving off the tarmac, and decide it's wiser to stop for a proper look and to breathe the tranquil high perfecting air. No pylons. No trash. No developments. So much tourist stuff is over-hyped and when you get there you find crummy holiday development, and then you come across something like this which isn't flagged and flogged, which is not a national park, which is just a region where man and nature have colluded to produce a unique scenic wonder.

I drive on in a mood of fulfilment and affirmation. I could drive for ever like this. But on the left a placard stuck in a field catches my attention. Think nothing of it. But here's another. I slow down.

Save the Waitaki. Hell … what are the buggers planning now? For God's sake, please don't mess this up with your insane greed! Doomed beauty, obviously I'm driving through doomed beauty, and I recall the essay by Huysmans in which, contemplating the contamination by industry of a river smaller than this, he imagines the tortures of the river nymphs whose agony he describes with sadistic relish. The cut-off point for this perfection of beauty is a place called Kurow. After Kurow the dams and pylons take over, with all the attendant mess, and of course those cruel artificial lakes. It's all repulsive through here now. And this no doubt is what they're planning for the perfect bit too.

At Otematata I stop for a cup of tea at a café with black Formica tables and chrome chairs. I ask the woman what *Save the Waitaki* means and she says 'They want to build a canal there and put six hydro dams on it.'

'They've already done that up here.'

'Yes, and they want to do it down there.'

'Who do?'

'The water company.'

On leaving the dams behind, the landscape improves again, bedecked by splashes of pink and blue lupins … Twizel is where we now are, entangled in yet another hydro-electric complex, and where is the turn-off for Mount Cook? That's where I'm heading by the way, Mount Cook. Here it is … Well, that was Twizel – which didn't live up to its name. Scrabble in a bag of mints. I feel crushed by what they're going to do to the Waitaki Valley. A morose and anxious fug fills the car … hup, hup … That was extraordinary. No, not the doomed Waitaki Valley – which was already an hour ago – but something that's just taken place. It's uncrushed me. Wind back the film. Let me explain – and in the present tense. I do keep flipping between past and present tenses, I know; that's how it is, how it has to be. Firstly, ahead of you on the road, above

the car bonnet, a sliver of electric blue appears. As you advance the
sliver expands, and you realise it's water. Slowly a blue lake is rising
in front of you, rising up as it were out of the floor of a stage, and
even on an overcast day like today, the blues of its waters are
radiant, seemingly lit from beneath, the blue light pouring upwards
out of the lake, as though you have come upon the mythic source
of blueness itself. By chance I've driven into the throbbing, absolute heart of the nation. That's what it feels like, this huge lake of
living light which has risen up before me. And the heart of the
nation is blue.

∾

Mount Cook, the Hermitage Hotel, Wakefield Wing, Room 434. I
have arrived in another country and am surrounded by crowds of
Japanese. Most of the staff are Japanese and some of them can't
speak English. There are Japanese channels on the television.
Hotel signs are in Japanese as well as in English. There is Japanese
food on the menu. Among the few non-oriental guests I hear only
American voices. It produces a sense of dislocation, not entirely
unpleasant, to find myself in another country without having
made any obvious move to get to one. My room is on the top floor
with a window looking on to … Matthew, my English porter, says
it looks on to Mount Cook, but the view is all cloud and rain, and
one can't see anything at all.

'Has it been raining long?' I ask him.

'It's been raining for days.'

A card on the desk reads (ungrammatically) *Warning. Our
mountain parrot, the kea, may appear to be friendly, but please do not
feed them. They can inflict a nasty bite and have the potential to be
very destructive. Do not leave any personal items such as shoes, cloth-
ing, cameras, etc. on your balcony as the kea will not hesitate to destroy
them.*

This hotel has a confused layout. Everyone, including the staff, is somehow adrift. It's like an anarchic film-set where we're all playing a part, and come the evening there will be the shout 'Go home, everybody. Filming starts again at 8 a.m.' The coffee shop and grocery shop close at 6 p.m., plunging the place into deeper mystery. There is beauty to this total rain, total cloud. It adds to the filmic, dysfunctional quality. You can't see anything through it. We've all expended great effort and spent lots of money in order to be completely buried in rain and cloud. Where is Mount Cook? Apparently it virtually nuzzles the hotel. But I can't see a thing, and the light is fading at 9 p.m. Nonetheless, though I can't see it, I can *sense* it. Sort of coming at me through the plate glass, a massive floor to ceiling rock-face.

Turning back into the room I decide to try the Akarua, Wine of the Year. Its alcohol level is 14.5 per cent, far too high. No wine should be that strong. Is it going to be one of those black treacly ones which are the horror of the New World Wine Experience? I only really like French wine … Screw top, not cork. I know that's OK because they've done studies. Pour … it is a very dark beverage, the black hole of Calcutta in a glass. You can't see through it even when holding it directly in front of a lamp. That amount of suspension is not good for the liver. Smell is figgy but slight – a quality nose but extremely understated, no real sensuous pleasure in it, no premonitory evocation, some faraway memories of old Burgundy possibly. Perhaps it will open out … Sip. Oh yes. All parts of the tongue brought alive. But it tastes young. It needs time to discover its own possibilities. At present it is garish and tense. The tongue come quickly alive, yes, and then it's quickly over. Second sip – a nice pinch in the side of the cheeks, but the moment it leaves the mouth and descends to the stomach it's over. So I should say that this wine is like a dark room in which one divines all sorts of things which remain conjectural. It is too adolescent and surly and turning away from me and it comes too soon. So I see no reason to modify my conviction that France is wine, elsewhere is drinking.

Do you know how to check the quality of red wine? Fling a glass of it on to a clean white tablecloth. If good it will produce concentric rings; if not it will produce a uniform stain. Try it at Claridge's next time. Well, Bunny, here I am, and instead of flinging my goblet I raise it to you beyond the wall of rain, beyond the wall of rock, beyond the sky, and want you to know that I miss you very much and perhaps you'd keep an eye out for me because, judging by the Japanese news on the telly tonight, or by any news any day for that matter, the world has flown off its spindle and things are getting pretty hairy down here.

≈

Reading *Pickwick Papers* on the bed. Hilarious. An on-the-road book. It reminds one of that first on-the-road book, *Don Quixote*, with Sam Weller as Pickwick's Sancho Panza. Dickens began *Pickwick Papers* in the reign of William IV, but by the time the last part was published, in November 1837, Victoria had been on the throne for four months and Dickens was never so bawdy again. I'm also charmed to note that there's a character in it called Mr Jinks, a name I'd never come across until my stay in Devonport.

≈

The cloud has lifted, the sun is out, and Mount Cook is visible through a gap in Mount something else. This morning, attended by grey warblers, I went for a walk along the Hooker Valley with a Japanese man. He was very polite, and not only that, his politeness somehow took a sotto voce form that was unnervingly seductive. He explained to me how the Japanese use a computer-keyboard and said 'It is far more likely that people will become like computers than computers will become like people. If the computer adds to our intelligence it must therefore add to our stupidity also.' He had beautiful teeth and a red bowed mouth and for a Japanese was unusually hirsute. When he came back to my room for tea, he showed me how hairy his wrists were. Nothing sexual happened, but the way he came so close with his courtesy and good manners, whispering so near my body, was enchanting and remained with me for days.

~

The stark, geometric Mackenzie Country. A road fringed by lupins crossing miles and miles of tawny grass, and the far horizon making a complete circle of low crests pinched with snow. When I phoned her in Menton, Sandy Boyle said 'The Mackenzie Country is as empty as hell' and it is, but I've stopped the car on the gravel shoulder and got out to discover that it's not inhospitable. The temperature is warm and the air is soft. Birds sing merrily. In the distance glints a tin homestead with a clump of trees beside it.

~

At a shop on the shore of Lake Tekapo I buy some possum-wool gloves. This settlement has resisted exploitation and it would be a good place to stay if I came this way again, because there's an amusing military camp here with cottages in pretty ranks. Nicholas Chevalier, staying at John Hay's station in 1866, painted a watercolour of Lake Tekapo sheltered by lilac peaks beneath a pale blue sky. In his picture all is treeless and ethereal, with a handful of tiny homesteads indicated on the lakeside. The view is barely different today.

~

One thing you always notice is the freedom of the children, which has exuberance but no spitefulness in it, and their physical beauty too, which fades into an unkempt adolescence and which the mature adults do not usually retain except in their eyes. The wide clear independence of childhood remains in their eyes. I'm thinking of this as I walk round Geraldine with all the children pedalling hither and thither on bicycles. Geraldine is a small town and after all the scenic grandeur I've lately endured, and the heavy weather too, I feel as though I've entered the Home Counties. The River Waihi flows through the town, and the woodland along its banks smells damp. Wild irises grow in impacted masses beneath beach, chestnut and willow. These introduced European plants they call 'exotics'. The place to live is up on the Downs where a number of old houses are found in steep gardens between which animals graze. The style there blends Texas hacienda with hill station Raj. Maybank, Chartwell, Burnlea are the sort of names those houses have. There are many plots for sale. Whether the Downs' enchanting blend of native trees, English country gardens and undulating farms can survive mass marketing …

∽

I've booked ahead into the YMCA, the only place in Christchurch which could give me a run of six nights. Never stayed in a YMCA before. The weather is highly volatile, boiling one minute, freezing the next. Indeed the weather pattern over both the North and South Islands is very uneven – for example 29 degrees in Napier on Saturday, 15 degrees a few miles down the coast, and snow in Invercargill!

In Geraldine it's drizzle as I take the road towards the Peel Forest with Led Zeppelin's first album scorching the speakers and my bum churning in the seat to 'Dazed and Confused'. Samuel Butler came here in the time of the Aclands, and the Aclands are still rattling round inside the Mount Peel homestead, its gables roofed with

13,000 slates. The forest itself is another of those rare native rem-
nants. It hangs on steep hillsides threaded by smoking mists. Science-
fiction fronds and arthritic evergreens drip upon the car, but it is too
soggy to get out so, while eating a currant bun, I contemplate the bee-
tling Rider Haggard effect through a watery windscreen.

I can see what drew Butler hither. And I can see what drove him
away again. The road turns to gravel and I find myself in the
Rangitata Valley, which has a sour look – don't want to continue
to Mesopotamia – really don't want that – it's 'orrible up that way
– fuck me if that ain't a mudslide – turn round – divert to Arundel
and the Rakaia Gorge, which is convulsing in fog. Going to play
that Zep album again.

∼

My room at the YMCA has a good position overlooking Hagley
Park, which does something to ameliorate my foul mood. The first
thing I noticed about Christchurch is – look, I'm really sorry about
this, I know I keep going on about it – but yes, they've destroyed
Christchurch too. Cathedral Square is a visual disaster zone. Still,
it's the only piazza in the country in the social sense. Just before
my arrival it was the site of National Penis Day. Which, plus the
green preserved banks of the Avon winding through the streets,
gives Christchurch an urbanity unique in New Zealand. It feels
like a city you can use. Also it's flat, which is a help.

Since the town is built on a grid of wide and immensely long
streets, the last thing it needs is a one-way traffic system, so the
City Council has given it one. The cars simply *fly* along, with no
mercy for walkers. That's another reason for the urbanity: Christchurch is terribly fast. You hear people cursing each other at traffic
lights. Young men on skateboards throw up two fingers. 'Your
mother takes it up the bum!' I heard yelled in my first minutes –
not at me, thank goodness. The boys from the city's famous schools

shout 'Wanker!' at their enemies on the opposite side of streets, safe in the knowledge that they'll never be able to cross the speed-way for a fight. The people have spontaneity, madness and sexiness. They dress more smartly than other New Zealanders too. Clothes aren't covered in words. Men wear shorts only for sporting activities. As I was dragging myself into an oncoming wind along the degraded stretches of Oxford Terrace, a dandy of all things came bustling towards me. He was in a cream suit and had long white hair which, since the wind was in his rear, was blowing up in a fine aurora. Who was this eccentric aesthete so eager to reach his destination or escape a pursuer?

≈

I'm fed up. I'm fed up with smashed-up towns. I'm fed up with beauty spots covered in shacks. I'm fed up with sloppy food. I'm fed up with 10 a.m. check-out times in hotels. Two things every hotel owner must observe: white cotton sheets and check-out at noon. They do all right on the former, but the latter, it's ridiculous to expect rooms to be vacated by 10 a.m., it's persecution.

≈

And I'm fed up with people being fat and ugly and covered in tattoos. I'm fed up with unwashed hair and spotty complexions. I'm fed up with my own company. I'm fed up that the locals never go *beyond*. Anyone successful appearing on radio or television repeatedly makes down-home cringes, honky-tonk obeisances to ordinariness, to prove that he or she has not got above themselves. No one is allowed to *soar*. Physical courage is taken for granted among them. Bravery is admired. Real daring of the heart or mind is distrusted or simply off the radar. Am I feeling homesick? Am I missing London's infinite variety? The only person I know of who lives in Christchurch is Viscount Bolingbroke but I have no phone number for him.

~

How in this stew of splenetic negativity I discovered the architect Peter Beaven I cannot remember, but when he turned up for our appointment at the café, I said 'I've seen you before.'

'It's not impossible. Where?'

'Oxford Terrace.'

He was the elderly aesthete I'd seen battling against the wind.

'It's so sad what they've done to this town,' I tell him.

His blue eyes light up. 'You think so? I'm glad. Few people notice. Christchurch had a very third-rate mayor, a woman, and a man called Miles Warren told her "There's nothing here worth saving except the two cathedrals." This did untold damage.' But Peter rallies, pushing back his long white tresses. 'Come!' And we're off on a tour of the city.

'Have you heard of the United Services Hotel?' I ask.

'Have I heard of it! The question is – why have you heard of it?'

'Because it's where the Oliviers stayed.'

'The Oliviers!' beams Peter. 'In the 1940s a friend and I were students in Auckland on forces' bursaries and we went to see the Thornton Wilder play. At one point Vivien Leigh had to step out of the frame and confide something to the audience across the footlights, and so, very scantily clad as a French maid, she walked down to the front where my friend and I were sitting. My friend said in the middle of her lines "We're having a great party to-night. Will you come?" And Vivien Leigh stopped what she was saying, looked down and said "I'll be there!" and then continued with the play.'

'Did she come?'

'I don't think so. But it was the way she carried it off.'

'So where is the United Services Hotel?'

After his happy recollection, he is crestfallen. 'It was a building of real quality in Cathedral Square. Oh, we tried so hard to save that building! It was put up in 1884, Port Hills trachyte, with pillars in Scottish granite. It was pulled down in the 1980s and it took a lot of pulling down too. They kept bashing at it but it wouldn't give way. The ANZ Bank is on the site now. It's such a shame because that whole side of Cathedral Square was very beautifully built.'

'Do people here understand what the word "quality" means?'

'A very good question … '

Peter tells me he's seventy-eight years old, which I can hardly believe – I'd've lopped ten years at least off that – and as we stride from street to street I point to one hideous new building after another. It turns out that almost every one of them was designed by the villainous Sir Miles Warren. Peter looks apologetic and says 'I'm afraid I was at school with him.'

'But his buildings can't manage the simplest attributes of good design or benevolence.'

'Oh dear, I'm afraid you're right. But look at that lovely little church over there. It's by Benjamin Mountfort, a nineteenth-century architect of the first rank. He did most of what's really special in Christchurch, including the black and white university buildings which we only *just* succeeded in saving from the bull-dozer. Mountfort didn't simply import gothic into this country, he made a highly original play with it and created a local idiom that is absolutely distinctive. Its smallness for a start and its boldness – and his comfort – people love to be around his buildings and rub up against them.'

'I'm looking for an exile and wonder if you ever came across a man called Lord Bolingbroke.'

'Kenneth!'

'You have?'

'Of course. I know him very well. Or did. He's fallen on hard times and I've lost touch.'

'I thought since he lives in Christchurch he'd be rather fun to meet.'

'He would. And more to the point he'd love to see you – because you're from England.'

'What sort of hard times?'

'Not very well. And not very rich – the problem was that being a lord he had lots of women after him, and he was quite happy about that, but as we all know women have to be entertained …'

'I have an address for him.'

'Really? Who gave it to you?'

'I got it from *Burke's Peerage*.'

'How sweet. Then use it.'

'What, just turn up unannounced?'

'Yes, just turn up. You can do that in this country. He's a delightful man. Really delightful. I'm sure he wouldn't mind.'

~

Christchurch's old university buildings, reprieved at the eleventh hour, have been converted to an arts centre: shops, cafés, restaurants, handicrafts, theatre, and in this rambling cultural depot is Rutherford's Den, the cellar wherein Ernest Rutherford's first experiments into radioactivity got going. There is a recording of Rutherford's voice addressing an audience of Germans in the 1930s. He has a very slight New Zealand accent which makes me think that the accent derives not from Cockney but from that of the southern English working class, what we now call Estuary English. 'Out' pronounced 'eart', 'now' pronounced 'near'. Rutherford died in 1937, the year that Karl Popper arrived, and the air would have been buzzing with it. Popper admired Rutherford, Peer of the Realm, President of the Royal Society and Nobel

Prizewinner for Chemistry, as a man passionately devoted to objectivity. But though there is plenty of Rutherford around this arts complex, there is nothing whatsoever of Popper. No mention at all of his name. And yet it was here that Popper, the apostle of personal freedom, wrote his greatest book.

My endeavours in tracking down a connection did in the end produce Dr Roy Holmes. He'd been a medical student in his first year when the Hiroshima bomb was dropped in August 1945, and he said that on the day following this epoch-making event, Popper gave an address in the Great Hall of what in those days was known as Canterbury College. Dr Holmes transcribed it at the time – it's never been published – and he promised to put it in the post to me.

'The Registrar of the college had got to hear that Popper was writing a book,' continued Dr Holmes. 'Popper was only a humble lecturer and they didn't usually write books. It was a period of wartime shortages and the Registrar said to Popper "I hope you're not writing this book on university paper." To be honest, Popper wasn't liked. He applied for a chair and was turned down in favour of a nonentity. He applied for a chair at Queensland and was again turned down – in favour of someone who had only just completed his Ph.D. This was despite the fact that Popper had quoted Bertrand Russell and Wittgenstein as references! Nobody else could come anywhere near that.'

'Why was he rejected?'

'It frightened them off. He was too much for them, he had big ears and a funny accent, he was Jewish, he had a reputation for stirring up the pot.'

'Is that why there's no memorial to him here?'

'There's a writer's plaque – or used to be – on the house where Popper had his study.'

'Where's that?'

'In Montreal Street, opposite the Dux de Lux restaurant.'
But I couldn't find it. Probably it's been demolished.

≈

Curious how one's judgement can alter with mood. A few days ago
their refusal to soar infuriated me. But today this refusal to be
impressed by anything has an appeal: English phlegm raised to the
level of Zen contentment, of smiling stoicism. But passion does
exist: I heard real honesty in their parliamentary broadcasts on the
radio – vigorous and candid confrontations – there and on the
rugby field. Their rugby All Blacks thing is a bit overdone. They
load it with more than it can rightfully carry. Is it rugby that makes
them emotionally autistic, or is it emotional autism that drives
them to the escape of rugby?

≈

To the glossy, curvy Christchurch Art Gallery, where I discover
Tea-trees and Creepers, Cape Schank, Victoria, 1865 by Nicholas
Chevalier, a picture with dramatic lighting effects, the Empire as
high adventure. In my pursuit of this unknown artist, whom I first
encountered in Invercargill, I have another stroke of luck; the
gallery shop is flogging off old catalogues of a Chevalier exhibition
for two dollars a piece. Chevalier is one of the most delightful and
unknown personalities of the Victorian age, and his career is an
example of an often overlooked state of affairs: we like to think we
invented globalisation, but the educated classes in the nineteenth
century were extraordinarily cosmopolitan and their experiences
highly multi-cultural.

Nicholas Chevalier was born in St Petersburg in 1828, to a
Swiss father and Russian mother. His father was factor on the
estates of Prince Wittgenstein, aide-de-camp to Tsar Nicholas I.
The young Chevalier studied painting in Lausanne, architecture

in Munich and art in Rome. In 1854 he sailed for Australia in search of a brother who'd gone missing in the goldfields there and moved on to New Zealand in 1865. A self-portrait done in 1857 shows a bohemian type of artist with gypsy tendencies, a type which endured into living memory in the person of Augustus John. From beneath a wide-brimmed fedora, which gives a soft spin to the whole composition, Chevalier's black hair falls to his collar and covers half his ears. The full beard hides the mouth and chin but above it light-brown eyes shine with questing intelligence. The face is sensitive and manly, the head flawed only by ears that are lobeless. How often one comes across that detail, spoiling a lovely head: ears which can't wait to rush into the neck.

Chevalier's journeys through the South Island were unprecedented at the time. Somewhere in his wanderings he'd already picked up a wife – Caroline Wilkie, niece of the painter David Wilkie – and she wrote a full diary account of their bumping over hill and dale with paint and brush. The local newspaper, the *Otago Witness*, reported that in eight months Chevalier travelled 3,600 miles and visited nineteen lakes.

The curator of the Chevalier exhibition was Neil Roberts, who is now the Senior Curator in Christchurch, so I ring him up and he tells me that 'Te Papa has a lot of Chevaliers but of course they're not shown. Te Papa has been an all-round disaster but it was so expensive that nobody dares admit it.'

'I've realised that there's a lot of sentimentality around in this country,' I reply, 'Rousseau's noble savage stuff, the idea that it was a Garden of Eden before the Europeans arrived and wrecked it.'

'Yes, it's nonsense, but politically motivated, you see. The Garden of Eden – if by that you mean the Land of Plenty – was created by the British. Maori society was brutal. It wasn't easy for a Pacific island culture to live in our cold climate. They were very warlike and always fighting each other because resources were scarce.'

(Perhaps this is the point to interject something else that's on my mind. People talk about the European conquest of the world and how Europeans should apologise for it as though the conquered were pacifist and morally superior to the conquerors. But conquest was everybody's game in those days – it's just that some were better at it than others.)

Neil Roberts said there are a lot more Chevaliers in Melbourne and quite a few in the Royal Collection. So when I returned to England I wrote to the Surveyor of the Queen's Pictures about what was held. The Royal Collection has five oils, many watercolours and several albums of pen sketches. The oils are large ceremonial records, such as *The Review in Windsor Great Park in Honour of the Shah of Persia 1873*, which hangs in Buckingham Palace. *The Coral Seller, Tahiti* is exceptional in being an intimate work and is tucked away in the Equerry's Passage at Sandringham.

Sketch albums, before the age of photography, functioned as souvenirs. I went to look at one of Chevalier's in the Print Room at Windsor, that covering the marriage of the Duke of Edinburgh to the Tsar's daughter in St Petersburg in 1874. The sketches incorporate detail of lace and jewels, uniforms and decor, and since the wedding was in the middle of winter there are many snowy scenes too, including a funfair set up to celebrate the happy event. The depictions of big-dipper rides, sleighs with blue and magenta upholstery, theatres and mock castles, coats of arms in colour transparency, illuminations of pink steam and beams of green light, demonstrate Chevalier's exquisite skill and quickness.

But I was astonished by the state of the Print Room itself, which is in fact three rooms installed beneath the Royal Library. The neo-Jacobean scheme was commissioned by the Prince Consort, but it looks like the mail-order department at Harrods on a hectic day, clogged with unsorted material, packing cases, trolleys and bubblewrap. Quite frankly it was a disgrace, but possibly the view from the windows across the playing fields of Eton to the M4 motorway and the rubbishy skyline of Slough has discouraged them from keeping up any sort of style.

Chevalier moved permanently to London in 1870, setting up a studio at 5 Porchester Terrace, north of the Park. In later years his ability to paint or draw was interrupted by gout of the right hand, and he and Caroline travelled to Madeira for long sojourns to relieve the condition. By 1895 he'd all but ceased to paint and retired to Wood Road, off Sydenham Hill, where he built himself a Swiss chalet. His last years were spent concocting poetry, which he set to his own music, organising for the purpose an amateur orchestra in which he played second violin. He died in 1902.

∼

Yesterday the boys of Christ's College celebrated the end of term in grey suits, round-collared shirts, and ties of horizontal black and white bars. Today they are walking away from the school pre-cincts in T-shirts and shorts, dragging suitcases on wheels towards the long summer holidays. Outside the Arts Centre a trumpeter is playing 'Jingle Bells'. The shops are tricked up to the nines in glitter, tinsel, cotton-wool and other simulations of the cold and frosty morn. But it's still only November. What do they do at Christmas – celebrate Easter? I'm heading towards the Rose Garden in the botanical gardens of Hagley Park.

A well-to-do group of Indians is moving among the yellow, orange and crimson flowers. Their clothes exactly complement the rich clusters of blooms, and their tinkling chatter animates the scene. They move away, leaving one of their number reading a book on the grass beneath the hedgerow not far from where I'm sitting. We start to talk and though he is wearing a baseball cap, red top, khaki jeans and sunglasses, it transpires that he's a monk, a member of the Hare Krishna group, and is staying in their

Christchurch ashram for six months. When he takes off his sun-glasses out of politeness I see he is extraordinarily handsome. There is something Nepalese about the eyes, but he says he's from Bihar. He's also a vegetarian, and celibate.

'Is it easy to be celibate?'

'No.'

'What will you do?'

'I've been thinking about it.'

'Have you decided anything?'

'Not a 100 per cent – but I think I must marry.'

'Will you stop being a monk?'

'No. We have two ways. The higher way: you can't marry. The lower way: you can.'

'And you can't stick to the higher way?'

'I can't for much longer. I think I'll go crazy if I do.'

'Have you found a particular person?'

'No. But when I decide I'll find a girl and ask her.'

'And if she says no?'

'Then I'll ask another – and another – until one says yes.' He laughs.

'Are you allowed to drink?'

'No intoxicants of any kind.'

'Masturbation?'

'Not allowed.'

'They are very harsh. Does the juice come out at night?'

'Yes, sometimes it does.'

'All this denial – and you are so beautiful.'

'Oh … thank-you.' He's chuffed that I've called him beautiful. 'Are you married?' he asks me.

'No. And I don't have a male partner either. I'm a sort of monk too.'

'You are celibate?'

'No! I think celibacy is an absurd affectation. God must be really fed up with religion. Religion is forever holding God back as though He were a naughty little boy.'

The monk's lips move silently.

'Anyway, for me sex and love are not always the same,' I tell him. 'If you don't have sex you feel more and more uncomfortable, and if you do have it you feel more comfortable with the world around you, because it's a natural function. Sorry, I'm giving you a sermon.'

'I agree with it. Except that if I were married, sex and love would be the same.'

'I have only one rule. If it's beautiful it's good, if it's ugly it's bad.'

'I think it is a very good rule. I like your rule.'

All the time we are talking, his left knee is juddering on the grass, vibrating up and down, but he ignores it entirely as though this loud statement from the knee were nothing to do with him. He is bursting with desire – not for me in particular but for connective release in general – but he is obedient to the rule; the tension between the two – he didn't realise that I could see it so clearly – is very erotic. The eroticism of bondage. He would ejaculate at a touch. And so, by now, would I.

∽

'By the way, you are very sunburnt,' observed Peter Beaven as we launched out on a second hike round town. Back at the YMCA I had a look – I *am* very sunburnt. It was talking so long with the monk in the Rose Garden that did it. It was one of those typical sunny days here – freezing in the shade, hot in the sun. So you sit in the shade to avoid the sun and start to feel cold, and sit out on the grass and start to fry. That's how it was and now my face and forearms are tomato red.

~

Sunday morning drive to the Banks Peninsula. I feel low. My head is not firmly on my neck and shoulders. No obvious reason for it, except that Sunday has this lowering effect, the lowering into religious submission, something I quite like when in London as it takes the city briefly off the boil. But I don't like it here. And it is at this point that I wish to tabulate some provisional thoughts on religion, rather formally expressed – as they should be. But these are largely for myself, so do skip if you wish.

1. In reference to the development of the reasonable in ancient Greece, Bryan Magee in his book on Karl Popper writes 'When man no longer shared the death of his theories he was emboldened to venture. Whereas before, the entire weight of intellectual tradition had been defensive and had served to preserve existing doctrines, now, for the first time, it was put behind a questioning attitude and became a force for change. The pre-Socratics concerned themselves with questions about the natural world. Socrates applied the same critical rationality to human behaviour and social institutions. There began that runaway growth of enquiry and resultant knowledge which almost sensationally differentiates the civilisation of ancient Greece, *and its legatees*, from all others.' Italics mine.

2. In other words, people who believe devoutly in a religion suffer from certainty, and certainty is a form of stupidity. Because religion is tautological, it leaves men vulnerable to outside information. Religious fundamentalists are the most insecure people in the world. They live so close to rage because reality refuses to conform to their fantasies.

3. Popper: 'Novelty cannot be causally or rationally explained,

but only intuitively grasped.' Lichtenberg put it another way: 'Left to itself, reason can lead to nothing else.' This suggests that anything new is a leap of faith or, as I should say, of the imagination. So the open society prospers through maverick input. The open society, the open mind, the open road, this is what we've been dealing with.

4. If religions are saying there is that which is greater than man, this is obviously true. We didn't create ourselves. It's when they take the next step and try to militarise our minds that I reject religions. Yes, we need God in order to escape from religion.

5. We can never know a fixed reality because we can never be outside the thing of which we are an emanation. What we can do instead is be intimate; then we are involved in movement, the reality of which is not external.

6. I am by temperament a pacifist. But I am not a utopian. The world can be a very hostile place. Sometimes I have to steel myself against my own pacifism in order to survive at all.

7. Words have limitations. In fact that's what a word is, a limitation. Anyone who believes in one book is wrong.

8. People confuse holiness with religion. The two rarely have anything in common.

9. A religion can be beautiful when it is weak. Religion creates rites and stories which help people navigate their journey through the mystery in which they live. But when religion is strong it is always ugly. When religion takes people over, the truth becomes purely emotional: truth is what people want to be true.

10. Theology aside, I'm a great fan of the Salvation Army.

11. Every so often in history whole populations become hysterical and, like individuals so afflicted, are unreachable. All you can do is protect yourselves from them. Often only the tip of the

iceberg is visible – you could have gone down any street in Munich in 1938 and been given coffee and a piece of cake with a warm smile and come away saying what nice, ordinary people most Germans were. Does this mean Nazism was harmless? I once read an article in the *London Review of Books* which said that Stalin was better than Hitler because at least Stalin was working for a good cause. A terrifying statement.

12. Jesus wasn't a family man. He was single and hung out with marginal figures.

13. The Archbishop of Canterbury recently made a plea for toleration between Judaism, Christianity and Islam, saying 'We are all children of Abraham.' Is there a story more revolting than that of Abraham preparing to murder his son because he heard a voice in the clouds? A surrender of reason even to the extent of murdering your own innocent child. Jesus wasn't Abrahamic. His was a new message of love and peace. Christianity would have been a great deal less unpleasant if it had never adopted the Old Testament but had stuck simply to the Four Gospels of the New Testament.

14. Who knows what the ultimate reality is? The bishops and ayatollahs know nothing more about it than you or I do. They have the nerve to call their presumption humility. Any society directed by clerics can only be a terror: the Aztec system of politics.

15. The British Government introduced a law making incitement to religious hatred a crime punishable by prison. History reminds us again and again that religions have many hateful aspects – it is chilling that to say so should become a criminal offence.

16. Gibbon, *The Decline and Fall of the Roman Empire*: 'The various modes of worship which prevailed in the Roman world were all considered by the people as equally true; by the

philosopher as equally false; and by the magistrate as equally useful. And thus toleration produced not only mutual indulgence, but even religious accord.'

17. The Goncourt Brothers said in their journal 'If there is a God, atheism must strike Him as less of an insult than religion.'

18. The other day someone asked me if I believed in God. It has become a trick question. 'God' is one of those shut-down words. I am not a rationalist. I think the universe is like a brain, not like a computer, and a brain is alive, dynamic, its chemical composition altering from moment to moment. I know that an imaginative, intuitive, emotional engagement with reality is as vital as reason to comprehension. Anyone who has ever fallen in love knows this too. I was thinking the other day of how many times I've fallen in love – fallen in love properly. It is six times. I need to be in love to give interest to my days and a muse to my work. But it must be a person. I could never fall in love with an idea. People have said falling in love is like a sickness. But falling in love with an idea is a much greater sickness.

19. As an artist, I feel that art is not doodling and filling in space, that there is an ultimate coherence in reality, that the highest form is a unity. Does this make me a closest monotheist?

20. I'm a great one for lighting candles in churches. Is this the acceptable face of pollution?

21. I like the pick and mix approach to philosophy and religion. Why should we have to swallow bullshit whole?

~

Sumner is nothing special, but Lyttelton is, reached after coiling across the back of the peninsula, and the very danger of the road has forced up my spirits. Lyttelton is the port of Christchurch, loaded with maritime vapours in a jawdrop setting, but I stop only

to buy the Sunday paper. The corniche drive continues through
Governor's Bay in swerves of sea-green, lavender and sky-blue,
studded with red and yellow dots of flowers. The scenery might be
characterised as a hybrid of Hebrides and Riviera before tourists
arrived in either. The smell too reminds me of the South of France,
pine and palm and drifts of heavily scented flowers. One grasps
echoes in order to position oneself, but they are only echoes. Where
in fact am I?

I stop to check the map, then reverse and turn off to Cashmere.
Which is where Popper lived, at 14A Westenra Terrace, and the
house is still there, tethered like a balloon to the top of a bluff with
a commanding view over the Canterbury Plains to the Southern
Alps. Perched in anguished bliss, Popper was no doubt reminded
a little of his Austrian homeland, since Vienna too sits on a plain
with snow-topped mountains beyond. The Southern Alps are
ranged along the horizon like a line of overlapping bell tents set up
by an expeditionary force.

~

I have now received from Dr Holmes a contemporary newspaper
report on that post-Hiroshima lecture, 11 August 1945. Popper's
tenor is histrionic. The world as we have known it has come to an
end. A complete break with all past history because man now has
the power to destroy the whole world in an instant. Popper thinks
forms of dictatorship will be much more likely as it will be necessary to control with an iron hand this new destructive force of
nuclear energy. 'Are coalmines and oilfields of any value now? Is it
worth expanding car factories if in a year's time the motor car as
we know it will be as obsolete as the stagecoach?' Very little of it
makes sense. Shows you how wrong the great minds can be.

To be fair, Popper wrote to the *Christchurch Star-Sun* immediately, saying that he'd only been suggesting possibilities. 'I must

insist upon this point as I have, in various publications, attacked historical prophecy as a kind of intellectual charlatanry.' Why therefore did he indulge in it? And ... 'finally, concerning the moral struggle of mankind, what I said was that this is the struggle for freedom, i.e. for the limitation of the power men wield over their fellow men.'

In his autobiography *The Unended Quest* he wrote 'I had the impression that New Zealand was the best-governed country in the world, and the most easily governed.' And elsewhere he writes 'There was no harm in the people: like the British they were decent, friendly, and well-disposed.' Both Voltaire and Goethe stated that England was the best-governed nation and the wisest model for other nations in the future. By this I assume they meant that a political system is worthy of admiration to the extent that it can feed and clothe its citizens and protect them from harm and injustice. But in England now, a teenager, say, murders a woman for a tenner. The cry goes up – how ghastly, how did we fail him? A psychopath blows up fellow citizens on the Tube and voices are heard – we understand, it's our foreign policy. Hardly a month goes by without some official body telling the British what nasty racists they are. The drone of governmental rebuke is incessant and personal relationships are increasingly conditioned by legalistic calibrations of deeply invasive specificity. Yet in the broad scheme of things the British obviously aren't racist because they've handed over huge chunks of their cities to impoverished people from the third world whose lives have been transformed as a result. Indeed people quote this as an example of that English toleration which so infuriated D. H. Lawrence. On which subject Graham Greene, referring to Norman Douglas on Capri, remarked 'Even his enormous tolerance had limits. He loved life too well to have patience with puritans and fanatics.' Just as the noble ideal of fair play can leave one defenceless against those who won't play the

game, so toleration may degenerate into appeasement. Cyril Connolly said one of the best things on appeasement: 'A tiger does not
become a vegetarian because you throw it more and more
carcasses.'

~

I was flicking through Christchurch's *The Press*, the best newspaper in either North or South Island. Its motto is *Nihil utile quod
non honestum*. Excellent: societies which don't put a high value on
honesty cannot be democratic and will be ruled by gangs, for the
only alternative to democracy is rule by gangsters. Here in *The
Press* is a nice example of honesty: sex for sale. And among the girls
putting themselves forward in its Personals column are sprinkled
a few boys. I pause at one who describes himself as 'bisexual, early
20s'. After a shower and a cup of tea I ring the number. He picks
it up right away and sounds very normal. In these circumstances
normality is the most thrilling, the most sexual quality of all. One
hundred NZ dollars for an hour. We arrange to meet outside the
museum at 5 p.m.

'How shall I recognise you?' I ask.

'I've got fair hair. Sort of short and a bit spiky. And
sunglasses.'

'I've got long fair hair. Too long. No sunglasses.'

I go for a walk in the botanical gardens to distract my collywob-
bles. At last. I'm going to unbutton a Kiwi fly.

That sun is killingly bright and I am obliged to adopt sunglasses
after all, as round and round the gardens I slowly wheel, willing
the clock towards the hour but apprehensive too. What will he
look like? Shall I fancy him? Will he find me awful? Will it be
hamfisted or embarrassing or a flop? Smooth the long locks back
behind the ears. Silly hair. Must get it cut. I am looking at flowers
but don't see flowers, I don't see anything, my head is a box of

bees. There he is. We shake hands. I'm burbling. Can't judge him yet. Swirling in politeness and new impressions. However, as we ascend in the lift of the YMCA I register his full red lips, his bashful look, and notice a little tuft of hair in the centre of his breast where his shirt is unbuttoned, and a soft surge passes through me. Suddenly I know this is going to be wonderful.

Davey, twenty-two years old, is a lovely natural kissing sturdy young man. Big square hands and feet. Muscular shoulders – no worked stomach, simply flat – strong haunches and legs. Shy smile. The tuft of hair on his breast is matched by a little goatee on his chin. 'I have that,' he explains, 'because if I take it off I look too young.' Trickle of hair down from navel. Greenish brown eyes through which pass alternating flickers of uncertainty and mischief. Handsome. Very.

'There you are.' I put the money in his trouser pocket – I usually get rid of the money at the outset on such occasions – and said anything goes but no anal.

The encounter, being the discovery of a brand-new person, was alert, uncertain, nutritious. He was very fastidious about keeping it to safe sex and overshot the time purchased by a further hour. After the biz we had a cup of tea and some cake with the sun warm through the window on our naked skin. He told me he'd been an electrician but gave it up, his mother is English, he's had four girlfriends and two boyfriends and now doesn't want any partner at all. Alas I can't buy him again because he must leave for Wellington tomorrow, but I feel grounded and content and awake. Davey was typical of the local lads, nothing spivvy or swaggering, notably straightforward, boyish and affectionate, and also typically – behind the carefree veneer – the sense of something deeper and less happy, a man who is looking out into the world with a certain unease, which is very attractive. He left me his email address. I am aware of having described all this much too quickly.

Directly Davey had dressed and gone, I returned to the botanical gardens because I didn't want to be left alone in the room where we'd been together. I was light-headed, light-footed, oozing easily into the spaces around me. This time I did notice the flowers, I noticed them very much, and in the Rose Garden moved slowly from bloom to bloom giving each my full attention and judging its scent and colour. My favourite rose – I didn't see the name until afterwards – was called 'City of London', followed by 'Ginger Rogers' and 'Charles Dickens'.

∼

Tomorrow I must leave the YMCA, which is booked solid from 1 December. So I move to the Merivale Court Motel in Papanui Road. Which seems fine.

Spoke too soon. Screwed to the porch beneath my room are bells which scream every time the phone rings in the office. Mr Hock, the owner, says the previous owner, 'a British lady', was deaf and wanted to catch the phone if she were anywhere else on the property. I asked if he'd mind deactivating them so I'd not be woken at 7 a.m. or in the middle of the night. He said the only way was by unscrewing them and this he would gladly do. He agreed that the noise was very piercing but remarked, with a quizzical frown, as though he too found it highly curious, that in the six months he'd been running the place no other guest had mentioned it.

Mr Hock is Malaysian, slightly built but clearly a cut above your average motel owner. He used to run a Malaysian bank in Fiji and studied for an MBA (Master of Business Something) in Belgium, 'so of course we went to London a lot'. They followed their children here, who are in Christchurch schools.

∼

Deb Nation and her husband Andy entertained me at their house in Bishopsworth Street. Vaguely sensed some children around but it was only the three of us and a slinky cat. Baked fish (groper – *not* grouper, she emphasised – I queried the point again – she was decisive: it was groper – but I'm still not satisfied), asparagus, red and yellow peppers braised in olive oil and balsamic vinegar, new potatoes, green salad. I'd been longing for simple, delicious food like this for weeks.

'If you're interested in the Old Vic Tour,' she said, 'you should meet Elric Hooper.'

'Mr Theatre in this town,' said Andy. 'He can also tell you about Fellini's rent boys – he's very funny on that subject.'

Deb said 'I asked Lesley Beaven why she married a seventy-eight-year-old man and she said because the sex is *so* good!'

I asked 'Why is the suicide rate so high here for young men?'

'Because the sex is so bad?' suggested Andy.

'Because,' replied Deb, 'boys think they must only have feelings about rugby.'

At the end of the nineteenth century Durkheim said that suicide was the product of social isolation.

'I think it is more accurate to say emotional isolation,' Deb suggested.

'Funnily enough,' I say, 'the most uptight males seem to be Maoris. Even in all-male saunas they hide when they change and don't mix. And I've observed the same behaviour with Muslim chaps in England. They seem to live in mortal terror of someone glimpsing their genitals. No eye contact, no chat. I want to talk to a Maori. Properly. Like a human being. But they won't even look at me. Why won't they? Is it because I'm off-putting or because they are shy or because they are angry?'

We're eating outside under the pergola from which the garden descends to white rose trees, a pond and native shrubs.

'We'll never find out the answer to that question because we're not allowed to put it. "Young man, are you shy or are you angry?" Don't ask. Your hair looks good,' she says.

I had it cut this afternoon by a man she recommended, Michael Hamel.

'He's won lots of prizes,' she says.

'Not for his own hair,' I reply. He had matted dreadlocks. White men with frizzy blond hair shouldn't do dreadlocks. 'And he was in clown's clothes.'

'What sort?'

'Candlewick trousers.'

'Yuk.'

'And green shirt and red gingham waistcoat.'

Pudding is tamarillo in syrup with chocolate ice cream. Tamarillo used to be called the tree-tomato but Deb says that's not smart enough any more. As I leave, she raises her arm, gives a slight tug and presents me with a fruit which has yellow rind and absolutely no smell. 'It's a loquat. It's not ready yet,' she says.

∽

Decided to chance it and use the address for Lord Bolingbroke in *Burke's Peerage* and found myself outside a prefab divided into lettered sections. He was letter A. I think it was a wing of a nursing home, or sheltered housing. Couldn't quite get the set-up. And yes, he came to the door. Momentarily I thought it might be a son: tall, grey wavy hair, dressed in blue denim with a red polo shirt. He stooped slightly to look over the top of his specs with a twinkly eye. I apologised for troubling him. Peter was right – he didn't mind in the least. 'But if you want to meet I have to collect myself. I've just come back from shopping and what with the Parkinson's–'

'Forgive me.'

'No, it's all right. I was at the gym this morning and I'm absolutely buggered.'

We arrange that I should call for a drink at 6 p.m. on Thursday and I give him my phone number.

~

Peter Beaven was expatiating over the telephone on the loveliness of the Banks Peninsula. I agreed. He said it's remarkable and I must see more of it. I said I shall. He said it was the handiwork of two volcanic eruptions. I asked if they were eruptions of two volcanoes or two eruptions of the same one. He said the former and added that he is reading Wordsworth to keep his mind in trim for his next visit there. He said his wife Lesley is a super cook and we should meet next Friday at five and eat at a restaurant called Tiffany's at six. Oh. No home cooking then. And such odd timing.

~

Lord Bolingbroke rang me about our meeting tomorrow.

'I've woken you up. I'm sorry,' he says.

'That's all right.' I say. 'What time is it?' My bedroom fails to come into focus. I scramble blearily for spectacles, which elude me.

'It's eight o'clock.'

'In the morning?'

'Yes.'

'Is there a problem?' I ask him.

'No. I just wanted to tell you that it's all right to park on the grass.'

~

The people of this country do not have parties. At least I've never been invited to one, or even heard of one that I wasn't invited to.

Cafés and restaurants, it seems, have replaced parties. I rang Elisa in England. She said that seven members of the Firle Bonfire Society have been arrested for racism because they made a bonfire effigy of a gypsy, and that she's going to the Bad Sex Party tonight in St James's Square – I had to ring London to hear the word 'party' again. She asked me what I was doing and I said I was going to have drinks with Lord Bolingbroke. She asked 'What's he doing there?' I said he's been here for fifty years. She said she played Bolingbroke in Shakespeare at school.

≈

A deep fatigue claims me. Really I've stopped inside. After my visit to Bolingbroke's I intend to – I must – lie horizontally for a few days. Travelling on the road can do this. It's the new impressions pouring in day after day, week after week, and needing to be processed. You just can't sit up straight any longer and have to call a halt to allow rumination and digestion to take place. So I ring Peter Beaven and leave a message on his machine cancelling our dinner at Tiffany's on Friday and I deeply regret that. But sometimes there's no choice: you simply stop and that's all there is to it. When I was nineteen and in Istanbul, a man said he'd like to organise a party for me and a Swedish boy I was travelling with. The Turk said 'You'll be sure to come?' 'Yes, we're sure.' 'Because I'll invite some friends and we'll have bottles of Coca-Cola. So we'll make a good party and you really will come?' 'Yes, we'll definitely come.' But back at the Gulhane Cinar the Swede and I had overdone the speed and Romilar cough mixture and we hadn't slept for two days and simply conked out and never made it to the party. We returned to the spot the following day to apologise and explain, but couldn't find him. To this day I feel bad about letting that Turkish guy down. Shame that Davey the rent boy has gone to Wellington. He was the most glorious shape.

≈

Mrs Hock, cleaning my room, said 'Don't you find it slow here?'

'That's one of the reasons I came.'

'I find it slow. Malaysia very fast.'

'Malaysia wasn't fast when I was there in 1975.'

'Now yes. Many big roads. Here very slow but Malaysia very fast, very jetset.'

Sounds vile.

≈

To Lord Bolingbroke's, 6 p.m., December the 4th. I survey the grass and park on it with great deliberation. He's still wearing his blue jeans but this time with black Oxford shoes and a blue shirt, and he's holding up *The Seven Ages of Paris*.

'Got this from the library.'

'My brother bought me that last Christmas.'

'Any good?'

'Not brilliant but OK.' And I hand over my offering of the Akarua wine. 'It won top prize this year.'

'That's very kind. But you shouldn't've brought anything. Do you want to open it?'

'No, no, it's too heavy.'

'Would you like white? I've done some cheese and biscuits – to lessen the pain.' He pops into the kitchen. On a powder-pink sofa with cream fringes are collated piles of documents associated with his existence: one concerning the ancestral seat of Lydiard Park in Wiltshire, another of photographs and letters, a third with a file on top labelled Presidents of TAANZ. In the bookshelves sit a number of thrillers and reference works.

He re-emerges with a plate of small crackers, each with a sliver of Brie-like topping. 'Isn't Paris marvellous?' he enthuses. 'I lived

there with a girl for nine months after the war. That was before I
went to New York, where … well, like most English people I considered America the great home of democracy, but when I arrived
I got a telephone call – this was in 1948 – from a friend of my
mother's called Gladys Garthwaite. She said she'd got me invited
to a small luncheon party as a welcome and a car would pick me
up. So I'm dressed for a quiet little lunch. A huge car pulls up,
chauffeur driven. We arrive at this *enormous* place on the Hudson
with at least six tennis courts and another huge identical car in the
drive moving ahead of us. I mentioned this to the chauffeur who
said "The Duchess has a whole *fleet*." I thought – Duchess? It
turned out to be Anna Gould – hugely rich – who married the Duc
de Talleyrand and restored his family fortunes.'

'Where did her loot come from?'

'Her father was Jay Gould, the American railway king. She had
two English butlers and there was a trio playing music. I found
myself being introduced to about forty luncheon guests and when
Anna came down – she was very ugly – one of the English butlers
who was pouring my g & t said "Sir, you see Mr So and So over
there, he's after the old girl's money." The lunch started and one
old lady encrusted with jewels, called Mrs Kavanagh, said across
the table "Oh, Mr St John, you English have such *beautiful* complexions." But that wasn't it, it was that I was permanently red
with embarrassment, especially when the whole table stopped
eating in order to examine my face – I was only twenty.'

'It's amazing,' I say, 'how we still remember our blushes. I used
to blush a lot and thought it a terrible weakness. I still do blush but
became reconciled to it when I was in Germany in my twenties – a
woman there said "Do you know what's the most attractive thing
for a woman? A man who blushes. It is so exciting, this revelation of
feeling in a man, the control barrier gone." And I now see it like
that. I've never really clicked with New York. How did you find it?'

'I loved it! We went to a restaurant where Humphrey Bogart and Lauren Bacall were dining. He was pissed up to the eyeballs and throwing rolls at the waiters. Thinking of Mrs Kavanagh again, she sent me an invitation to the last night of the Metropolitan opera and she turned up in the box with an armed bodyguard but still "lost" in inverted commas an emerald bracelet. It was in the *New York Times* the next day, *Mrs Kavanagh once again loses priceless jewels.*'

'For the insurance you mean?'

'Let's say she was … wily. In 1953 she got hold of my number in London and wanted a seat in the Abbey for the Coronation and asked "Would it help if I front up with ten thousand dollars?" That's almost quarter of a million in today's money. But she didn't care. The Coronation at all costs!'

'When did your title come to you?'

'It came to me in 1976 from a cousin called Vernon. He had no children and liked chasing butterflies. I was in Sydney at the time and in the club a member asked me "What will your maiden speech be about in the House of Lords?" I thought a moment and said "Syphilis in the Solomon Islands."'

'Was it?'

'I never made it. I was going to, but Tony Blair decided to abolish us.'

'Er … but you had over twenty years before that to have a go.'

He offers the plate with the snacks. 'Yes, I know, but I was working hard beforehand. Did I tell you I founded Atlantic & Pacific Travel? We had branches all over this country and a branch in Sydney. At one point I had a hundred people working for me. It's still going.'

'Do you still have an interest in it?'

'No, unfortunately. I wish I did.'

'But how was it you came to be here at all?'

'Well, you see, my first wife, she was from Christchurch and her mother was dying, so we came out in 1955. When I arrived there was no wine or anything like that. If you wanted wine it came from South Africa. This country was a revelation to me because I'd been living in places like America and the West Indies. I said to my wife "Where can we go for coffee?" and she said "I think there's somewhere near Cathedral Square" and when we got there they poured this brown chicory stuff out of a bottle. In my hotel, I rang down for breakfast, just coffee and some bread rolls, and the woman on the other end said "You can't have it in your room, you've got to come down," so I went down and was about to sit at one of the tables and she said "You can't sit here, you've got to sit over there with all the other people." And it went on and on like this. Christchurch can still be stodgy and English.'

'I think it's quite a sexy town. It's got some streak of –'

'Christchurch has more massage parlours than anywhere else here.'

'And do they have parties?'

'Yes, I go to parties. I went to a good party the other day where we were all up to one in the morning boozing.'

'I don't like getting up too early.'

'Yes, I hate the mornings too.'

'But you rang me at 8 a.m.'

'Yes, I'm afraid I woke you up. You said "What time is it?" in a forlorn way. But I thought you might go out and I wanted to catch you.'

'I've had to cancel a dinner for tomorrow evening. I feel so guilty about it. That's from my parents, who thought you may be at death's door but you never cancel. It was with someone called Peter Beaven. Do you know him?'

'I know him very well. Nice man. Good talker. He'll understand.'

'I'll flop completely for a few days.'

'You seem all right.'

'Oh, I'm all right!'

'I was going to suggest you contact him since you're interested in buildings. I knew Eric Beaven too, his father. We were in Vancouver on a business delegation together and Eric said to me "Now, Sinjy, you'll be representing us on television. The car will collect you at seven in the morning." Ugh – awful – seven in the morning to appear on television – a definition of hell.'

'This name. Boll-ing-brook–'

'Actually the correct pronunciation is Bull-ing-brook. Not many people know that.'

'Really? I'll pronounce it that way from now on. Bull-ing-brook. To score a point over others.'

'And it was originally spelt with a "u" too. It was a family name of John of Gaunt and … and … of who? Oh God, I *must* get myself mentally organised.'

To further this he picks up a pamphlet on Lydiard Park and flips to the front where his family tree is laid out. As he starts to explain the lineage I lose him – I simply cannot retain genealogies in my head and never could – but he ends up 'So that's how we got to Henry VII', as though subsequent events were a doddle.

'And when did the house go out of the family?'

'1943. It was by then in the most dreadful state. But recently I had a letter from Miss Sarah Finch-Crisp, who's in charge of it for the Swindon Borough Council, saying that it looks like they're getting five million pounds in a lottery grant to do up the house and park. Miss Finch-Crisp is very keen.'

'Do you have a son and heir?'

'Yes. I have three sons. Unfortunately the eldest has Down's Syndrome and has been at the Rudolf Steiner place since he was eight. He's very autocratic and comes here in a taxi. My wife and I settled quite a lot of money on him so that he would be all right and when he dies we arranged that it will go to the Rudolf Steiner organisation. I have a second son who is in Australia. He's not in line because he was born before I married my second wife. You know how strict they are. My third son is in line and he's in Japan.'

'How many wives have you had?'

'Only two. My father had four.'

'Was he a playboy?'

'Not quite. He was sent down from Oxford for knocking off a deer in the park.'

'That would've been Magdalen. I was at Magdalen.'

'Yes, that's exactly where he was. Afterwards he was sent off to grow coffee in Kenya, did well in the war, Military Cross, the First War that is, lived to be eighty-six. He took off for the South of France when I was seven or eight and I didn't see much of him after that. Please, have some more of this Riesling. It's not bad, is it.'

'Very good. One thing I've been on the track of – a good local rosé.'

'I love rosé! It's a good drink, as you know from the South of France. Used to be a good one here called … called … '

'Gibbston Valley? That's fabulous. You must get some in. Did you go to the South of France because of your father?'

'Not really. Everyone goes if they can, don't they.'

'People say it's been ruined and of course it has. But it's still got something, especially at our end, round St Tropez.'

'I loved St Tropez in the late forties. In those days you could buy an enormous house at the back of Cannes for £5,000. But the problem used to be getting the money out of England. The Treasury sent agents down to the Monte Carlo Casino to see if anyone was, you know, betting out of proportion. I remember coming out of the casino with Doris Orr-Lewis and we saw a curious character

lying in wait and Doris looked down at his feet and said "Regula-
tion boots! I'd know them anywhere. He's a Treasury agent."'

'My dad took me to the casino at Monte Carlo and I was shocked
at how unglamorous it was. There was only one room left where
you had to wear a jacket. And he said "Well, if you want to do it
properly, you must come with us to the Palm Beach at Cannes."
Where they still had the orchestra playing, champagne in buckets,
evening dress. Have you been to the Palm Beach Casino?'

'Not lately, no. What's-her-name, the mother of David Milford
Haven, she was a real fixture at the Monte Carlo roulette tables.
She'd shout *voleur!* Claiming someone was stealing her winning
bet. In those days the croupiers had to be damn good because you
didn't have coloured chips for different bets. She was famous for
shouting *voleur.*'

'Are you saying she was trying to con them?'

'Well – she was Russian … '

'I love the Russians, but with Russians you very often never
know.'

'Precisely. I knew you'd get my meaning. The portrait of me on
the floor over there, that was done by a Russian. Pavlov. When I
was eighteen.'

'You were bloody good-looking.'

'I've told Lydiard they can have it when I'm gone. When I was
in the travel business I had the general agency here for Intourist,
and about the same time I was involved in the spy game, sort of.
At a bar in Sydney I got talking to a fellow who said he was at the
Russian Embassy in Canberra. Three weeks later I got a visit from
someone at the British High Commission who said "You do realise
who you were speaking to – Smirnoff! The First Secretary at the
Russian Embassy!" I hadn't the faintest idea about Smirnoff. The
British agent went on to ask "What did you glean of his sex
life?"'

'They put that question?'

'Those very words. What did you glean of his sex life? I ask you. How is your drink going?'

'Fine. Have one of your cheese biscuits.'

'Thank-you very much.'

'And what *did* you glean of his sex life?'

'Nothing at all. I had no interest in Smirnoff's sex life. Have some more wine.'

'I'm driving. Are they hot on that here?'

'I'm afraid they are a bit.'

'I got fined in Dunedin – for facing the wrong way. A bit much I thought.'

'I have a young girlfriend who has a bottle of bubbly and drives off with an apple at the ready.'

'What does that do, counteract the alcohol?'

'Psychologically. If they stop her for, you know, odd driving, she takes a bite out of it and says sorry, I'm just eating an apple.'

'I don't get it.'

'Took her hand off the wheel.'

'Ah. You seem to have a lot of girlfriends.'

'I do like women.'

'I like men – for that sort of thing. Christchurch is better for young men than the other towns.'

'Is it? I'm glad to hear it.'

'My problem is that I'm attracted to rather mischievous people.'

'I do know what you mean, yes. I'm going to the Tango Ball on Saturday.'

'Are you – will that be mischievous?'

'I hope so. It's somewhere in Manchester Street. I love the tango. I first danced to it in the Monte Carlo Casino and loved it immediately.'

'So you go to the gym, you've got a touch of Parkinson's, you love women, you love the tango–'

'And I've had a stroke.'

'Good Lord. I'm thinking of the leaning. There's a lot of leaning in the tango.'

'I'm not always completely steady in the leaning. But I'm not bad. It's mind over matter. That's what I always say – mind over matter.'

'My mother hates growing old,' I tell him. 'She lives alone now. Hates it. The machinery breaking down. The loneliness.'

'Mind over matter, tell her – and change your attitude. Go out. You have to go out. I love going out.'

'Yes, she goes out a lot.'

'She should have an affair then,' he advises.

'Lovely, yes.'

'Why I say that is because recently I was at a party where I was one of the younger people present.' (He was born in 1927.) 'The host and hostess were in their eighties and were celebrating well, er, I don't know if they got married, let us say their new union, and they were so *happy*.'

'Who are your friends in Christchurch?'

'Mostly women in their fifties.'

'How did you discover the facts of life, Kenneth?'

'I can't remember. But probably quite early. I do remember when I was at Eton entertaining some girls in my room from a nearby school – Ascot or somewhere – and my housemaster found out and he was furious. "St John, you've been entertaining loose women." "No, sir, *loosed* women." He wrote to my mother and said "Your son is turning Eton into a province of Mayfair!"'

'I'm still interested in your Riviera period. I'm sort of hung up in my investigations on the late forties, which extend to about 1953, a forgotten period. I love forgotten things.'

'Well, one place I used to go was the Bar Felix on the Croisette. Felix was a Corsican and the bon mot scrawled up, I remember it to this day, was *Alcool tue lentement – on s'en fout – on n'est pas pressé.* Alcohol kills slowly – we don't give a damn – we aren't in a hurry anyway. I was at university in Geneva so I spent some time around France.'

'I interviewed Sophia Loren in Geneva. Like a lot of these women, she's more beautiful in the flesh. The screen makes you look bloated.'

'Do you know – yes. I thought the same when I danced with Rita Hayworth.'

'You danced with Rita Hayworth? I adore Rita Hayworth.'

'Once I worked in the Bahamas as a sort of PA to Sir William Garthwaite. An interesting character. Left school at fourteen, made a fortune in shipping. We were cruising back to Europe and Rita Hayworth was on the boat. The old boy said "Go on, get stuck in," so I went up and said "I believe you're Miss Hayworth" and she said "Yes, I am" and I said "Would you have this dance with me?" and she said "I'd love to." Very beautiful, wonderful dancer of course, but not very interesting to talk to.'

'You tried.'

'Yes, I tried, but she had no conversation.'

'You seem to have worked all over.'

'I have a bit. What really tested my mettle was taking charge of a Mediterranean cruise for Mr Goulandris when I was twenty-four. It was a nightmare. Cabins double-booked, passengers fighting, food shortages. I thought if I could survive that I could survive anything.'

'Where was your mother from?'

'Yorkshire.'

'What did she think of your coming all this way to live?'

'She thought I was just going on holiday.'

'And fifty years later you're still here. Don't you miss England?'

'Not really. In many ways I'm a product of the Antipodes. And there are still many connections.'

A copy of the *Spectator* lies by his feet. Looking about I ask 'What is the arrangement here? Is it a nursing home?'

The prefab is in a tonic position beside the River Avon but he has only two small rooms.

'No, no. You thought it was a nursing home? It's just an ordinary apartment. I wanted something that was no bother.'

It must have been difficult, his reduced circumstances, but there's not a trace of bitterness.

'Like Graham Greene,' I propose. 'He used to write with his back against the wall in a small flat where he could take everything in at a glance. He didn't want wings or corridors, they unsettled him.'

'Yes, I understand that. When I think of how they lived at Lydiard at the end, the roof half off, creeping down stone corridors trying to stop the candle being blown out.'

'No electricity?'

'The house wasn't wired. No gas either. The place was lit entirely with oil lamps and candles when the family had it. I used to have a holiday home at Geraldine.'

'The Peel Forest.'

'Yes, that's where it was, in the Peel Forest. There was a little stream running along by the property and one day it turned into a raging torrent, the build-up was simply unbelievable. We pulled three dead children out. It was the most appalling thing. And the place was wrecked. I had to get rid of it.'

I'm looking at a black-and-white photograph on the mantel-shelf.

'Can I ask you who that is?'

'My brother. When he was in the Life Guards.'

'He looks like a sensualist too.' (Fruity face with dark eyes and thick lips.)

'Yes, he was.'

'Does it run in the family?'

'I think it does, yes. He was in the tea business in India. He died not long ago. And so did his son – from melanoma.'

'Very nasty.'

'Do cover up. I do.'

'Is it useful being a Lord here?'

'Sometimes it is. A little maybe. But I tell you what is much better if you go to Asia – being a Sir. For some reason the word "Lord" doesn't impress them, but if you are Sir Somebody that goes down very well. As you know, I'm also a baronet so I tend to use that in Asia.'

He saw me out to the car. 'I love the river here,' he said. Willows along the side of the road tickle the water's surface. And he waved me off, not turning in until after I was out of sight.

~

(Embedded footnote. Anna Gould's first marriage was to Boni de Castellane, one of the stars of Proustian Paris before the Great War. His abuse of her and her money was always very stylish. With the railway dollars he built the Palais Rose where the avenue Foch meets the Bois de Boulogne, to a design by Sanson, principal architect of the mansions of *belle époque* Paris. In 1897 Boni gave a ball for Anna's twenty-first birthday, inviting 3,000 guests and spending a third of a million francs on it. Eventually Anna tired of his arrogance, infidelities and delirious expenditure. Taking their two sons with her, she left him and they were divorced in 1906. Two years later Anna married Boni's cousin, Hélie de Talleyrand-Périgord, Prince de Sagan, a more sombre and kindly man. Boni, who was left destitute, became an antique dealer. With typical aplomb he published a volume of memoirs in 1925 called *The Art of Being Poor* and died in 1932. Anna eventually returned to America and died in 1961. Her heirs sold the Palais Rose the following year and this, one of the most beautiful houses in Paris, was demolished in 1969 by developers.)

∾

Rang Helen, who runs Scorpio Books, and asked her to send *To Noto* to Kenneth St John (the name he generally uses hereabouts) and she said 'Poor lovely Kenneth!'

I also asked her to send *A History of Facelifting* to Peter Beaven and she said 'Jocelyn Beaven was just in the shop.'

'Who's she, his daughter?'

'No, his wife.'

'I thought his wife was called Lesley.'

'He's been living with Lesley for four years but they're not married yet. Jocelyn is wonderful. She plays the piano beautifully. She's so intelligent and so tall. Lesley is very short.'

'I've not met Lesley. Or Jocelyn.'

'You'd love Jocelyn.'

'I'm meeting Elric Hooper. You probably know all about him too. I want him to be naughty.'

'He *is* naughty. You won't have to make him be.'

∾

At long last. Putting up my feet. Letting my eyes fall shut. Not bothering to go anywhere. Relaxing. Snoozing. Snacking. Lying on the bed. Buy a copy of *The Press* from a nearby garage. The New Zealand police logged 45,000 cases of violence last year, most of them caused by the lost redundant boys. If boys are on the way out, it would appear that the dark-skinned ones are on the way out first – a redundant species, the human male, coinciding with redundant cultures. Black American music has been one of the delights of my life, but hip-hop usually sounds like the enraged howling of men trapped in their own idiocy; the murder politics of radical Islam can be viewed as the death rattle of the castration complex; and reading the statistics for violent crime here reveals that a greatly disproportionate number of young Maori males are involved. These are perversions of prowess. But the problem remains: how can such men from traditional societies demonstrate their prowess if fate is against them?

Yet it seems the destiny of men is no better in advanced communities. Academics from the universities of Leeds, Vienna and Ottawa, with the assistance of the World Health Organization, spent a year looking at data on 200 million men in seventeen countries across the developed world, and they concluded that being male should be classified as a disease. Men in such countries are more prone than women to die from cancer, heart disease, strokes, skin and blood and digestive illnesses, and from suicide; they are also more likely to be killed in accidents and car crashes, and are more at risk from mental illnesses.

What's more, increasing numbers of men all over the world are parasitical on women for basic survival – this is often the reason for their underlying hatred of women.

Turning to the next page of the newspaper – how cherubic. A picture of the Kiwi buddha Rinpoche, smiling with a tin of biscuits, the first High Lama born in the southern hemisphere. He's ten years old and was discovered in Kaukapakapa three years ago when the Dalai Lama recognised him as the reincarnation of one of the pantheon and took him off to the foothills of the Himalayas. Rinpoche is mad about cricket as well as biscuits. I must give Bernard and Daisy a ring. I'm supposed to be visiting them. They live near Picton. I know them from Herefordshire. And Matt, who lived in Bronllys on the Welsh side of the border, is also supposed to be turning up. At the moment he's somewhere in Australia.

～

This is Spencer Park Beach on the other side of the River Styx. I am walking through the silver trees that grow upon the dunes. Inland lie salt marshes. From dark clouds a tornado funnel spirals down, miles off. The air is hot and still today, the kind of heat which makes you realise that air is matter and not a void. The only sound is made by birds' prattle and the quiet crashing of surf. As I rise over the dunes and skid down towards the ocean, the scent of seaweed sharpens. The beach is empty except for a small group of people very distant. They are indistinguishable from driftwood until a child dashes towards the water or a flash of yellow towel brings them alive. Two teenage surfer boys come jauntily over the dune carrying their boards and are absorbed soundlessly into the scene.

～

Elric Hooper. A place for everything and everything in its place: rows of art books meticulously shelved, ranges of CDs in alphabetical order secreted in specially constructed drawers, Buddhist bits and pieces positioned with dustless accuracy, and Elric himself shaven-headed in Indian cotton pyjamas, his day-wear.

'When you said you wanted to come at tea-time I was a bit confused, because we don't have tea in that sense. For us tea is an evening meal at six. So I wondered if you were inviting yourself for a meal.'

'No, no, not at all!'

'Well, I wasn't sure. So in case you were I bought two fat buns.'

He pushes the buns in my direction as though the merest glance would make him put on weight. I expect he's very ounce-conscious. I mention Rome. He worked with Zeffirelli, not Fellini.

'I was introduced to Noel Coward in the via Veneto,' he says. 'Someone rushed into the café and said "Have you heard? Brian Epstein's blown his brains out!" A pause. Noel Coward piped up "He must've been a very good shot."'

I mention how Christchurch is good for boys and he says 'Really? It's like the lighthouse keeper not seeing the light.'

'Do you have a partner?'

'No, I'd be impossible to live with.'

He partook of Swinging London. He was in Lionel Bart's *Twang!* He worked with Olivier at the Old Vic. He came back home in 1975 to direct plays. But he won't let himself go. Elric naughty? I mention John Osborne living in Clun and he quotes a chunk of *A Shropshire Lad*. I mention the Old Vic Tour 1948 – ah – 'I saw it!' he exclaims. 'Here in Christchurch.'

(Yes, the troupe were in this very town on September the 26th 1948, the day I was born.)

'Did your parents take you?' I ask.

'Oh no, they weren't those sort of people. I took myself. I must've been eleven, twelve. It was at the St James, which is still the best theatre in Christchurch.'

'I think I passed it. Painted a horrible dark colour. Religious?'

'It was out of commission and bought by the House of God, but it's now for sale again. I saw *The School for Scandal* there and what I remember about it was they had a vision curtain.'

'A what?'

'It's a gauze curtain with painting on it and the actors are positioned behind their painted selves. The light comes up, the curtain goes up, the actors come alive. It's very effective but considered old hat now. The Oliviers were royalty; 1948 was the year he won the Oscar for *Hamlet*.'

'Which is the worst *Hamlet* I've ever seen. She was in *Anna Karenina*, same year. Music by Constant Lambert.'

'Costumes by Cecil Beaton.'

'You don't have a New Zealand accent.'

'I let it go.'

'I think standard English is coming back, but at the moment they're not allowed to teach it in English schools. These days the best English is spoken by foreigners.'

'That's so sad.'

'I can't always understand what people are saying here.'

'Me too! The telephone operator – I sometimes have to ask them three or four times. Because the vowels are all confused in our accent. What people don't realise is that not only is standard English, received pronunciation, the easiest to understand but also – and you learn this very quickly as an actor – it is the most euphonious and expressive. It has the widest range of sounds.'

The problem began when it became impermissible to propose that there be a proper way to pronounce English. The same philosophy later renounced the correction of grammar and spelling, even in examinations. Therefore, in English state schools at least, English cannot in effect be taught. The worst form of child abuse in Britain is letting children leave school unable to read and write. A recent survey establishes that 47 per cent of sixteen-year-olds in English state education have not reached minimum competence in reading and writing English. This is because mental rigour has itself been deemed abusive, making it impossible to train young minds. We seem to be going from the age of the common man to the age of the zombie. The only possible reduction after that is the elimination of the species altogether.

~

The Banks Peninsula manages to be both severe and voluptuous, as though someone threw a cloth of jade-green velvet over the entire thing. Its fertile slopes were once wooded, but in the second half of the nineteenth century millions of feet of timber were cut down to build Christchurch and the slopes subsequently seeded with cocksfoot, a tough but shiny strain of pasture grass from England. This has enhanced the complexity of light and shadow created on the surface of the exposed, crinkled hills.

Akaroa, occupying a concealed site on the peninsula's southern shore, was for long a French outpost, and the switchback access road also has the French-style driving. They swoop on to your rear bumper, throwing up their hands in exasperation as though you have no right to exist. En route I listen to the gardening correspondent on National Radio: 'Summer has arrived, Wayne, and isn't it paradise? Suddenly the garden is drenched with flowers. The great balls of my giant hogweed are ready to burst! It's the biggest thing you can have in a garden, more than ten feet tall, and a big cartwheel of white, Wayne, over your head, and now that my garden is mature – maturity is so important, isn't it, Wayne? – I've decided that paradise on earth *is* possible. What I call the Christmas rhododendron – something *virginibus* for those who want to buy one – it's just *gorgeous*, Wayne, smells like a lily. Here's a bit of a stocking stuffer for floral fanciers, a bit of froth and bubble for Christmas – *Astrology and the Garden* – what sign are you, Wayne? Libra. You're a rose! I'm Aries, a tiger lily, so watch out, Wayne. I know it's all been exploded now but do you think we're compatible? Petal guru Jane Packer has a very *modern* book out and that's not meant as a criticism, it's the best flower-arranging vol. I've come across in a long time, but you won't find *one* classical abundant arrangement, and there's a lovely page in thirst-quenching red – did you know the Dutch spend more money on flowers than anyone else in the world?'

I'm not sure why she describes red as thirst-quenching; maybe she drinks blood. If ever a small town deserved the epithet of 'heavenly' it is Akaroa. Orchestrated in blues and greens and embosomed in hills, Akaroa straggles along the water's edge of an inlet created by the sea flooding the crater of an extinct volcano. It is designed for pleasure, with palm trees and jetties, groups of coloured buildings and waterside walks, and yet the mood is rustic. It is invaded by farms. It has boats but is not yachty. It has the French finesse but without irritability. It preserves a high proportion of its historic architecture as though that were the most normal thing in the world. It doesn't have the silence usually found in small towns here, but is complicit, playful and talkative. After sitting for ages in the warm sun on the cricket green, I sauntered over to a shop called Pot Pourri, painted pink. They were playing 'Spanish Eyes'. I bought a large piece of Russian fudge. The woman who made the fudge, when I asked her why it was called Russian, shrugged her shoulders and said 'That's just what we call it.' But there *must* be a reason. She wasn't interested in any reason, had never bothered to enquire. Propping myself against a post of the pink verandah, I wait to watch the world go by. But it doesn't go by. All is calm and quiet in the sun, with flowers.

His Button

My journey has gone pear-shaped. It's been a fair swim until now, but suddenly it's no longer possible to stay where I want to stay because everywhere is filled with Christmas and New Year bookings. In other words I've driven slap-bang into their summer high season. So I'd better stop writing-as-I-go, until I've found out where I'm going.

~

December the 15th. Dammit, I'm back in Auckland and living at the Windsor Hotel in Queen Street. The idea was to spend Yule in Golden Bay with Bernard, Daisy and Matt, those friends of mine from Herefordshire. But now I'm alone in a big art deco bedroom on main street and waiting for Matt to arrive here. It wasn't supposed to be like this.

~

What happened was – I left Christchurch on a sunny morning to drive up to Bernard and Daisy, who were hanging out over one of the spectacular Marlborough Sounds. On leaving the Merivale

Court Motel, Mr Hock added my phonebill to my room-charge and the total came to $388. His eyebrows shot up. 'This is very, very good number!'

'It is?'

'388 is the best possible number!'

Though I fancy I'm not superstitious, his announcement lifted me and made me inquisitive.

'Long life and prosperity!' he exclaimed.

'But why?'

'In Chinese world three is long life and eighty-eight is maximum prosperity. So 388 is the best number you can have!'

Goodee. The car hummed merrily through Domett and Parnassus. Up and down, in and out we went, sustained by sushi and Russian fudge, National Radio, swinging tunes from Hutch ... *I'm sure you'd hate to hear ... that I adore you, dear ... for you'd be so easy to love* ... and Amon Tobin's *Supermodified* electronica – 'Get Your Snack On' – 'Deo' – 'Rhino Jockey' – 'Keepin It Steel' ... A little before Kaikoura there was a break in the wall of hills which hides the sea, and with heart-in-mouth effect the road reeled directly on to the Pacific Ocean. Waves toppled against my right window and snowy mountains pushed their faces against the left. Impetuously the coastal margin expanded or contracted, now wider, now narrower, mile after mile, shoving one more or less against the rushes of surf. And to my amazement, along this stretch of coast, there were no holiday homes. At a high empty point I decided to pull over and change into shorts but halted in the transition, removed everything and walked naked in the open air, exposing myself to natural life. Ahead and into the distance were miles of turfy shore fringed with the diminishing lace of Pacific rollers and the affectionate breeze licked and caressed my entire body, every part of it, yes, from now on it would be shorts, shorts, shorts, lovely brown legs, naked in bed, soft summer. *Sand in my shoes ... calling me to*

that ever so heavenly shore ... deep in my soul the thundering roll of a
tropic sea ...

A caravan on a lay-by. From it an old hippy was selling crayfish
so I bought one for my lunch and one for Bernard and Daisy later
on. The hippy wrapped them in newspaper, along with lemons and
tartare sauce, against a backdrop of crags. It must have been here
in the late 1970s that the Kaikoura Lights manifested themselves,
a series of anomalous illuminations and radar sightings spotted by
two cargo planes flying down to Christchurch. Some of the phe-
nomena were filmed by the crew. To this day there has never been
a prosaic explanation. But I note that flying saucers were first
reported in 1947, which led to UFO sightings taking over from the
sighting of fairies. Until the aeroplane age, fairies were always the
things to spot.

Further on I find a more cosy lay-by, unwrap lunch, and pull
and chew the crayfish. I'm eating the ocean, swallowing the view,
and I'm in heaven – again. Joseph Brodsky said that St Petersburg
suited lonely moods because the city itself is lonely. I would say the
same about this country. Loneliness suits it. The pleasures of
encountering people are all the greater for knowing that at any
time you choose you can be reabsorbed into the nourishing, healing
loneliness. I jot down the following on my car pad: 'I'm not an
egalitarian. I believe that some freedom somewhere is better than
no freedom anywhere.'

~

In radiant sunshine the Pacific switched its moods between mighty,
sluggish and frolicsome, as the landscape too modulated through
phases of rock, hill, dune and cliff, with the ocean coming at you
blue & white from different directions all along. People who know
about such things say this drive is better than Big Sur. From time
to time a narrow vista would shoot deeply inland.

Around Blenheim everything got dreary, suburban, plucked clean by agriculture, but at Picton ranks of wooded hills fell down into the sea like tidal waves of trees. Picton is romanced by the arrivals and departures of boats between the North and South Islands, and even has a whiff of William Hodges and Tahiti in those forests flying upwards, but is otherwise entirely modern so far as I could see.

Bernard had given me meticulous instructions. Turn left ... round another roundabout ... sharp right ... up and around – ooo, yes, we're on the Queen Charlotte Drive. I think this is famous. It certainly should be. It's the corniche above the Marlborough Sounds, in and out, up and down, a Brucknerian counterpoint of vertical forest and horizontal water.

Bernard is – well, I'm not sure what he is. In Herefordshire he's known for owning a windmill and inventing an oven. Here, I believe, he sails a boat and chops things with an axe. Either way he has remarkably good muscle-tone for a seventy-year-old. Daisy is his ex-wife. But she often behaves like his wife. He lives in a sort of tree-house overlooking a Sound and had warned me about the turn-off and approach. 'Rev hard, and whatever you do don't stop.' My tin car slithers and squeals. Tyres burn. Rubble and earth fly out sideways. Are we ascending, or careening laterally to a plunging death? As I brake urgently before a pile of logs, red-faced and sweating and terrified, Daisy's voice trills 'Bernard's not very well.' I think the car is level. Level-ish anyway, though everything else is at a most peculiar angle. I look up out of the open window. Daisy is leaning down from a platform. She says Bernard's having a drink with the neighbours. But he must've heard my racket because, beard first, he parts a pair of bushes and most of him emerges.

'So you found it then.' He's smiling his slightly anxious smile. 'Have I?'

'Seems so.'

I'm standing on a small apron of rock abutting the house, and stretching my arms and legs. The smell from the car's engine is intense.

'This is amazing,' I say, scrambling towards Bernard and shaking his hand. And it is. Like a Chinese landscape. 'But I hear you're not well.'

'I've lost my sense of balance.'

'Recently?'

'On the plane.'

'There's a name for that.'

'And I can't go on the boat.'

'Incredible.'

It's odd seeing them at home in this context. I don't think Daisy's very well either, judging from appearances, but I don't want to open that subject. So I hand them the newspaper of crayfish and a bottle of wine. 'It won an award.'

'How lovely.'

'The wine did.'

'We can have it this evening. Would you like a cup of tea?'

'Rather.'

Hope it's strong. I need a strong cup. It was a long drive. The house is a kit of green metal, brown wood and sheets of glass. But it's not exactly a bungalow because the living floor is reached up a tall flight of wooden steps and there's a lot going on underneath it – Bernard's axe room for example.

'Have you got over the jetlag?' asks Daisy.

'Yes. I've been here two months. Have you got over yours?'

'Yes.'

'How long have you been here?'

'Two days.'

Actually I don't think she has got over hers. Or maybe she's just worried about Bernard's balance. Her smile, like his, has the anxious vibe. And the tea's not that strong.

'There's another Duncan here,' says Bernard. 'Duncan Rutherford who lives near Nelson and is in his nineties.'

'Is he a –'

'Yes, great-nephew. He has an incredible collection of vintage cars in a warehouse, over a hundred of them, and his principal occupation is going round pumping up the tyres.'

'My goodness.'

'One car he's owned for seventy-nine years.'

'Owned it personally?'

'Yes, personally.'

'Wow.'

'And another – it's not a car – the family acquired one of the very first motorised tractors in the country, in the early1900s. He still has it and it still works.'

'Gosh.'

Are we gelling? Is Christmas still on the cards? What was mooted in Herefordshire is now a different kettle of fish.

A wild bird flies in through the open glass door and Bernard feeds it from his hand. He pushes back another glass door – the whole side of the room is sliding glass and leads on to the wooden balcony, which goes all round – and we walk out and sink into the cosmic Chinese vista, suspended like characters from *Peter Pan*.

Bernard points across the void. 'That's my boat.'

'The black one with the poop?'

'I wish it were. No, the little one to the left of it.'

'Who lives there?'

I indicate an arrangement of red pagodas on a promontary, peeping above the leaves.

'I don't know. Somebody important. I can't go on to my boat. I stepped on the plane in England right as rain. When I stepped off

here my balance had gone. I'm going to see a specialist in Christchurch on Thursday.'

'What happens when you step on your boat?'

'Everything goes slushy. I can't get my bearings. I get dizzy.
Sometimes it happens without stepping on the boat. Did you come
through Picton?'

'Yes. Wonderful situation. Is there an old quarter?'

'Not any more. They've pulled down the Terminus Hotel,
which was one of the few remaining old buildings. Just a few days
ago they did it. Quite a job getting it down. The building was so
strong.'

I knew there was something mephistophelian about this place.
The Marlborough Sounds are intensely beautiful but there's something – is 'evil' too strong a word? Louring, maybe.

'That's what frightens me about this country,' says Daisy. 'No
taste. When you go into their houses and see what they've done,
it's all very cosy – but no taste.'

Perhaps she hasn't got in with the right crowd. Shirley O'Connor
had taste and so did Deb Nation.

'Where are you staying next?' asks Bernard.

Er, that was sudden.

'I've booked into a gay farm at Takaka,' I reply.

'Sounds fun.'

'These gay places aren't really me. But I thought – why not
while you're here.'

'Shall we ring up Matt?' suggests Daisy.

Matt is on a farm somewhere in Australia doing a bit of dry-
stone walling. Strange to say, a person answers the phone at the
Australian end – and they've heard of him. It's perfectly logical but
seems so improbable. What's more, they say they'll go and get him.
He's in the bunkhouse. It's like we're phoning a John Wayne film
or a Glen Baxter cartoon. 'You talk to him.' Daisy, with a faint

blush on her cheeks, quickly hands me the receiver as though it were infected, and snatches her hands back into her lap, where they twitch.

Matt and I are soon laughing. He's going to fly from Melbourne to Christchurch then up to Nelson. He'll email me some dates when he knows them. Bernard looks nervous – I think he's worried about the phone bill – not to mention the arrival of Matt the virile young Yorkshireman into their Christmas.

Bernard and Daisy, they inform me, soon after the phone call is terminated, are spending Christmas somewhere else. Right-o. So that's that. Now they've made it clear, the atmosphere relaxes a bit. And with a slump I feel dog-tired. We leave it that I should rent a place in Golden Bay, which is a few hours west of here, that Matt should come and stay with me there, and that Bernard and Daisy will join us for the New Year – maybe – or something. None of it sounds very festive.

'Hope Thursday goes all right at the doctor's. Will you have a brain scan?' I ask Bernard ... The light turns violet ... While Daisy prepares dinner, the sound of Bernard going at something with an axe rises up from below.

Can't sleep. My bedroom is freezing.

~

Takaka Hill is made from lavender marble and it is the great natural barrier which confers on Golden Bay its seclusion. Driving down the far side in a low gear one descends into a sort of secret land-scape that feels somehow ... different. Takaka itself is a cute town, with long-hairs in jeeps trailing blond children in and out of a wholefood café where magical forms of massage are offered on pinboards.

I've only once before stayed in a gay hotel and that was in Brighton, where I was disconcerted by the all-male gentility. So I was in two minds about trying out Autumn Farm, and this uncertainty wasn't helped when on my arrival at the establishment a well-meaning, faintly odd-looking man in his forties, whom I didn't know from Adam, greeted me like a long-lost friend. He introduced me to his partner who was working in the garden, and showed me to a room in the old wooden house. The room was large and beautiful, with a double bed whose counterpane rose like the plump bosom of a contralto at La Scala.

'Very nice,' I muttered.

'Try it out,' he said.

I seemed to sink for ages before coming to a halt. It produced a slightly sick feeling, being eaten by a piece of furniture. Unfortunately the beautiful bedroom was next to the communal kitchen, so there'd be no sleep after 7 a.m. Even the gays in this country get up at dawn. A hunk past his prime lolloped into the kitchen and sat steaming with a grin.

'This is Greg. This is Duncan. How was your run, Greg?'

Greg splays his legs to ease the pressure inside his running shorts.

'Brilliant,' he says.

Am I supposed to fuck him? Is he supposed to fuck me? Are we all supposed to fuck each other? Shall I be considered a party pooper if I don't at least plonk for one of them? The obligation to bond pervades the atmosphere like superglue and somehow this is not dispelled when the owner reassures me that 'At Autumn Farm everyone is free to do whatever they want whenever they want.'

Oh God, no. I can't take it. It's entirely *my* inadequacy of course, my insecurity, call it what you like; they're extending thick tendrils of friendship, lianas of high-octane hospitality are snapping round my ankles and wrists and neck, and I just can't take it, my whole nature is in rebellion against this over-familiarity from strangers. And the all-maleness, as at Brighton, gives me the creeps. I've fallen in love with many males but it's been females who've kept me going in this life and it feels funny without them. If only they'd sprinkled a few dykes around, it might've helped. I can do all-male environments at school, in prison, in clubs, in bogs and in changing rooms and Turkish baths, but in hotels, even small ones at the Shangri-La end of the earth? Can't do it *here* anyway. And I can't stand the idea of everyone on top of everyone else in some kind of tacit conspiracy. To put it another way – I have nothing in common with these guys – and don't fancy any of them either. I'll put up with almost anything if I fancy someone. Before you can say Jack Robinson I've mumbled an excuse about being too close to the kitchen, jumped in the car, fled down the drive, out the gate –

And ah ... breathe an easier air. I believe I've just had an attack of homosexual panic, the thing that judges say excuses the murder of gays by violent thugs. And when I come round from my 'turn' I find myself in the blankest possible motel at the end of Takaka high street in a huge impersonal room with several beds. The television is on and it's purveying meaningless pap and I'm making a cup of tea in my bland, totally characterless kitchen. There are no undercurrents or overcurrents here whatsoever, absolutely none and I am able to subside into the deep and thankful calm of complete anonymity in no-place.

Later, with more tea and a Kit-Kat perched on my left knee, I pick up a book and snuggle in for a read. It's called *The Godwits Fly* and is by Robin Hyde, who was a woman. She was very beautiful, more so than Katherine Mansfield, and the opposite kind of writer: effusive rather than selective. I see from the Introduction that she was born under another name in Cape Town in 1906 but the family moved to Wellington soon after. Never married. Two illegitimate children; one died at birth when she was twenty years old, the other was adopted. Several breakdowns – of course – in the 1930s led to her volunteering to enter a mental clinic where, as Ivor Gurney had done in his, she experienced an exceptional burst of creativity. Tucked up in her supervised attic, Robin wrote among other things her novel *The Godwits Fly*. It is the story of her upbringing and I read through it in the next few days.

The first half I didn't enjoy much, despite the vividness of the scene-setting, because I'm allergic to books with the word 'Daddy' in them. But I can recognise that it's one of the finest evocations of family life ever penned. Even when horrible things happen, the iridescence of the writing drenches the scenes with beauty. The text is rich food and mustn't be rushed. She often ventures into the surreal. Her morality is unconventional. There is even a gay scene, quietly done but definite. It is not a family saga, she doesn't tell you a story – she tells you everything. There is an emotional completeness even to the most incidental characters which calls to mind D. H. Lawrence in his earlier, Nottinghamshire works. The second half, recounting the heroine's more independent involvement with the world around her, held me more, and yet I have less to say about it. The book builds to a powerful climax, before dipping in subtle resolution.

By the late 1930s Robin Hyde's work had been attracting notice in London and she decided to make the long journey there, to her spiritual, literary home. Scraping together what money she could, she booked a sea-passage with most of it. Her ship left Auckland for Hong Kong on January the 18th 1938. It so happened that on the very same day in London a farewell party was given, at an artist's studio overlooking the Thames at Hammersmith, for W. H. Auden and Christopher Isherwood. Those two young, already international celebrities were sailing in a direction opposite to that of the obscure Robin Hyde. She departed alone, but through the fashionable farewell party in London about 250 guests passed in the course of the night, including Benjamin Britten, E. M. Forster, Eddie Marsh, Rose Macaulay, Cyril Connolly and the Spenders.

Auden and Isherwood had announced to the press that their objective was the Sino-Japanese war, and this could explain Robin Hyde's sudden decision in Hong Kong to divert to China, rather than continue directly on for England. Being a left-wing dreamer, she may even have hoped to meet the cocky pair, and possibly did, since she too scrambled her way to the Sino-Japanese war front and sent reports back to New Zealand newspapers.

Robin Hyde finally reached England in September 1938, ill and desperately impoverished. She occupied a caravan in Kent and stayed with Charles Brasch outside London before moving to Notting Hill. On August the 23rd 1939, after less than a year of struggle in the city of her dreams and hopes, in a bedsitter in Pembridge Square, she killed herself. They usually say she died of benzedrine poisoning, but that doesn't sound right. She was a benny writer and the fact that the police found much benzedrine in her blood and two empty fifty-tablet bottles of benzedrine on a wardrobe shelf is not a surprise. There was also clear evidence that she'd tried to gas herself in the oven and I expect that was her chosen exit. By this time, Auden and Isherwood had flown again, this time to the USA, where they would be able to view the horrors of the war in Europe from a distance. When the Auckland writer Frank Sargeson heard of Isherwood's escape to the USA he wrote to John Lehmann that he thought it the most courageous thing imaginable: perhaps that is the kindest way of looking at it – as an act of daring – but Sargeson is the master of New Zealand gothic and Isherwood's move wasn't wise. Subsequently Isherwood wrote little of artistic importance except *Lost Years*, a candid erotic journal published after his death. Isherwood wouldn't have considered *Lost Years* a proper book, but its spontaneity and untidiness are aspects of its value. Indeed it's a superb example of unfinished art. The unfinished is closer to life since everything in life is unfinished, and this is especially relevant to a work like *Lost*

Years, which is a sexual autobiography. Auden's is a more complex case. Auden continued in ambiguity and returned to Europe when the war was over.

~

Next day I paid a visit to the Takaka tourist office. I was looking for a small house to rent for three weeks until early January, so that I might settle down for a bit and organise our New Year house party. I felt I'd been on the run for ages. When I put my head on the pillow I sensed my hair still streaming into the breeze behind me. Only two properties remained vacant. On checking out both I found suburban developments underway in their vicinity. No thanks. So let's move on to Collingwood, named after the illustrious admiral who was second in command to Nelson at Trafalgar. The Jinkses of Devonport had told me that Collingwood is 'unspoilt'. Well, let's find out. Buying a paper in the Takaka Bookshop my eye was caught by *The Paedophile and Sex Offender Index*, which is published annually by a private organisation. It lists offenders by name, district and profession. I wonder if this makes the offenders more or less sought after. I can imagine them pulling a lot of trade that way.

On driving north along the coast from Takaka the road got better and better and I began to think – don't count your chickens – but yes, this might well be *it*. The final dream destination, the sublime spot *off the beaten track* to end with. One always travels hopefully of course and the hope is to find a place which is not only habitable but also *authentic* and about which one can be selfish and claim it wholly for oneself. This is my discovery, my perfect little corner, keep off, keep out, don't spoil it, but here I am doing what writers and artists have been doing for centuries, blowing the secret. First you have the native inhabitants who want to move out of the old houses into new ones. So the writers and artists buy the old ones. Then the general bohemians arrive, then the middle class who restore property or build fancy villas, then developers turn up with big ideas, followed by the mass invasion. In my own experience it's a process I've observed swallowing up Goa, Phuket, St Tropez, Hay-on-Wye and Notting Hill, while in the past it happened to Taormina, Capri, Tangier and countless others places, so it looks as though the world has more or less run out of perfect little corners off the beaten track. If the process can be halted at the middle-class stage, the upside is that it prevents the old houses from falling down and the shops improve. But with mass invasion come the blocks of flats and the chain-stores and all is lost.

As the road ran over a causeway and curved to the right, I seemed at last to leave the holiday world behind, the world in which there's a brochure for everything. A line of pohutukawa trees stood like a row of portly guardsmen. On an impulse I stopped the car and got out to examine their blossoms, which resemble small fibre-optic bursts the size of a powder puff, each scarlet filament tipped with a dot of yellow. After the causeway the landscape ascended and became lush with tree-ferns. The absolute rule of this country's landscape is that wherever you find a tree-fern growing naturally will be a lovely place. The tree-fern is a true aesthete. It simply can't bear to grow anywhere ugly.

Well, yes, I do have to say – and why is it that I can't prevent myself spreading the destructive news? Because to do so, I suppose, would be to cancel the whole point of exploration and having brought you this far it's simply not cricket to abandon you – I have to say that as I reached Collingwood I did have the rapture, the tingling sense of a hope fulfilled, of having attained an ideal objective. It wasn't doomed like the Waitaki. It wasn't famous like Akaroa. It was my personal version of breaking through to the silent steeples of Angkor Wat, or more accurately perhaps my little Darien moment since it was characterised not by architectural but by natural splendour set off with a few small buildings here and there.

The situation of Collingwood is superb and unusual but not overpowering. There are limitless sands on one side, an estuary on the other and, further back, jungly King Kong hills. Old photographs in one of the shop windows illustrated that its tiny main street, which is a cul de sac where the State Highway 60 ends, once had numerous two-storeyed buildings, many gay with double verandahs one above the other. Only one of these buildings survives, the Old Post Office, but its presence anchors Collingwood to some time and place and gives distinction to its roofline as you approach. Collingwood suffered major fires in 1859, 1904 and 1967, so its depletion of original architecture is forgivable. Almost anywhere else, even in South Wales, this cul de sac termination of State Highway 60 – which is a very wide space – would have become a communal village square, laid out and preserved. But not here, where it is merely an aggregate of structures by the roadside with a holiday camp hunkering down at the end. Still, Collingwood is terribly attractive in an unfussy way and I want to have my three-week halt hereabouts. With that in mind, I check into the Beachcomber Motel, where I can stay only until Saturday because it's fully booked thereafter.

Another motel, another bed. Sat on the end of it and finished the last piece of Russian fudge. On National Radio my ears twitch – they are talking about fuckshen. It takes me some time to grasp that it is the opposite of non-fuckshen. I'm bushed. I'll do a reccy tomorrow.

~

Hills of native forest descend into the sea, with narrow paddocks on shelves. Lustrous sands stretch to the horizon when the tide is out. Old goldfields hide syrupy lakes and are reached by secret

dripping gorges overhung with ferns and crossed by a wooden
bridge. Becalmed inlets ooze beneath screaming birds where
beaches of baize-green fend off the distant rage of the sea. Rocks
stand like sculptures. Wet woods resonate in pensive depths to the
call of the bellbird. I had found my destination. This little area,
north of Collingwood to Farewell Spit, and west into the forests
and valley of the Aorere River, was what I'd been journeying for
these past months.

But as in so many romantic encounters, though I very much
wanted it, it didn't want me. Not a bed to be had through to New
Year. Anne-Marie, the owner of the Beachcomber, said she'd try to
help but it was blank after blank. She says she's heard of an empty
place out at Rockville and will get back to me. I do want to rest
awhile. I've been travelling for so long. She does get back to me –
the house at Rockville is currently occupied by a farm labourer.
She has another idea, a half-finished house near the river – and
will get back to me again. Her assistant, Sean, lies on the floor
beside the spin dryers, smiling and stroking his tummy button. He
seems to have the answer to everything but never divulges. Can't
sleep. I'm lost. And today I'm irritable. I'm soured by rejection.
Today I find everything *naff*, even the birds along the seashore,
what's so special about them, just naff birds on sand.

... I drove out to Rockville. It was a humid day. Cloud threaded
the clambering forest. I stopped at the Early Settlers Museum,
which sounds as though Rockville might be a town but it isn't, just
a few houses and farms in a fabulous location. The museum was
open but unattended, an old dairy co-op in a field of abandoned
tractors, ploughs, steam engines and harvesters, and I am the only
person for miles around. Several concrete warehouses, pitted and
stained, were interlinked. The items inside were not labelled or
cleaned up much. This added to their interest, as though the
strong, steady, sunburnt hands which worked these obsolete

machines brought them here and left them behind only yesterday. Museums acquire objects, but here every acquisition has come with its attendant ghosts, and the ghosts are susurrating. The roofs of the warehouses creak in the muggy breeze. I keep thinking I hear someone walking about. They are always ahead of me round a corner or behind me in another hall. I hear them moving things, shuffling away or closing a door. But they are always out of sight. I look but find nobody. I try to walk quietly, peep round walls, catch them before they give me the slip and move out to the yard, but I never succeed. I hear them but I never see them. The only living things I do see are birds nesting in the roof. They send down little gusts of concerned sound. Outside I stare at some bladed relic red with rust. Behind me in the distance, clouds pour across the high hillsides like forest fires. There is much forest round here. That's how I like it. Plenty of wood cover. It's too good round here to last. I know they are coming to destroy it. I can hear the chatter of their plans.

≈

Anne-Marie, middle-aged, skinny, closely cropped hair, pert in manner, orderly in behaviour, tight little top, tight little bottom, is still looking for a house for me and came near to success with a cockle farmer who was going to move out of one property and later move out of another, but though I waited all afternoon for him in hazy, agitated expectation, hoping he would put flesh on the bones of this perplexing idea, he failed to turn up. Anne-Marie clacked to and fro across the gravel of the courtyard, going about her business like a Gauleiter in a concentration camp, but the cockle farmer didn't drop by or telephone. Outside the low cloud merges with sea fret, making a turbid mist. The air is clammy but cooler now.

≈

Pakawau Beach is silver in the afternoon light. A young man is squatting there on a log. He is motionless in a cream top and the hood of it is drawn over his head so that who he is cannot be seen. Becalmed I write some doggerel:

> Pierrot on a silver beach
> Switches off his mobile phone.
> With penknife he divides a peach
> And swallows all, including stone.
> The kernel in his stomach bides
> Its time until the winter snow
> And with the freezing of the tides
> Puts forth antennae sharp and slow.
> These needles break out back and front,
> Above, below. Into the night
> Pierrot floats and with a grunt
> He turns into a satellite.

~

I've moved to the Skara Brae Motel, run by Pax and Joanne Northover. It is not what it sounds but embowered in a garden and a good example of 'the bay villa'. This charming name for the characteristic Victorian residence of New Zealand suggests a villa overlooking a bay. In fact it is a villa with bay windows and it's one of the great abodes of the world, like the English Georgian terrace house or the French apartment. The bay villa is always detached and in its own garden, usually one storey, two for the rich, and constructed from wood. They were usually put up by speculative builders working from pattern books and there was great variety, an expression of Victorian frivolity after the severe classicism of the Georgians (it seems that human nature cannot be denied, and the more sober public life becomes the more outrageous the architecture). The villas were originally painted in buff colours but today's schemes are prettier: blue, primrose, pink, apricot, stone grey, white. I've forgotten what colour the Northovers' house was, and didn't take a photograph to remind me. But I do remember that they were braced for Christmas, with not one but two Christmas trees in the beflounced sitting-room.

Again and again I find myself taking the road north of Collingwood. It begins with a chain of small bridges across the estuary of the Aorere which bring you beneath a wooded ridge embellished with fernery and grows more and more unusual, until this scenic rock 'n' roll throws up its hands and goes minimalist, sand dunes fading to the horizon in fifteen miles of diminishing humps which slide at a gentle gradient beneath the quietly lisping sea. All along here the godwits live, coffee-coloured and white, long-billed waders probing for sandhoppers and molluscs, crustacea and marine worms, whenever the retreating tide exposes the hissing flats, whether it be day or night, until the autumn arrives in March and, after some days of mounting agitation, the godwits stream off in one cloudy, whirring mass of 15,000 to 20,000 birds, for their summer breeding grounds in the tundra of Siberia. A few of their number stay behind as an over-wintering flock, but how these are chosen or how they choose themselves remains a mystery. These left-behind or stay-behind birds do not breed but, loth to be omitted from the ongoing story altogether, they discard the summer feathers and adopt the chestnut plumage of wedlock.

Where the car-track peters out on the rocks, overlooking the awesome parabola of Farewell Spit, is where we come to a stop, the very furthest point of my journey and exploration, the place at which the dot pauses, draws its breath and with a rush accelerates into infinity.

There is an extraordinary café here. It has good food, spacey electronic music, a view to the end of the world, and Jeff.

A teenager. He is the coltish boy, carefree and smiling, who is standing upright with steady gaze at the end of this long, long road from London, who represents let us say not the collapse of a type but our sentimental hope that the doomed male may reconfigure himself in a new light. Jeff is blond but they come in all complexions, the good-natured boys, the intelligent few who aren't trapped in malice. The only future for the male: the good guy who can make a go of it. Isn't it time that being rude and thick became unfashionable?

Jeff is merely glimpsed. He brings me my coffee and cake and we talk about the music which is quietly ruffling the air, while he slowly transfers his weight from one foot to another. He told me the name of the album but I forgot to make a note. I go back the next afternoon, bumping my little white car up the rocky track to the café at the end of the world, wanting to know what the enchanting, elusive music was, wanting to interview him for this book and ask him why he is so peaceful and lively and courteous and smiling and free all at the same time. They say he's not working today. I leave tomorrow. They tell me his father runs the nearby farm and I should find him there. But I don't try. Perhaps it's just as well. To lead him into complexity might well obstruct what is good in him. Let us leave Jeff to his private triumphs, his self-forgetting pleasures, his beauty.

~

All drives hereabouts have the privacy of trees. There is a particularly cinematic road along the Aorere Valley, through Rockville and Bainham and up to Fifteen Mile Creek, and on the day I took it the whole landscape was moving in and out of a mist like spectral echoes of Devon dislodged to the tropics. The blue cottage! I found an empty blue cottage facing the road, just past Bainham before the tarmac turns to gravel. It was a perfect square on a rising meadow, its wooden walls weathered to powder blue, with a low pyramidal roof weathered to pink. Its front door had a single window on either side. Smaller outbuildings of the same bleached colours were scattered about among bushes and a few Scots pines. On the ragged lawn out front, a detritus of planks and beams had been piled in bonfire shape. Extending behind the house, the escarpment turned ever gloomier, from lime green to a sepulchral blue, as the meadows became loose woodland and then thick forest where low mountains faded up into down-plundering mists. Could I perhaps rent this cottage?

I went back to Langford's Stores to enquire – closed until Monday. I stopped at a farm to enquire. A grey-eyed man with huge shoulders was hosing foul-smelling muck off a sward of concrete.

'It's empty, yes. But it's gonna be shifted. Everything disconnected. But there's another blue cottage which is empty – about five Ks along the gravel road.'

I'd forgotten. They use kilometres.

'Is the road OK?'

'Piece of cake.'

I went there – saw a bluish hut on a far bluff – would that be it? Then it vanished from sight and I could never find it again. Stopped at the little bridge of Fifteen Mile Creek in the middle of the forest. Its banks were overhung by damsel-haired plants and the fickle rivulet ran on uneven stones sending up a variety of consoling murmurs. Lovely soft English rain comes on. The lowing of distant cows echoes like phantoms. Well, I found my blue cottage but it *shifted*.

~

I am all the time on this journey gravitating to the east coast, to the feminine coast, to the Pacific side, the side of sunrise, newness, beginning. Everywhere I go I am caught in a curl which puts me down on a beach on the east side. There is something bitter, I sense, about the coast facing west. The wind and rain come at you. The fierce seas are borne up on the Roaring Forties and further south the glaciated fjords impose daunting obstacles. It was in Auckland, visiting Tony Ogle, that briefly I broke through to the west coast. And at the base of Farewell Spit I found I was able to do it for a second time.

The car yanks me over on a flicking route and deposits me in a small sheltered compound in wild terrain. The rest must be done on foot via turf ridges and heaving dunes. The landscape is tough. The rock is striated. Blasted patches of vegetation hunker in cracks. Everything is scarred by tempestuousness. And when finally I break through, trundling down a dune to the shore, the sea rushes at me in bucking bronco mood. The sea is nasty. No smooth rollers on Wharariki Beach but muscular waves confused and fluttering this way and that in clashing undertows before lurching and spitting at me. It's blowing a gale and the sand is swirled, its patterns constantly reshaped. The dunes themselves are wandering imperceptibly, shifting their atomised and ghostly bulk. The sky, sea and sand merge in swathes of chilling paleness, and dead centre, out of the inhospitable fume, rise two black rocks of diabolical outline, up to their waists in turbulence, standing offshore like the guardians of hell. I think it's time to leave.

∽

Over the phone I book my flight from Nelson back to Auckland. On the Northover's computer I send an email to Matt telling him to fly to Auckland and not to Nelson. I hope that's clear – basically we'll have to Christmas it out somewhere at the top of the country. This car – the smallest, cheapest Toyota – has performed very well. After my back scare in Dunedin I purchased a hot water bottle from a chemist, half filled it with water and left it in the car because its value was not from heat but from support and movement. Placing it in the small of my back, the vibrations of the car caused its contents to tremble, giving the lower back an ongoing and subtle massage, particularly beneficial on long drives. When I checked the car in at Nelson airport I'd driven nearly 9,000 kilometres since Invercargill. A group of surfing boys were flying with us barefoot. Small thirty-two-seater prop plane. The air hostess said 'Hi, folks!' Clear, cloudless, sunny blue flight. No wonder they like corrugated iron – the land is corrugated as you fly over it.

~

Being back in a large cosmopolitan city was thrilling. Although I don't want everything to vanish in soup, I realise I couldn't live in a mono culture for always, I'd miss the chemical excitement of miscegenation. Actually I need both aspects in my life back home – the excitement of London as the world city, but also a need to be reassured that timeless England continues to exist, because without that reassurance I get panicky.

Auckland airport, which seemed so small on arrival from London, now seemed big. The buildings and motorway on the approach, which first struck me as modest, now looked the acme of urban weight and sophstication. My taxi-driver was from Hong Kong. He wanted to know how much money you can make from writing. That's all they ever want to know. I told him – none. After which he lost all interest in me and drove on in silence.

My first task was to check emails at the internet shop. Matt had changed his dates again. Now he was flying from Sydney to Auckland on December the 17th – blimey, that's tomorrow! I'm giving up on trying to organise things. Perhaps Matt won't show – he'll meet someone and take off in a different direction – isn't that what everyone does these days, keep it all ultra-temporary, in a flux of permanent revision and update? – and I'll be obliged to spend Christmas by myself in this Windsor Hotel, Queen Street. That's what I told David Jenkins when I rang him in London, and he thought it sounded a marvellous prospect. People with children often view the idea of spending Christmas alone as akin to nirvana. Matt mentioned he wanted to go to Thailand at some point. Everyone in Auckland seems to be going to Waiheke Island for Christmas.

The Windsor Hotel used to be a bank. It's a 1930s building of quality and has been remodelled with great attention to detail, retaining the curious brass window openers. I've become a huge fan of art deco architecture since arriving in this country – it's the rococo of modernism. My attraction perhaps began as a drowning man clutching at straws, but now I really delight in its classical balance and the jazz frills with which it trims itself. We never had much of it in England (or much of rococo either, for that matter).

My room is large and high with two double beds and tall windows on two sides framed by floor-length curtains. The furniture is of dark wood upholstered in green brocade. There is a small kitchen as you enter and a bathroom attached. Check-out time is an hour later than the customary 10 a.m. – almost chic. But I'm not checking out. I've booked three weeks and shall be in great comfort and make myself very much at home, beginning with a good long soak in the bath and contemplation of my balls slowly churning in their sack.

~

To the Centurian Sauna in Beresford Street – wish they hadn't spelt it with an 'a' but they do things like that out here. A Maori in the changing-room puts his towel on before taking off his underpants, and then slips the pants down and puts on a bathing costume under the towel and keeps the towel on as well. Shall I ever see a Maori cock? When I left England, Jonno, an old chum, said 'The Maoris are very good-looking but be warned.'

'What, they're a bunch of cut-throats?'

'No, no. They suffer from China syndrome.'

'What's that?'

'Small willies.'

I don't mind small willies in the least. I don't mind big willies either. The Greeks considered a small willy to be an essential attribute of male beauty because much of the time Greeks went round naked, when obviously a large one flopping about would be more of a distraction from the harmonious whole – though their genitals were not necessarily free, for on occasion in ancient Greece, athletes and other public performers used a form of penile infibulation in which a clasp was used to close the foreskin and draw the penis over to one side (this can be clearly seen on a statue of Anacreon found in the Sabine Hills and now in the Glyptotek, Copenhagen).

There are three Maoris wandering about the Centurian Sauna but they are not talking to each other or to anyone else, and all three are wearing long swimming shorts while everyone else goes towel-draped or unclad. Not that there's much larrying going on, though there are private closets available for the purpose. The premises are very dark indeed, with only a few tiny red lights glowing like dots. I must feel my way … When I get back to the hotel the question of Maori sexuality is raised again. They weren't always so prudish. The local newspaper carries a report on the remarks of Bishop Vercoe, whoever he is, that homosexuality did not exist in pre-European society. The thickness of these bishops! A Maori representative, in contradiction, cites recent research giving 'clear evidence that pre-European Maori sexuality was far more accepting of sexual diversity and difference than is the case today. We know that the imposition of a Western way of looking at the world, based on Christian concepts and beliefs, was responsible for an erosion of traditional practices and values. This was especially so in relation to sexuality.'

Right on, brother. Put those bloody missionaries in their place. But what this doesn't explain is why the colonised – it is just as true in the West Indies and Africa and India – hold on to the Victorian view of sex long after the colonisers have junked it. As for Muslims, I'm told that due to the extreme division of the sexes the people are very bisexual in their own countries but become super-straight when they move to the West – presumably because they are no longer confident of transgressive behaviour remaining unspoken of in an open society.

~

I have been in touch with the campaign to save the Waitaki Valley from destruction by the water company and have written letters to various newspapers. Maybe my position as an outsider, with no vested interests, will carry some weight. The letters do get published and provoke further comment.

~

My God, Matt's here. His flight from Sydney was early. And he turns up at the hotel looking fit and tanned.

'Did a lot of walling. Incredible heat,' he says. 'Flat grass all the way to the horizon.'

So much for Australia.

He's staying in the pink house in Emily Place which I was moved to photograph months ago so unexpected was its charm. Trust Matt to find the prettiest billet in Auckland *by accident*. I'm clearing out some books.

'Have you read that?'

'It didn't grab me,' he says (it's *The Golden Bowl*). 'Yeah … ' he adds after a while, à propos nothing. Matt's eyes have that odd expression they sometimes have, intense but neutral as though his eyes are drawing breath, breathing in, combined with a hint of a smile which is suppressed and never actually blossoms. It's some kind of amalgam of interest, pleasure, anxiety and disbelief. Quite often it resolves itself in a short but genuine belly laugh breaking out, though not on this occasion.

'Would you like a drink?'

'Have you got any juice? This place is soft and dreamy. It's like walking on a mattress.'

'And Australia wasn't?'

'Australia was hot and stony and dry and dusty and speedy. There's a cannabis shop in the basement of your hotel.'

'Is there? I thought there was a bar down there.'

'Yeah, it used to be a bar. But they closed it and it became a cannabis shop.'

He knows everything already. We went to the Hilton for drinks and a snack supper which took ages to arrive. The smiling robots kept saying 'Your food will be with you shortly' and nothing happened. And Matt kept saying 'Yeah …' out of the blue and nothing else, sometimes rubbing his hands together, 'Yeah' and rubbing his hands. When the food turned up he went into his private chuckle and said 'Conrad and Lawrence went to Australia but they didn't come here.'

'Samuel Butler came here, and Trollope and Mark Twain. And Blaise Cendrars.'

'Didn't George Bernard Shaw come here?'

'Yes, he came, the same time as Krishnamurti I think, in the 1930s. Shaw preached here against democracy and in favour of totalitarianism.'

'Fuckin' windbag,' he observes.

'I'm so much more pro-American since September 11th, aren't you?'

'There's a poem by Auden, I can't remember which one, a long one though, in which he says radicalism and extermination have always held hands.' He rubs his hands together, and this time gives the short belly laugh too, looking down at the floor. He's the world's best-read dry-stone waller. Honestly, he is.

'I visited Bernard and Daisy,' I say.

'How were they?'

'Not well.'

'I'm supposed to be going down there.'

'Will you?'

'Am I supposed to be going down there? Did they say?'

'They didn't say. But they're not on for Christmas.'

'Oh.'

'I understand. They're in a different context here.'

I remember when I was living in St Petersburg and friends would fly in and say let's party and I, up to my eyes in something else entirely, would simply gawp at them because they hadn't real-ised they'd arrived on Pluto.

'Do you fancy Waiheke for Christmas?' I ask. 'It's an island. Not far away.'

'Sure ... Why not,' he replies.

≈

Sex. It's not a four-letter word. Matt is off doing some exploring – and I have discovered the Den. It's in Wyndham Street across the road from the Windsor Hotel. The ground floor is a shop selling sex toys to straights but the basement is a dark labyrinth of nooks and cells where males hover for anonymous encounters. There are never more than two or three down there. The fewness of customers makes it sexier. As I slide to a halt in this diffused city

I find myself wanting lots of sex and this is the place which is most convenient for it. I haven't had much since London and lack of sex gives me malaise. One of the things about going it alone is that you lose not only the touch but also the *smell* of people close. These things – touch and smell of one's fellow humans – are vital to mental health. At last the sex-on-tap problem has been solved. Many racial types find their way down there. Race and type are very important in sex. I like to try all sorts of races and types: it's an absolutely fascinating pastime, probably the most fascinating there is, the endless lure of the unknown and the untried, because you at once discover that everyone is different, shifting from the species to the race to the type to the individual and back again, through interactive layers of reality and fantasy which under other circumstances would be called prejudice. In sex all forms of pure racism and racial mixing flourish fruitfully. Would anyone prosecute a white woman for saying she only wanted a white baby? Of course not. Alternatively could anyone deny that having sex with someone from another race is an incredibly rewarding experience? Only a fool would.

The Den's basement resembles a small abandoned factory, derelict and vandalised. Everything is painted black and the blackness is deepened by the glow from a television set showing porn videos in a corner cell with black sofas. Holes pierced in the walls of the cell reveal the back of the head of a single spectator within. As tentatively I push through the hanging strips of black rubber which form the entrance to this inner sanctum he looks up. His trousers are open. His penis is erect, its swollen head hidden by a long foreskin puckering over the top, but he isn't touching it. His arms are spread either side of him along the top of the sofa and, having registered me, he leans back, slides his bum slightly forward and looks up at the ceiling in a posture of self-offering. Coloured light from the video glimmers over him. H. G. Wells said that the

Novel would decline and be replaced by Candid Autobiography. Well, he's been right about that. Most of the fiction which is rated these days is written in the first person singular as faked Candid Autobiography. But this is real autobiography and I'm not faking anything. And sex of course is the great subject of the modern arts; not sex generally – but sex specifically. But perhaps I shall not tell everything here, not because I'm abashed but because sex and secrecy are intertwined. It is unsexy to have no inhibitions under any circumstances. Besides, sex is about switching to another, non-social, more animal level of consciousness. It doesn't come in paragraphs. On the other hand if one is an artist wanting to include the great modern subject ... the man on the sofa is I guess in his late twenties, heavily built with strong hairy haunches. He stands up and pulls off his T-shirt and pushes down his trousers and mumbles 'Whatever ...'

We went for a drink afterwards, which is unusual. He was a seaman from Liverpool, working on one of the boats docked near the Hilton Hotel. He sails away tomorrow.

∼

Reading Strachey's *Eminent Victorians* for the first time since my adolescence, I can't recall a single thing of it, but that is nearly always the case with me. The moment a book is finished it plunges to the bottom of the well. Gladstone wrote to Cardinal Manning, after their rift, 'As and when they move upwards, there is a meet-ing-point for those whom a chasm separates below.' I suppose that's why there's no racism in the jetset. Went down the Den again – no one else there. I shunted listlessly about the maze, watched some synthetic American porn – I think American porn is the least sexy – and after almost an hour of waiting for a fantasy to come down the steps I left and returned to the Windsor Hotel to finish off 'Cardinal Manning'. That's so typical of travel – just when you think you've found a place, you haven't. Perhaps it's typical of life now – just when you think something's happening, and you're on a roll, it isn't. The stone never rolls uphill of its own accord. It has to be pushed every inch of the way. That's the price of individuality.

~

Matt has the hots for an Australian girl who is staying at his pink hotel. He says she's an alternative therapist.

'Has she tried any alternative therapy on you?'

'She hasn't even tried any, er – what's the alternative to alternative therapy?'

'Um … therapy?'

'Yeah, none of that, no.'

I took him to Flesh, a nightclub with a chatty Russian barmaid whose massive breasts were laced up in a leather bodice. Matt took the Australian alternative therapist the next night and she wandered off into the shadows and he couldn't find her again and went back to start *Eminent Victorians*, which I've passed on to him. This book is built on the quiet but deadly exposure of the extraordinary religious beliefs of Strachey's four subjects, beliefs that gave them the exceptional strength to do what they did. Even in 1918 when the book was published it must have been like reading about the preposterous superstitions of cavemen; and yet these absurdities, like any strongly held conviction, yielded highly practical results. Four subjects who believed in mumbo-jumbo but whose achievements were all *worldly*. Why does real piety always have something repellent about it?

~

Matt says that the softness and dreaminess of this land are making him giddy. I suggested he look at soft and dreamy Devonport and he comes back saying he wants to look round Portsmouth – in England, that is. He's never been to Portsmouth and feels the lack.

'Do you have a type?' he asks.

'No, I don't. But at the moment I'm into unkempt and dysfunctional.'

'Yeah, that'll do.'

~

The Den – young blond local about twenty and very short – not at all unkempt and very certain of what he wanted to do – mutual sucking. I don't mind very short. My relationships as well as casual pick-ups have been various in the extreme. How I choose a sexual partner is never predicated on the austerity of categorisation and yet is usually a definite thing – I feel a click of desire for one person and not for another. Occasionally people grow on me. But usually it's the other way round, which is to say I fancy someone then cool off if it doesn't go anywhere. But the aggregate of these encounters produces no identification of type, except that as I've grown older I go with younger. When I was young it was more the other way round. I think this is natural, nature's way of transmitting experience. Circumstance has something to do with it too: ordinary life for example is much sexier than a singles bar. But as for falling in love, as distinct from having sex, I can only fall for an intelligence which can challenge me and equal me. This means that my love affairs have been wonderfully rich and unsatisfactory. I've never fallen in love with anyone taller than myself. As tall, yes. Taller, no. Women like tall men. They are not turned on by short men, who remind them of boys, so short men have to win on personality, which they frequently do. This short man in the Den today tucks very nicely into my arms. A randy little number he is. But he wouldn't speak. I murmured some horny stuff but his vocal faculty was switched off. His silence was absolute and necessary to his sexual excitement. I say 'local' but since he didn't speak I couldn't be sure. He might easily have been a tourist. Who knows who he was.

≈

Matt has rented a car, an old white Merc, and after a few mistaken turn-offs we find the jetty at Half Moon Bay and drive on to the 10 a.m. ferry to Waiheke Island. The weather is mild but overcast and the beach apartment, when we arrive at Onetangi, doesn't present quite the hot 'n' buzzy Christmas atmosphere one was expecting. The resort has only a smattering of folk. You see, I've still got my English head, the word 'holiday' means crowds, packed in like sardines, bumper to bumper, stiflement. Onetangi Beach is family orientated but not overdeveloped and is planted with pohutukawa trees in red blossom. Matt sits on the sand in swimming shorts, rubbing his muscles, gazing out across the South Pacific, and says 'Yeah. I really want to check out Winchester and Portsmouth.'

≈

Next morning he's through the sliding glass door, across the road, down the sandbank and into the sea. Freezing no doubt. I mosey over the road half an hour later and flop for a sunbathe, should the sun come out. Matt leaps in corkscrews again and again so that the surf slaps into his back, but when it's obvious that I'm not going to join him he emerges from the waves like a Hooker's sea-lion and rolls in the sand beside me, giggling and kicking his sandy feet in the air.

'Which did you identify with when you were young, cowboys or Indians?' I ask.

'Cowboys,' he says.

'I identified with the Indians. Every single time. It was automatic, a soul thing. Do you think it's a gay thing?'

'Dunno. I identify with Gordon of Khartoum,' he says, adding 'Perhaps identify is too strong a word.'

'It's the most brilliant of Strachey's portraits.'

'It is.'

'I get confused sometimes between – I have this ongoing list of confusions, I put some of them in *To Noto* – I get confused between Gordon of Khartoum and Kitchener of Omdurman.'

'Kitchener lived on.'

'I know that. I get confused with their personalities. They were both gay.'

'Were they?'

'In that if-only-I-dared way. Tell you what impresses me so much coming out here – the astonishing reach and effectiveness of the British Empire.'

'Yeah, me too …' Matt nods agreement, brushing sand off the hair on his thighs. 'There are plenty of Mahdi relics at the Duke of Atholl's place in Scotland.'

'What are they doing there?'

'I've forgotten. This place reminds me of Bronllys.' Which is where his home is.

'What? Bronllys doesn't have a beach. It's in the middle of Wales.'

'But the way the hills look. Smooth and rainy. I'm not sure I want to be reminded of Bronllys.'

'I think we live in a world in which everybody's homeland is insufferable to them for one reason or another. These days everyone's homeland is beset with insoluble problems. Everyone wants to leave for a place where you needn't take responsibility, where you can just criticise. Life is shallower abroad. That's the great appeal. Everybody wants to be an immigrant. This applies as much to the rich Western tourist as to the poorest third world peasant, don't you think?'

'The sort of people wandering around here remind me of Bronllys.'

'Did you hear what I said?'

'It's the visuals,' he says. 'They're all white. And they can't connect up their clothes. They can't even make a T-shirt match with a pair of jeans. Pure Bronllys.'

∼

In the evening we turned on the television and turned it off again. I asked Matt 'Do you think you are uncomplicated in a complicated way or complicated in an uncomplicated way?'

He thought long and hard – he often does – fixed me with those candid blue eyes and said 'Uncomplicated … '

'In a complicated way.'

' … Yes.'

Another long hard silence before he announced 'Someone said I was lost.'

'Really? Who said that?'

'My psychotherapist.'

I didn't know he'd had psychotherapy.

'When was that?'

'In September.'

'Have you had it before?'

'No.'

'Why did you have it then?'

'Because someone said I should.'

'Who?'

'Belinda. It was when I was breaking up with her. And I thought – why not? Get someone else's take on it.'

'On it? On you.'

'Yes.'

'It's narcissism, psychotherapy is. Unless one is mentally ill.'

'I can live with narcissism.'

'You haven't quite broken up with Belinda, have you.'

'Not quite, no. But she's broken up with me.'

~

The skinny, small, young chap who runs these apartments is called Luke and he's always dressed in baggy shorts and flipflops and nothing else. He brought in a bottle of wine and said 'It's a bribe.'

'For what?'

'I want to do something.'

'What do you want to do?'

'Saw two pieces of wood outside.'

'But why the wine?'

'Because I told you it would be quiet.'

'How long will it take?'

'Four minutes.'

'That's OK, don't worry.'

But he gave me the wine anyway. New Zealand can be a noisy country – because the walls are so thin. But that was sweet of Luke. He is sweet. The way his shorts slip down to his pubes is elvish sweet. But our apartment – I had to ask for a rubbish bin and a frying pan. It said there was a washing machine but there wasn't. The video didn't work – since it's raining a lot of the time it would be annoying if we can't get in a few films over Christmas. No dustpan and brush. No iron and ironing-board. It was next door to an office with a high window between and a communicating door – no privacy. The office was being redecorated and the apartment stank of paint. So we moved to another apartment in a pretty garden courtyard behind the first apartment. There are short palm trees outside and ducks waddle in through the open glass door.

~

Matt is driving scorchingly fast round the bendy island roads using only one hand. He's sucking up the tarmac with hugely focused eyes. But orientation is not his strong point. At a T-junction he never knows whether to turn left or right. I choose and the old white Merc zips off accordingly. There are hibiscus bushes and white and purple agapanthus along the residential roadways, but I never got the hang of the island's attraction until we astroplaned over to the eastern half with its vineyards and open hills, Treasure Island coves and woodland. We stopped in Man o' War Bay and walked out on its old jetty. It could be 1850 apart from the car.

'But they don't have many stone walls round here,' he says.

'No. I thought that.'

'I was going to see if I could pick up a bit of work but … '

'If they're not into walls.'

'Precisely.'

~

It turns out that the girl whom Matt fancies from the pink hotel is now staying on Waiheke too, somewhere above Palm Beach, which is the smartest beach in the built-up half of the island, and Matt has arranged a rendezvous at a café called Sticky Fingers close to the water's edge.

'Can I come too?' I ask.

'Definitely. It's nothing like that. She wants to meet you.'

We are very late, which bothers me but doesn't bother him and certainly doesn't bother her. She's sitting under an umbrella with a bald old man of stature and vigour, a type quite common in this country. The man's shorts reveal heavily varicose-veined legs, again quite common here. Sportiness produces strong legs in youth and varicose veins later on.

The girl's name is Babs. Traveller, masseur, acupuncturist, smoker, drinker, of Welsh-Indian background, living in Japan but a citizen of Australia, Babs has been undergoing therapy since the age of thirteen. She is now thirty-five and possesses a faculty which may be observed in most experienced travellers, that of sliding in anywhere, of being familiar very quickly, and yet living behind a membrane where they cannot be reached. Intimacy and remoteness, friendliness and suspicion are mixed in her demeanour.

The man is called Arch and he's her landlord, with a house overlooking the beach. She found him on the internet only a week ago but they talk as though they were uncle and niece. Babs and Matt take off for a walk along the beach. Perhaps he'll have a crack at her, while Arch and I discuss duller things. Arch used to be a lecturer in psychology and engineering. I said it was a funny combination and he said it was basically attitudes to machines and accident prevention, though he'd also worked with the military. He mentioned a wife and kids but seemed to have done a lot of solo travelling in Laos, Thailand and Indonesia. We reminisced about Laos but he wasn't there when I was (which was when it fell silently to the Communists). I amused him with some of my sexual exploits. He was very mum about his – perhaps he had none, though that's very difficult to achieve in South East Asia. Played it close to his chest while seeming very jolly, open and relaxed. Matt and Babs returned sooner than expected and Arch invited us up to his house for dinner later this evening.

Back at our apartment to wash and change, Matt tells me that he made a pass at Babs while they were sitting on the beach. 'Yeah,' he says and cackles non-commitally.

'What did you do?'

'I stroked her back.'

'And?'

'She said don't do that.'

'Just like that?'

'Yeah. Hard and decisive.'

'Oh.'

'Frightened the living daylights out of me.'

'I'm sure.'

'She says she's a lesbian. Well, bisexual really. But a lesbian as far as I'm concerned.'

'She won't be funny tonight, will she?'

'No, no, nothing like that. I dunno. Maybe.'

'Will he be funny?'

'I don't see why.'

'I thought he was a nice chap.'

'He is. But why isn't he called Archie?'

I think a bit before saying 'Probably for the same reason that Babs isn't called Barbie.'

'What reason's that then?' Matt's eyes look up at me like a trusting little boy's.

Mmm. He's got me there.

With some difficulty he gets his old white Merc up Arch's drive, which is tight and steep, and wedges the car at the top. There's a sound of chopping from the kitchen. Babs is pottering about as though she's lived here all her life.

Arch has lit the barbecue outdoors. After roasting chicken legs and venison sausages, with a salad and large dish of new potatoes already prepared, and the wine opened which Matt and I contributed, Arch said 'Right. It looks as though we might have the beginnings of a meal.' He was full of this charming Kiwi understatement, a very English form of drollery which they take to extremes. We ate on the open terrace in the scent of honeysuckle, with candles steady in the starry twilight. Passing a jar of tamarind chutney, 'a speciality of the island', Arch said that in the Second World War New Zealand was the country which sacrificed the highest proportion of its population after Russia. Then the sun went down and Arch lit a brazier doused in petrol. The burst of flames floodlit us like a Fortnum & Mason Christmas window. Arch said that a line has been drawn down the centre of the island, beyond which Waiheke has been designated as rural. I said there's extensive replanting on that side as though some millionaire had bought it up and he said yes, that's John Spencer, who made a mint from paper mills. Arch said that when he first came, the island was very deforested but now there's a lot more leaf than there used to be, a *lot* more.

'Who's the richest person in the country?'

'Our richest person? I couldn't say,' said Arch, 'but the richest family are the Todds.'

'That rings a bell.'

'A friend of mine has shacked up with one of them in a new house over that way. I would've introduced you to him – he's very interesting and knows a lot – but he's pretty much absorbed by his new life.'

We sat at the table sipping red wine and took it in turns to tell ghost stories. Later Arch said that until recently in this country the division of the sexes was absolute. There was a man's world and a woman's world and the two didn't understand each other at all.

'At the same time, or perhaps because of this,' I say, 'the men were very homophobic.'

'Yes,' he says. 'Very touchy about anything like that. And as a result the men lived a life in complete stultification of the emotions and poured everything into hacking down trees and building up farms. There was a man called John Mulgan who wrote our great novel about this called *Man Alone*. He was one of our first writers to go to Oxford University and in the end he couldn't fit in anywhere and killed himself. But before John Mulgan killed himself he put it about that he was dying from a terminal disease.'

'Because he was ashamed to commit suicide for the true reason.'

'Yes.'

'Which was fear of life.'

'Yes. There was no terminal disease apart from that.'

~

Rain and wind. I ask the gardener what the name is of the attractive short palms outside our window and he says he doesn't know, he's from Belgium. Matt comes in from the sea, hangs his wet trunks in the bathroom, and wanders around naked sipping a cup of tea with the saucer held genteely beneath it. He usually goes for a jog and a swim before breakfast and into the sea again at teatime, throwing himself against the inpounding waves with abstract determination. He's particularly fond of swimming in the rain and says 'Swimming in the rain is even better than walking in the snow.' When I mention Arch's remark about war casualties, Matt replies 'Every country seems to claim their percentage loss of population in the war was the greatest after Russia.'

'Do they? Who else does?'

'I know the Scottish do.'

'Did you know that Scotland has the highest murder rate in Europe after Russia?'

'Always?'

'Currently.'

~

Confusions continued:

Virginal – spinet

Allan Ramsay – Henry Raeburn

Edmund Blunden – Basil Bunting

Lugano – Locarno

Meilleur – mieux

Sam Cooke – Jackie Wilson

Hay – straw

Raisins – sultanas

Motet – madrigal

Pessary – suppository

Lapwing – peewit

Hesiod – Herodotus

Pine tree – fir tree

Abscess – carbuncle

≈

That bell which rang at Arch's – it rings again and this time I have the recollection. The friend of Mike Horovitz's, the one he gave me the number of – she was called Todd and didn't she live on something called Waiheke Island? Let's have a go. I give her a ring and it's the very one Arch was referring to and she invites Matt and myself up for a drink at 6 p.m.

≈

Just got back from Jenny Todd's and open a rosé made on this island: Goldwater. 12.5 per cent. Correct pale colour of orangey pink. Nose: vague odour of running shoes and swimming pools soon fading away – it's not corked. Taste: nothing, no taste at all, with a faintly chlorine finish coming out of the blue. At twenty dollars a bottle this is incomprehensible.

When we got back to our apartment a builder was doing work in it. Luke had asked if they might do a couple of things to the apartment while we were out 'because the owner would like them done before he arrives', but it turns out to be a long list. The builder apologised and said he'd leave but he'd come back tomorrow morning. I said 'No, you won't come back tomorrow. This place has been let to us. Come back when we've gone. Come back when the owner is here.'

Jenny Todd's house had only recently been erected. It was in a compound with half a dozen others on an unspoilt peninsula and one gained access to this domain via a coded electric gate. There wasn't a single curve in Jenny's house inside or out. Pale grey, pale green, ivory white, in intersecting planes, with a peculiar front door: a large square on a central pivot. Matt immediately pointed out to me what was wrong with her front-terrace wall: the outline of breeze-blocks visible through the rendering.

'That's disgraceful,' he said.

'Ask her if you can do it properly.'

He glanced at me with serious eyes. 'I'd love to.'

Jenny was short with long dark hair, far younger than I was expecting, clear open expression, generous eyes and a good smile showing gums. She used to run an art gallery in Needham Road near where I live in London, and had a house in Artesian Road.

'Did you know someone called Elric Hooper? He used to live in Artesian Road.'

She appeared not to, though an anxiety briefly crossed her face, as though not to know someone might be problematic. Funny how many connections I'm finding in this country with my Notting Hill/Westbourne/Bayswater part of town. Laurence Olivier made his London debut at the Bijou Theatre in Westbourne Grove in 1924. It's now called the Twentieth Century Theatre and people throw parties there.

Jenny asked me where I'd been, how I'd got on, and I said that Kiwis were sometimes a bit odd with people who came from abroad.

She said 'A dealer I know brought in a painter from Europe and there was a strange kind of stiffness towards him, or even outright, you know, why are you bringing a European artist here, why do we need a European artist? But when he took the same artist to New York the response was totally different, it was "Oh, how exciting, let's have a look at this new European artist!" But when I was in America I found it quite … well, I'm quiet and they are louder and so when I reached London I breathed a sigh of relief and said thank goodness I'm home.'

Pink and yellow balloons bobbed on the floor in the draught. A man was sort of hammering, or *something*, in another part of the house. He came by at one point in a black shirt, dragging a box and nonchalantly nodded hullo without stopping. Jenny said she's marrying him next year. This must've been Arch's friend.

'You consider London home?' I asked her.

'Ah – the British,' she sighed. 'They have eight or ten layers of codes. You break through two or three of them and think to yourself "Hooray, I've arrived." But you are quite mistaken.'

'Peter Beaven was there.'

'Yes, he had an affair in London with a painter friend of mine but my friend said she was always aware of some other woman in the background.'

'That was probably his wife.'

'No, I don't think it was a wife.'

We're standing at a block in the open-plan kitchen. I pull the rim of skin from a coin of salami. She smiles the smile of small perfect teeth in healthy pink gums. 'Are you around at New Year? We usually have quite a few people in at New Year.'

As we left the house through the square glass door on a pivot, Jenny said 'This door is driving me mad. I tried to have it changed at the last minute but it was too late. I'm always letting people in on one side and inadvertently knocking people down the steps on the other.'

She pointed over to the right, where her neighbour had planted a whole hillside with native bush.

'A man's done a lot of this at the other end of the island,' I said.

'Yes, John Spencer. He made a fortune out of toilet rolls.'

'Look at that grotty wall,' Matt observed once again of the breeze-blocks, as he turned the Merc in the drive.

'I'm glad you didn't say anything about it.'

'No, one couldn't say anything about it but I'd love to rebuild it.'

He didn't say anything about anything, stood there in massive alert silence, sucking it all in, every single drop. Matt fancied her.

≈

Conversations with Goethe by Johann Eckermann. I've been looking for it for years and found a copy of the Everyman edition in Jason's Bookshop in Auckland. A Berlin friend of mine said 'Goethe was the last good German.'

'What do you mean?'

'He was the last *calm* German. After his death it was all Wagner, Nietzsche, Hitler, hysteria, remorse.'

Here's something apt. Goethe says 'Each traveller should know what he has to see, and what properly belongs to him … ' But that is only half of it – there is also the necessary intrusion of the unexpected, and the growing realisation that it's all unexpected, that it's all different from what one had envisaged. But the imaginative interest has to come first otherwise all is random. Perhaps that is what Goethe meant. Goethe's twin gods were Byron and Walter Scott. Being a calm man he could enjoy their wild romanticism.

≈

Luke dropped by this morning to apologise for the building work.

I'm starting to fancy him. With him I didn't get the click of desire. Well, I did – but not at first. Yes, some people do creep up on you in wavelets. I ask him his age. 'Twenty six', he replies with that innocent Oliver Twist look. He tells me that some years ago John Spencer, the toilet-paper magnate, blocked off the gravel road through his property with piles of earth but the council forced him to reopen the route. John Spencer sounds terrific.

'You can quite often see his helicopter hovering over the island. The local council gives you ten native trees a year free of charge if you're a rate-payer,' said Luke, whose shorts are balancing very precariously on slender hips, his pubic hair prickling slightly over the waistband, and as he talks enthusiastically his tight abdomen goes in and out. I long to give the shorts a tug. Cloud breaking up. Sun coming through and retreating again in peremptory explosions of light, like someone opening and closing blinds. By the afternoon the weather is sunny and hot.

≈

It's Christmas Eve. Matt is trying to crack nuts without a nut-cracker. This evening we tried a couple of bars in the main townlet, Oneroa, but we were the only people there. Everywhere booked up but the island deserted – what sort of game is that? So we went to Video Ezy and chose three films: *Crash*, *The Golden Bowl*, *Heavenly Creatures*. The Maori (I'm speaking to one at last and with eye contact!) cashier said three films would cost us twelve dollars but five films would only cost ten dollars with the bonus of keeping them for a whole week.

'Are you sure you've got that right?' I enquire.

'Yeah. Special offer,' and he repeated it.

So we added *Bridget Jones's Diary* and *Mulholland Drive*. I've seen them all except *Jones* and *Bowl*. Peter Jackson's *Heavenly Creatures* is magnetic; he uses the landscape of the Banks

Peninsula to create myth; but he's produced nothing adult since, just as Alan Parker's debut *Midnight Express* was followed by rubbish. When Hollywood gets hold of these weak sort of men – artistically weak, that is – all turns to dross. But it's an old problem: Theocritus, Greek poet born in Syracuse about 300 BC, complained in his sixteenth idyll about the evils of commercialism. I hate the mass market. I've never seen, eaten or read anything from it that was worth the effort. I love excellence – élites – exceptions – experiments – enigmas – esoterica. When the hype says you must see *this* film, you must buy *that* car, you must love *this* pop star, don't. Do something else. Gravitate to the obscure.

~

Christmas Day. In the morning Dame Kiri Te Kanawa is on the box from Coventry Cathedral, with boys' choir and symphony orchestra. Matt presents me with a little bronze smiling Buddha he bought in Geelong. This is where Buddhism wins hands down over the other religions. It's based on a smile. In fact it hates being called a religion. I give Matt some Dirty Knees shower gel. Find the religion in that one.

For lunch I cook fillet steak and we drink a bottle of champagne as the Queen, dressed in a suit of royal blue, delivers her Christmas Message standing between two armoured Red Cross vehicles in the barracks of the Household Cavalry at Windsor.

'How long before we have a black queen?' I wonder.

'Yeah … ' he gurgles with his feet up on a sofa.

'It could be quite soon. One of the princes might marry a black girl. Their mother died with her Muslim boyfriend.'

'Last Christmas I went to see my father in Halifax and on my way back I had to go through the Paki area. It was about midnight. A gang of these lads started talking to me. They said "You look down on us, don't you?" I was a bit drunk but I didn't want to rise to the bait so I made small talk. They spoke Urdu among themsleves and English to me, and while we were talking – it was a bit tense – I realised they were picking my pocket. They took all my money, about fifty or sixty pounds. But that always happens, any white kids passing through get their bikes stolen, their money taken.'

'And nobody calls the police?'

'If the police tried to do anything there'd be a race riot. Everyone accepts it.'

'Can't we talk about something less depressing on Our Lord's birthday?'

'Are you religious?' he asks.

'I like visiting churches.'

'Don't you think religion can be a force for good?'

'Of itself, no. Whether someone is nice or nasty has nothing to do with whether they belong to a religion. Ethics don't need voodoo. Are you religious?'

'Not really. I went to a synagogue in Cracow.'

'Are you Jewish?'

'No. But I had to put a cap on. I felt very self-conscious. There was me and one other person, and a telly in the corner playing a film about life in the ghetto before the war.'

'There's a fantastic Hindu temple in Wembley. Why isn't there Hinduphobia?'

'Hindus are OK,' he says. 'They can have a laugh. Their women are a whole lot more attractive too.'

'I think the Islamic religion panders too much to male pride – since men are more violent than women, this makes good government hard to come by.'

'The big mistake of those Islamists is attacking everybody, not just us – Chinese, Indians, Russians, Thais, Filipinos, Darfur – and they attack each other too.'

'A black guy I know says there's trouble from them in Senegal.

He said "What's the matter with the Muslims? Can't they live with anybody?" Do you know what I think? A massive infusion of petrodollars has woken Islam from a five-hundred-year coma and it's thrashing around in stupefaction.

'What's weird is that Europe made it illegal for itself to control the resulting influx.'

'Oh yes, hardline Islam has set up big time in Europe. Many years ago in Berlin, Heiner Müller said to me "Europe has a death wish". I disagreed with him then. Now I'm not so sure. Thank God China is a secular state.'

'China will form an alliance with Islam to secure its oil supply. Both are anti-democratic.'

'Please can we change the subject?' I hear myself beginning to whine.

'OK, the progressive civilisation which gave Europe its eminence is the one that's destroying the planet. Socrates is responsible for global warming.'

'From religious lunacy to industrial lunacy – that's not changing the subject, Matt.'

'We have to look things squarely in the face.'

'Do we? Karl Popper told Peter Munz that Plato's crime was to believe it possible to know what people deserve. But I think religion is far more to blame for that. Religion is entirely about what people deserve. Is there any more champagne? Actually we need the three of those Greeks. Plato for the arty dreamers, Aristotle for the science boffins, and Socrates to get them in bed together.'

Matt gleefully rubs his hands together. 'If you like. But none of it makes any difference. I'm afraid catastrophe is hardwired into the destiny of the planet.'

'What a cheerful little determinist you are. Why is that?'

'Because we must remember that man's capacity for foolishness has no limits. Not even the law of survival can defeat foolishness.

You were saying you are no longer interested in the cultures of hot countries.'

'That's right. Scandinavian drizzle now has all the allure previously enjoyed by tropical sunshine. I never want to travel to a hot country again.'

'Do you know why?' he asks.

'Because—'

'I'll tell you why. Because the tropics will be the first to go. The migration from the hot to the temperate regions has already begun. So the question is – where do you draw the line? You can forget all that Geneva shit. We'll have to mine the beaches and man the clifftops to keep them off. Are you into survival or death? You're gonna have to decide because in the coming world whole populations will go to the wall. That's the name of the game now. Survival. You said the great modern subject is sex. No way. It's survival, mate.'

'I thought you said foolishness was bigger than survival.'

'It is. But it's not a subject.'

'Personally I'm going for hedonism. I want to unhook and enjoy my remaining years as pleasurably as I can. I want my sense of pleasure to survive.'

Matt glowers and says 'My urine's very dark. It's so green it's almost brown.'

'Have you seen the Ninja Tunes album?'

He raises his eyes. 'Natural blondes are predicted to become extinct by the year 2200 AD.'

'The compilation one – I put it on the arm of that chair. Look, are you trying to wreck my Christmas?'

'I'll open another bottle.'

'Aren't we supposed to protect biodiversity? Anyway, who says so?'

'I think it was a Norwegian scientist.'

'In historical terms 2200 is next week!'

'Yeah, not long to go now.'

'Maybe science will save us.' I locate the CD beneath a newspaper and slip it into the system. 'After all, Denmark is the most popular source for sperm donation. What I'm really looking forward to is the genetic modification of embryos. When parents can choose the complexion of their offspring, racism will be dead, skin colour will be depoliticised, whites will no longer be able to presume, blacks will no longer be able to hide, and people will be exposed for what they are.'

'What we really need,' says Matt, 'is to develop new economic models based on fewer people, prosperity deriving from population reduction. Nobody's working on this.'

'Nobody?'

'Nobody.'

'You mean there's a gap in the market there?'

'Absolutely. Not a soul working on it anywhere.'

'Then you should give it a go.'

Having attempted to explore somewhat the complexities of twenty-first-century life, we both unleash disturbed sighs and I have a little bop on the spot – 'Music for Body Lockers' from Chocolate Weasel – while Matt, finishing off his glass with a smack of the lips, jogs out of the flat and throws himself at the sea. Onetangi Beach faces north. If you swam off it and kept going, the first land mass you'd come to would be Alaska. In the evening we watch *Mulholland Drive*.

~

Boxing Day. The weather lady on television says 'It's a very bad time of year for hay fever sufferers, especially with privet flowering in the north.'

Matt says 'I had this dream last night.'

'You shagged a reindeer.'

'I haven't remembered my dreams since Sri Lanka.'

'And what did you dream about in Sri Lanka?'

'I can't remember,' he says. 'But I remember that I remembered them at the time.'

'And last night?'

'I was in this empty ruined house. Broken pillars. No roof. On one of the bare walls was an equation … Do you want to know what the equation was?'

'Yes, what was it?'

'Zen equals zen minus zen.'

'Ooo … Do you think it's true?'

'I think it's very true.'

'So do I. At last. The truth.'

On television the Derby is being run at Ellerslie racecourse, and Matt asks 'Should I visit Bernard and Daisy?'

'Bernard's very worried about his balance.'

'Maybe it came back over the holiday.'

'Ring them and find out. Oh no, you can't.'

'Why not?'

'They're not there.'

~

Next day we return to Auckland. The noise of seagulls above the Windsor Hotel is like strident howls of laughter. Matt is pacing about, panther-like. I say 'You need a good larrying, you do.' I've been urging him to go to a massage parlour. Clearly he wants to. But won't. Probably he doesn't want to pay. It's not really shyness or penury. It's that he doesn't want to hand over money for a *sensual* experience. Very English, that.

~

Matt is suffering. We talk in a bar and walk and talk in another bar. He's not been here long but he's at the end of his tether. I'm shocked. It wasn't obvious.

'No, well, I've had to go along with this no-worries, mate stuff. But I can't go along with it. It horrifies me.'

'Why?'

'Because I've got worries.'

We are in the Jackpot Bar, another bar full of drifters, single men, backpackers, who've floated in on air-rafts and who are already quite far advanced in invisibility.

'Australia made sense,' he says, 'because I was there for work. But this place doesn't make sense. Why am I here?'

'Because I'm here and Bernard and Daisy are here.'

'Is that it?'

'I agree it doesn't sound very much. Can't you say to yourself "I'm seeing the world"?'

'This isn't the world.'

'It's more than that. It's the end of the world. You thought someone would hand you meaning on a plate. But they haven't. Everything drifts to a halt and fades away here.'

'Stop it, stop it! I haven't felt like this since the early 1990s, knocking around Aberystwyth, in and out of work.'

'You haven't shown it.'

'No, I didn't want to. It's a ratty, white-noise desperation, uncomfortable prickly low-level despair and terror.'

My God, he's shitting pineapples.

'Terror of what?'

'That you're not going anywhere. That you don't matter. That you don't *exist*.'

'What's the solution?'

'That's what I'm racking my brains over.'

'You've come here. You've come as far as it's possible to go. And you've found that you don't exist.'

'That's it. You feel that when you come to the end of the road you'll be able to define yourself. But it's the opposite. You disappear.'

~

John Mulgan's books are out of print. He only wrote two and I find secondhand copies of *Man Alone* and *Report on Experience* in Jason's Bookshop. Mulgan was born in Christchurch in 1911. He loved Greek, rugby and sailing. He studied English at Merton under Blunden and took First-Class Honours. There's a photo of him at Oxford, most of his buttons undone, fair curly hair and a broad natural smile, a classic of open-shirted handsomeness. In *Don Quixote* Cervantes uses the simile *teeth as white as peeled almonds*. That dates Cervantes. Today's peeled almonds are yellowed and in cellophane packets. But if you take fresh almonds and peel them you will see that the simile is perfect, even down to the shallow grooves and the shape. Those are Mulgan's teeth in this photograph. Did anyone ever look happier and healthier? Everyone must have fallen in love with him.

The novel *Man Alone* was written at Oxford but not published until 1939. It is a link between Hemingway and the Beats. It has the lean Hemingway tone, leaner than Kerouac who never combed out a text. Mulgan writes 'There isn't any better country than this, not where a man can go about and get work, and stop when he wants to, and make money when he needs it, and take a holiday when he feels ready for one.' Disaster, when it comes in the story, is of female emotion breaking out and destroying the safety of taboo and reticence.

Report on Experience, a small volume of autobiography, was published by the Oxford University Press in 1947. There is a horror in finding oneself in the presence of a man who can never look through the eyes of realism; one knows instinctively these mad, fanatical people; you forget that philosophical crap about how no version of reality can be proved more valid than another, because when you meet someone who can't do reality your stomach tells you: it gets very jumpy. The opposite happens with Mulgan. He is not a fanatic. The voice is soothing: 'Educated and civilised men do not ask for faith and religion in their politics but go where the argument leads them,' he writes. What comes out of this book is goodness: the ability to know and say what you think quietly and clearly and with generosity. No wonder he had a successful war, working with the resistance fighters in Greece, ending as a lieuten-ant-colonel and awarded the Military Cross. He's been turned into a hero precisely because he wasn't heroic stuff. His manliness has the essential courage – and the equally essential kindness. There is a sweetness and courtesy and lack of cynicism in him, which are also national virtues in New Zealand and remain with me years after my journeying there, like a beautiful scent of wild ferns, blue irises, fresh hay …

Then it gets complicated. His great virtues somehow left him defenceless. He wrote in *Report on Experience* that New Zealanders live in their country 'as men might in a dream which will one day wake and destroy them … They roam the world looking not for adventure but for satisfaction … a queer, lost, eccentric pervading people … Those who are going and those who are staying have all the time within them this sad inner conflict and frustration …' and of the New Zealand soldiers he wrote 'Everything that was good from that small, remote country had gone into them – sun-shine and strength, good sense, patience, the versatility of practi-cal men.'

He'd scarcely finished revising this book when he killed himself with large doses of morphia. He did it in a room at the Continen-tal Hotel, Cairo, on April the 26th 1945. All Mulgan's commenta-tors say that though many people have put forward reasons for his suicide, his act is finally inexplicable. The day he killed himself was also the day before he was to be repatriated to his wife and family. Is this the answer to the mystery? If you read *Report on Experience*, if you contemplate the photographs of Mulgan, then yes, his suicide *is* extraordinary. The calming charmer must have been a deeply bewildered man. His inner needs were so threatening that he destroyed himself rather than act on them. Where is the evidence of this? So complete is his disguise that you cannot detect the evidence. There is no evidence except the act of suicide itself.

So, reading backwards, there must be profound dishonesty permeating *Report on Experience*, of which Mulgan himself must have been significantly if not wholly aware – he was no fool. In the end he betrays himself. He lies. He lies right through his almond *Don Quixote* teeth. And yet as you read the book and experience the man, you don't sense any lie. You are up very close and still can't detect any lying. Therefore this man is broken inside: the man who is false at the very moment when he seems to be his most genuine. I have since come across one other man like this in my life, English but similar background to John Mulgan's, not cynical, not a con man, not that at all, but something much stranger – the perfectly false man. He too has become a mystery that I can't solve, that I can't shake off. I hope his fate is better than Mulgan's.

~

There's nothing false about Matt. He is flying to Manchester tomorrow via Singapore, so this is his last night. The first thing he says when he turns up at my hotel is 'I had a very powerful dream last night.'

'Another one!'

'Yeah, enormous black and red clouds billowing, billowing.'

'Nazi colours.'

'Pretty much, yeah. Then I realised it was a city on fire, a city being consumed.'

'Maybe there'll be an earthquake here after you've gone.'

'That's what I was thinking.'

Is he serious?

'I've been longing for a tremor,' I say. 'But the earth hasn't moved a centimetre while I've been here. Not one tiddly jot.'

'Maybe you're in for a big surprise!'

'Do you believe in premonitory dreams or are you having a paranoiac seizure?'

His mouth hangs open in a curious way. Perhaps he'll turn into a werewolf. The hair on his forearms is erect. But I have since seen Gustave Doré's engraving of 1873 called 'The New Zealander': a man is sitting on the banks of the Thames and all around him London is in ruins. And suicide-bombers have struck London. One of them was arrested in a street near my home. It's all very close now. Terrorists letting off nuclear or biological bombs, it's very close.

We are walking along the Viaduct Harbour as the sun goes down. Though the Sky Tower looks gimmicky in photos, it's a brilliant success in reality, but what its floodlighting denotes this week – lime green – I can't imagine. Matt's bilious ontological vertigo perhaps. He pauses beside a sailing boat put up on the harbourside. It has a spiky mast reminiscent of a Norfolk pine, and a stabiliser hanging goitre-like from the bottom of the hull. And it's all in white. He flashes out a dark look and says 'That looks creepy. All white. In *Moby Dick* Melville says white is a more threatening colour than black.'

'Why did he say that?'

'Maybe because light is the colour of exposure. You can't hide in it. Fucking Tarkovsky.'

'The Russian film-maker?'

'Is there another?'

'Why did you mention him?'

'I think he's great. The future is dark.'

I let that go and say 'The future is green. Because there won't be any people left. I love individuals but I've gone right off people. Too many of the bastards.'

How many sodding restaurants has this Viaduct Harbour got? One after another and all new. The prattle of merry diners tinkles on terraces facing the provocative sunset.

Matt asks 'And do *you* like it here?'

'I do but it takes time to cope with the other-worldly feeling.'

I will *not* let Matt's nihilism bring me down and I plump for a restaurant with white Lloyd Loom chairs on Prince's Wharf. We're served by an efficient Russian girl, with a Peter Pan haircut, who says 'I want to go to London and live in Oxford Street.'

'But it's crowded with shoppers.'

'That's what I love. Crowds – and shopping.'

'Fish & chips for two, please.'

She came from Kazakhstan. Her father ran a computer business in the United Emirates. Her mother emigrated here. Matt fancied her.

'She's the first girl I've really fancied since I came away.'

'I thought you fancied the Russian barmaid in the nightclub.'

'She was sexy but too much.'

'What about Babs?'

'I only half fancied her.'

'And Jenny Todd?'

'That was interesting, the way we stood round the metal thing in the kitchen eating bits of cheese and salami and she didn't invite us to sit down. I never want to come back here again.'

'I thought you fancied the waitress.'

'The country, I never want to come back to this country again. I've got nothing to react against. I can't stand it.'

'Yes, we know, eat yer chips, you're leaving tomorrow, have a drink.'

He won't have a last-night drink, not even a beer. It's like he's afraid he'll vanish in a puff of smoke if he has so much as one beer. He says he's now booked his passage straight through to Manchester, not stopping in Singapore after all. But instead of this settling him, the closer he comes to departure the more agitated he becomes. It seems that what's horrified Matt is that there's no escape from personal responsibility.

'It's so funny, I checked out all the trains, buses, planes that would get me down to Bernard and Daisy's place – but I just couldn't do it. There was a force preventing me. Life's weird, isn't it?'

'Yes. But not that weird. You seem to have gone through the arsehole of an apocalypse.'

Maybe robust lack of sympathy can help. His head twitches. The Russian girl presents the bill and goes into a long account of the architectural importance of the house on the North Shore where she's living.

Walking back along the wharf, I say 'All that driving round Waiheke with one hand, that was weird.'

'That's normal for me. I'm sorry if it unnerved you.'

'No, I never once felt at risk, because your absorption in the tarmac ahead was total. The intensity was weird, the way you seemed to sink your attention into the road as a way of avoiding looking at where you actually were. It was the same with the sea – throwing yourself at it twice a day because you couldn't face your surroundings.'

'You noticed that, did you?'

'Perhaps you couldn't stand being with me.'

'I thought about that, but honestly it wasn't that. It was the terrifying sense of being at the end of the world and losing all sense

of who I was. This is the last time I'm going to say it – I'm so glad
I'm leaving.'

He says it at least three more times. Saliva glimmers on his
chin. As we pass the Lenin Bar he stops abruptly in front of an
iron pillar. Will he twist round and howl at the moon? I suggest
we pop in for a drink. By this time Matt can hardly speak. He's
seized up completely, wringing his hands, looking anxiously
about, his blue eyes almost black. I force an orange juice on him.
I've got painful indigestion from the huge plate of fish & chips.
I mention it.

'I never eat chips!' he exclaims frantically. 'Never! I ate them
all! Why did I eat those chips? Why?'

He didn't speak at all after that but drank his orange juice
silently, eyes flitting everywhere and nowhere, the hands writhing
over each other in incessant anticipation of that nameless, tranquil destiny for which he thirsted.

～

At last I manage to get hold of Sunny Amey on the telephone. She
was one of my Olivier contacts.

'As a young student,' she says, 'I paid what seemed to me a huge
amount to see the Oliviers in *The School for Scandal* in Christchurch. He was very good but I thought her voice was much too
high. The one I couldn't take my eyes off was Peter Cushing, who
played, I think, Joseph Surface. This was before he became famous
for his horror films. He glided about the stage in the most magical
way and I was *riveted*. I remember seeing him leaning elegantly
against a mantelpiece with his arm up and then I was told it wasn't
a mantelpiece at all, it was just a piece of painted cloth, but the
way he did it was so clever.'

'Did you ever see Vivien Leigh again?'

'Yes. When I worked at the Royal Court, we did a Feydeau farce,

Look After Lulu, directed by Noel Coward. I was the ASM. She starred in that – she was in a good space at the time and totally professional. I thought "Oh God, I must be respectful" because I'd heard that if she took against you she'd have you sacked. But she was charming and there wasn't the slightest problem. Olivier was still visiting her backstage, though the marriage had virtually come to an end.'

'When was this?'

'Late 1950s. The next production at the Court was *Hay Fever* and the star was Joan Plowright and there was a lot of hanky-panky with Olivier backstage. The press were *all over us*. So what we had to do was disguise someone as Joan to leave by the front entrance while she nipped out the back.'

Olivier was one of those highly eroticised men who flip into bisexuality. He is said to have bonked Brando. Or was it the other way round? Brando is supposed to have bonked both Larry and Vivien on the set of *A Streetcar Named Desire*. Larry was also supposed to have bonked Coward. It looks rather cheap when superstars bonk each other, as though they can't get out of the trinket box. But I suppose it's just working together really, equivalent to the quick office lay. Sometimes I regret not working in an office, having no colleagues.

'I know how tiring touring around can be. Are you doing it by yourself?' asks Sunny.

'Yes.'

'Even more tiring. And are you enjoying it?'

'I'm enjoying the continual spray of new scenes. But whether I like the country or not, I cannot say. It doesn't seem to be the important question.'

'Well, if you come back Wellington way, we'd love you to stay with us, and we can have a good old gossip.'

≈

So Matt has gone. Just like that. It's always 'just like that' with modern travel, as though someone waves a wand and the person who was with you day after day, sharing the small moments of your life, is erased in a second. I'm going too. But not just yet. I'm walking freely round the streets again, not in some tunnel of angst with Matt, and am re-engaged by the easy eye contact here. Only in Russia have I noticed an equivalent directness from the eyes. But in Russia it's more emotional; here it has the purity of water.

Matt certainly didn't find what he was hoping to find, what he is always hoping to find, some crystallisation of the self, and I haven't found what I was looking for either, the place of perfect exile unravaged by time. Of all those elegant hotels and theatres, where Larry and Viv strutted their stuff, virtually nothing remains: one light after another punched out. The delicate Victorian towns, where one imagined a life might be pursued free from ugliness, free from crime, free from pain, have been pulled down. It's been the art deco more than anything else which has carried the pungent sentiment of my past, since my first ever awareness of architecture was of the art deco cinema and shopping parade on Imperial Drive in North Harrow where once or twice the mischief took me and I ran laughing into the middle of the busy road, with cars screeching all around, my mother desperately trying to save me, and where the curious rustle to my left, which was the rubbing together of her thighs in their silk stockings, grounded me in peace on the walk home again. To be overpowered by nostalgia is so akin to love as to be, on occasions, almost indistinguishable from it. As love expands space, so nostalgia expands time. Of course nostalgia can never satisfy, which is fortunate since, if ever it did, it would amount to reabsorption by the womb and creation itself would be an impossibility.

∼

Tony Ogle dropped by the hotel with some pictures and invited me to a New Year's Eve party at Bethell's Beach. I'd have to rent a car, otherwise I'd be stuck out there, and I can't be bothered, but it was nice to be invited. Tony said he wants to move into portraiture and more explicit surf pictures and that Captain Cook first saw surfing in Hawaii and the missionaries put a stop to it as irreligious.

~

Davey, the boy I met in Christchurch, is now in Rotorua. He's sent me an email. He wants to drive up and see me before I leave. I'd love it and email back to that effect. These weeks staying at the Windsor Hotel, I've developed a certain routine. Up before ten, light breakfast, potter over to the Westfield Mall to buy food from the Swedish grocer and the seafood stall, newspaper, check emails in the Queen's Arcade, back to the hotel by which time the maids have usually done my room, write up notes, lunch, over to the Den for long, spacey, often frustrating sex sessions; bad sex can be good, it can be thrilling not knowing quite what to do, I can appreciate the value of frustration – a lot of great sex has been produced by frustration – a lot of great art too – and a lot of rubbish, because too much frustration is a killer, drives you mad, your cock goes up, goes down, refuses to go up, refuses to go down; I nearly ulcerated yesterday when a big Japanese muscle-boy decided to pull away just as it was beginning to warm up and *yes*, a bit later and *finally* a Maori lad in smart sporty clothes, with hard pencil cock (circumcised) sticking out of unbuttoned canvas fly, emerged from nowhere and reached for me, yes, at last, my first Maori and we were beginning to gel, the spontaneity was beginning to flow, and then I glimpsed his eyes, his uneasy flickering eyes, and there was a mutual glint of – of – of what? Of meeting, of interior touching, and this so disconcerted him, to spark beyond the physical to the personal, that he flipped off after someone else whom I hadn't noticed in the shadows but *he* had, he'd spotted the third, and moments after that he scarpered altogether – no, please don't go, you are fine and warm and I want to make contact and find out about you – but his footsteps tapped rapidly up the concrete staircase to the ground floor and he was gone for ever, whereupon the third loomed out of the shadows with an invitation but he wasn't me and I melted away into blackness.

What about me had repelled the young Maori? Was it the sense of exposure to another human being? Or something else altogether? Now that Matt has gone, my evenings are emptier. I've had lots of sex, mostly with language students, many of them oriental. At the beginning of this trip I asked Shirley O'Connor 'Why are there hordes of oriental kids in this town?' and she replied 'They come to learn English. But they are very disappointed when they get here to find themselves surrounded by others of their kind when they thought they were going abroad for a new experience.' So I'm a new experience for them. But it's all been pretty anonymous and I haven't met anyone with the earthy, giving charm of Davey, so it will be lovely to see him again.

∼

New Year's Day. Morning sunshine varnishes the city. *The Importance of Being Earnest* is on the telly. This 1952 film version is an inspired choice for the first morning of the year. Joan Greenwood as Lady Bracknell's daughter combines innocence with multiple-adultery voice. Michael Redgrave is luminous as Earnest, giving out some kind of life-force, yet hardly moving a facial muscle. His performance is a triumph of English charm, an artfulness enchanted with a dash of self-mockery. *The Importance of Being Earnest* is one of those creations which can persuade you that comedy is higher than tragedy, that above everything – if you are able to scramble up to it – is the cosmic joke. The high larking spirit of young airmen off on a mission – my father would say to his friends 'If I don't come back, you can have my breakfast.' They used to say that, that's how they were, the élan of the cavalier heart, the ability to laugh not only at oneself but at one's elimination. It's also the gambler's attitude, destiny hanging on a throw of the dice, and my father was a great gambler.

∾

The War Memorial Museum is a gigantic temple in Portland stone on top of a dead volcano in the centre of the Auckland domain which is their big park, but it's inaccessible without a car, not merely on the edge of town but also several ravines away. So I take a taxi.

On the ground floor are the Pacific halls. Statues from Papua New Guinea and Fiji. In my early twenties I had an affair with a Fijian rugby player. A girlfriend of mine once went to bed with him. They waited in bed together for me to arrive and said 'Surprise, surprise! Come to bed with us!' They thought it would delight me, until they saw my face. My beautiful English girlfriend and my beautiful Fijian boyfriend in bed together. It didn't happen again. I'd like to think I'd be more laid-back about it now and dive joyously in between them. But I wouldn't be. Jealousy has always been one of my big problems. I get emotional and possessive, my deeper feelings disturbed even when it's only a trick. In the Den I can find myself going through a whole love affair in twenty minutes flat.

A Maori war canoe, carved from a single trunk of totara and capable of carrying a hundred warriors, melds form and function so perfectly that its want of any misjudgement or clumsiness seems to render it weightless. A classic object clear as day. The Maoris may be hard to find, and even harder to engage with, but they don't strike me as a mysterious people. Perhaps I'd once imagined them wrapping themselves up in pride and romance and living close to nature in elusive settlements according to ancient mythological rites, but actually they go to the pictures and watch quiz shows and wander around eating junk food like everyone else, and any social problems they may have are not difficult to fathom. The mysterious people in this land are the original English colonists. What drove them and enabled them to create a social triumph on the opposite side of the world is a complete mystery to us now, when we doubt our every impulse, respect every culture but our own, seek wisdom everywhere but in our own origins.

On the top floor are regimental shrines and flags and stained glass, and an exhibition called Scars on the Heart, 200 years of New Zealand at war. Simple societies are often based on warfare and have warriors with spears. The English turned the warrior into a superior concept, the gentleman – and gentlemen were minced up in mechanised war. One of the soldiers returning from the Great War testified that 'I went home to a father, mother and four sisters and no one ever asked me what it was like. For seventy years no one ever asked me what it was like.'

Gruesome scenarios are here on display. Archive film of the Second World War in the Pacific pans across forest stretching limitlessly to every horizon (now mostly cleared). Maori soldiers, handsome and well-built, not fat in those days, are welcomed home with nose-touching and laughter. And here again is my father. Well, it's a Spitfire actually – and he flew Lancasters. But the association is instantaneous. When you're far from home, one's dead are just as alive as one's living. They are all equally away and equally near. So it's no surprise I've been thinking of my father on this journey. Not thinking *about* him or analysing our relationship. Nothing like that. There's nothing really to analyse – we had it all out with each other quite a while before he died. There was one last little thing I wanted to say to him and if I did, that would be it, there would be nothing left unsaid on my part. My parents were staying at the Llangammarch Wells Hotel in Wales and I joined them for dinner on the Saturday night, and said it, and after that my conscience was clear. My father looked very well that weekend. He died unexpectedly – in the saddle of course – the following Wednesday at the age of eighty. There were things I'd like to have asked and never did, but there was nothing further I felt I needed to say. And on this trip I've simply been aware of him and of the things I have in common with him. Though our parents didn't get everything right, they gave us love. They held us and kissed us and took us everywhere and called us darlings.

My father had come from a sterner world. He was the son of a mining engineer in the Nottingham coalfield. My grandfather William I never knew because he died of lung cancer in the 1930s, presumably brought on by coal-dust. I think he must have begun as a miner but I'm not really sure because my father never talked about him, except to say that he had a fierce temper and that I look like him. Apart from my father's mother in black bombasine, the Matriarch of Newstead, and a Fabian socialist and pacifist to boot, who came to live with us for a little while in Harrow at the end of her life, I never met anyone from his side of the family. He did tell me that his brother George died during the war from over-eating.

Tom Fallowell was an exceptionally entertaining man – if you went into a restaurant and heard laughter it would be at his table – and he wanted very much to get away from coal-dust and Methodism. When war was declared he was twenty-two, had passed all his accountancy exams, bought himself an Alvis and was thinking of taking a job in Calcutta. He had a good war. He went to flying school as an ambitious Midlands lad and came out of it with a Clark Gable moustache and a polished voice and all the RAF slang:

old boy, on the blower, pass the rag, what a shower, jolly good show, chocks away. This slang is one of the vivid memories of my boyhood and when I see Terry-Thomas in any of those films I'm always reminded of something in my father. As a flight-lieutenant under Bomber Command, the unit which suffered the greatest casualties in any of the forces, he lost most of his early friends. It was while he was stationed near Carlisle that he bumped into my mother, who'd been evacuated from London to Morecambe. She told me she tried to play hard to get but said it was hopeless, he was such fun, and they were married two months later.

After the war he couldn't take orders any more and, though very gregarious, he was his own man, hated clubs and organised groups, and wanted to run his own business, which, after some difficulties and rather surprisingly, turned out to be as a manufacturer of merchandising systems, with a wire factory in Reading. His many war medals and sporting cups – he played tennis for the RAF – were kept in old Smith's Crisps tins and eventually thrown away. He didn't talk much about the war, or the past generally. He preferred to live in the present and gamble on the future. But we didn't encourage him either. It wasn't quite as bad as 'Nobody asked me what it was like' but it was going in that direction. Adults talk about the Second World War far more today than they did in the 1950s – it wasn't only the Germans who took the amnesia option (but children were different: a fabulous, legendary cruelty, such as England had never known, filled my school playground with stories of German and Japanese atrocities). In the 1960s my father did good business with Germany and made German friends.

There was one particularly curious thing about him: his face always looked slightly wonky in the mirror. It didn't do so in photos or under any other conditions, but in mirrors it always did. It's not something I've ever come across in another person or have otherwise heard of and it remains a riddle to me. When as a little boy I noticed it and asked him about it, he was slightly bashful and dismissive. I vaguely remember being told that it was something to do with the war and I wonder if it was the effect of a facial injury he kept secret and which only showed up in mirrors.

Ours is a very small family. The only other male Fallowell I know is my brother. So when I was preparing this expedition, I googled our surname to see if there were any in New Zealand. There weren't. But I came across someone my father never knew about, an ancestor called Gabriel Fallowell, born in the reign of Elizabeth I. He was one of the founders of the Plymouth Colony in the USA, and went over from the East Midlands in the early seventeenth century. The Fallowells will soon die out in England, but maybe in America …

~

Davey hasn't got back to me. I've emailed him again but he hasn't got back. People are so tenuous these days and who knows what his life really is? The setting sun incarnadines the walls of my hotel room. Today's temperature at Darfield, near Christchurch, was a national record for January at 41°C (106°F). The electric blond light pours down over everything, penetrating everything. Yes, the two words I shall take away with me from this country are 'eerie' and 'poignant'. It feels a very old place, not young at all, though it was the last country to be discovered by the Europeans. This is part of its eeriness, that we are close to the prehistoric, close to Gondwanaland. And poignant is the bittersweet of being left behind, a yearning in the breast of this land of immigrants, whether of Maori or European origin, who have an apprehension not of having arrived in a new place but of being left behind in an old one. They are always standing on the ground, waving people off on aeroplanes.

There's a lot of comfort in Heidegger's grounded definition of existence: being in the world.

≈

Some African people are occupying a room opposite my windows but on the floor below. They keep their windows wide open and the curtains too and do their socialising, with loud gusting laughter, between four and six in the morning. After the third night of this I told reception I was not prepared to pay for another night without sleep – I have for some time been this hotel's best customer. They apologised, said they'd had many complaints from other guests too, have told the miscreants four times a night to no effect, but they are checking out today. I said why didn't you throw them out? They said they didn't want it to come to that. I said sometimes it has to come to that. Their room is a mess because they sleep all day and the maids can't get in. The woman sits by the open window watching television, laughing, laughing, until the man returns about 3.30 or 4 a.m. On the first two nights they had friends in and crates of beer. Last night there were only the two of them. There is nothing malicious about this couple. It is just that they cannot take it in that they are driving others round the bend, or that this should be a reason for them to enjoy life any the less. Yet there is something sad about the woman, accentuated by her piercing laughter which is more of a plaintive reflex to everything that's said. I've seen her naked in the bathroom, because she's pulled the blind up halfway. I've seen the man walking naked in the room. He is tall and of magnificent make. They are both, I'd guess, in their early thirties. They are the gods of insomnia. He is sliding into bed beside her now and having woken everyone else up they have a quick slithery fuck and fall asleep like babies.

≈

Davey rang! He's only just accessed his emails. He's coming to-morrow and now I'm easy. The other good news is that they've saved the Waitaki Valley. I've had an email from the campaign organiser saying the Government has refused the water company permission to destroy the valley for hydro-electricity. I've never understood why it's necessary to wreck the surface of the Earth for energy purposes when there is a limitless amount of ready-made heat beneath our feet. Capillaries driven down through the shallow mantle could tap the Earth's fiery core indefinitely.

~

I met Davey in the foyer of the Windsor and brought him up in the lift. The weather was heavy and overcast, and so was he. Some-thing was preying on his mind, which made him more handsome, and he'd shaved off his goatee beard. It was like a present for me, his shaving it off. The unselfconscious weight of his body was joined to mine in the narrow lift. Looking downwards as the cabin cranked upwards, he unfastened two buttons of his shirt. Some words in his ear made them hot and red. We did not hurry along the corridor to the room. We were drunk on the heat. The oblit-eration of all privacy was gradual and without panic and spread itself through time. That lovely dreamy look came into his eyes. The slow fever flushing breast and neck and face. And eventually we burst like taut tomatoes.

I asked him if he'd ever been in love and he said 'Yes, I think with my first girlfriend. When I was eighteen. I was all hunched over with a stutter. Pretty much a retard. She gave me the confi-dence to be myself.'

'She brought you out.'

'Yes. I never felt loved when I was growing up. My adoptive parents didn't involve me in conversations and I ended up hardly speaking at all.'

'How long did your first girlfriend last?'

'Until I was twenty.'

'Were you faithful to her?'

'Yes, I was.'

'When did you have your first male?'

'That was towards the end of our relationship. It was pretty much over. I felt I had to move on.'

'Who was it with?'

'Her uncle.'

'Was he "out" gay?'

'Very much so.'

'Did she know you did it with him?'

'No. But she suspected.'

'What made you do it?'

'I didn't for a while. Then I decided – if it gets hard, go with it.'

'Are you in love now?'

'No. I've got a young sister. She's the only person I'd sacrifice my life for.'

'You really love her?'

'Yes, but I haven't told her so with those words.'

'You should.'

Our dinner arrives from room service.

Davey eats his meat with quiet concentration but after a while pauses and looks up at me with one of those undeviating Kiwi looks which can be terrifying, with no innuendo at all, no layers of reverberation behind the eyes. He asks 'What's England like?'

'A cauldron.'

'I hope to go.'

'You can stay with me. Before I left London, my dentist said "England's not nice any more. It's got nasty."'

'Is that true?'

'No, but it's true of the cities. Civilised life in London is in tatters.'

He chews thoughtfully. 'But exciting?'

'Oh – magnificently exciting. London is the centre of the world. It's an immigrant city. A criminal city. A rich city. Incredibly sordid. The Cockneys have fled and so have the sparrows and now they've started to chop down the trees.'

He sips his beer. 'Sordid … in what way?'

'Everything is spat at.'

He ruminates for a moment before asking 'Why?'

'Because the barbarians have taken over. But they always do, don't they? I think it's called energy.'

He looks up with a glint of humour in his eye, chewing with lips closed. Seagulls yell outside.

'Have you ever fucked a sheep?' I enquire.

'No. But I know quite a few farmers who are into it.'

'Because they love sheep or just the convenience?'

'Oh, just the convenience.'

He smiles, sitting here, all warm, looking at me. We have stopped eating. We are looking at each other. We have stopped talking and are quietly looking at each other.

∾

NASA broadcasts on television the first ever photographs from the surface of Mars. They are beamed back by a rover named *Spirit* which has landed there laden with mechanical instruments.